Searching for the Promised Land

An Irishman's American Odyssey

Edward Deevy

The Liffey Press

Published by
The Liffey Press Ltd
Raheny Shopping Centre, Second Floor
Raheny, Dublin 5, Ireland
www.theliffeypress.com

A catalogue record of this book is
available from the British Library.

ISBN 978-1-908308-78-8

Printed in Ireland by Sprint Print

CONTENTS

Part Two

The Way Home

For my parents,
Michael Deevy and Mary Condren

Even with all the advantages of retrospect, and a lot of witnesses dead and gone, you can't make your life look as if you intended it or you were consistent. All you can do is show how you dealt with the various hands.
– Christopher Hitchens, commenting on
his memoir, *Hitch-22*

The way we are living,
timorous or bold,
will have been our life.
– 'Elegy', Seamus Heaney

Prologue

On that late summer morning I'm relaxing at home in Haverhill, Massachusetts. If I look out the window of my tenth floor apartment I can see the Merrimack River winding its last few miles on the way towards the Atlantic Ocean. It's a typical Sunday. I'm drinking coffee and simultaneously navigating my way through the *New York Times* and watching Gorbachev on C-Span, the public affairs network. It's the summer of 1991 and the Soviet Union is falling apart. It's a news junkie's weekly binge. On this August day the sun shines brightly, the light reflecting my mellow mood. The phone rings. It's Elsie, my sister-in-law in Ireland.

'Eddie, I have some bad news. Andy died last night.'

I freeze: *Andy is ... dead?*

She waits for the words to sink in. The sun still shines, the birds still sing, Gorbachev's mouth still moves. But the world has stopped. My brother is dead.

'What happened?'

'I'm afraid he ended his own life.'

It's like I've been hit with a sledgehammer. My brain seizes up and yet the questions spill out. How? Where? When? How are Mary Ann and the children?

The biggest one of all – why? – is too big for this moment.

When a sibling chooses to die, it makes you question everything. The shape of the past, present and future is changed forever.

1

As a result of an accident when he was a young man, Andy lived with excruciating physical pain. Even so, deciding to end his life was an act of such finality that all of us were forced to look at our family's history, to wonder about what seeds got planted early on and how they might have sprouted.

Andy's death did not come to define my life but it did throw it into perspective. I had been ordained a Catholic priest in 1962 and I had walked out of the ministry seven years later when I realized it was a matter of self-preservation. I had fought on the front lines in the civil rights movement in the American Deep South in the early seventies and then trained as a psychologist. I was 53 in 1991 and had weathered my share of crises. And yet when Andy died, it was as if I was stripped of all wisdom and understanding. I did not know which way to turn or what to think.

In the years before Andy's death I had sometimes considered the question of how family history influences our lives. In its immediate aftermath, facing with some fundamental questions about the past, I decided that I would try to figure out the extent to which my journey had been influenced by early experiences growing up in Ireland. At the time, I did not have the wherewithal to follow through on this and I put it on my long-term 'to do' list. The 'doing' has taken until now.

This is a story of one man's odyssey – personal, political and geographical – but also the story of a family and the father who moulded them. All families are fascinating in their own way because each encompasses the good, the bad and the irreparable. None of us can escape our origins – we have to live with them as best we can. While my story is not entirely typical I believe it has elements common to many Irish families of the last century – particularly the hold of faith and fatherland. My hope is that it is a story that throws a light on the transition from twentieth to twenty-first century Ireland, helps to explain something of our past, and captures a world that is now gone.

Part I

SETTING OUT

1.

Leaving Drumagh

In August 1962 I am a 24-year-old, newly minted Catholic priest, ready to set out for the New World. I am leaving behind my siblings and my parents. For generations before mine, the millions of Irish men and women who emigrated to find opportunity in places like Australia, New Zealand, Canada and the USA, it's been a one-way trip. An all-night 'American wake' – a party with drinking, music and dancing – marked the emigrant's departure. But with the advent of the jet age there's no longer a need to say final farewells. Emigrants expect to return. So my send-off party is limited to immediate family.

I was born in February 1938 and grew up in south County Laois in the townland of Drumagh in the parish of Mayo-Doonane. The parish is on the border with County Kilkenny and the nearest town is Carlow. I am the second in a family of seven – four boys and three girls.

My father, Michael Deevy, has three major passions apart from farming: his Fianna Fáil politics, his Catholic religion and Kilkenny hurling. He was born in Swithsheath, County Kilkenny in 1904. In his late teens he emigrated to New York and lived there for most of the 1920s and the early 1930s. He had various jobs, starting out as a labourer in a stone quarry and ending up as a bus driver with the Fifth Avenue Coach Company, a job he loved and talked of fondly.

5

In 1934 he had returned to Ireland, bought a house and a hundred-acre farm and married the following year. Despite his tough experiences as a young emigrant he always referred to America as 'the promised land'. My mother, Mary 'Molly' Condren, from the hills of Cruttenclough in County Kilkenny, was born in 1902 into a farming family. Originally my father had dated her sister, Irene, in New York and he met my mother on a visit home. She was a soft-spoken nurse who had qualified as a midwife in a Dublin hospital and worked in the community, delivering babies throughout the local countryside.

Andy is the eldest in our family. He was born in October 1936 and is the designated heir to the farm. After me come Mary (1939), Michael (1940), Rita (1941), Lena (1942) and Tom (1945). Our sister Brigid (1944) died after just a few weeks.

Like my siblings, I attended the local two-room national school in Mayo. Andy was pulled out of formal education at the age of 14, but as the rest of us boys were not destined for farming, we were sent to Knockbeg College, a boarding school located on the River Barrow outside Carlow town. Michael has recently qualified as a psychiatric nurse. After doing their leaving certs at St Leo's College in Carlow, Mary and Rita each joined the Sisters of Mercy in County Cork. Mary has trained as a teacher and Rita as a nurse. Lena is also pursuing nursing. Tom is still in school.

In my last year at Knockbeg I decided to go to Carlow College. It was one of the oldest seminaries in Ireland and had been sending young priests to various parts of the English-speaking world since the 1790s. Now I am getting ready to emigrate to the promised land of my father's recollection. With my six years of clerical training and the authority of my stiff Roman collar I think I am supposed to project an air of confidence, but I feel far from confident. I have no idea what the future holds, though for better or worse this farm boy is leaving his family to go to the New World to preach the Gospel.

On the eve of departure the family sits down in the parlour for the special dinner that Mammy has prepared. Of course, Mary and Rita aren't there – as religious sisters they are rarely allowed out of the convent, though they were allowed to attend my ordination ceremony and first Mass in June. None of us is interested in the food. My mother looks tired and preoccupied and an occasional tear rolls down her face. Daddy is unusually subdued. Normally he would dominate proceedings, sharing his opinions about local, national and international affairs, pronouncing on family matters, revealing future plans, generally being the centre of things. But today we are all heavy-hearted. Everyone had been looking forward to my ordination but now that its consequences have become real, the cost seems hard to bear. I feel awkward, being the focal point of this sadness.

'One of the priests from the diocese tells me I'll have two weeks' holidays each summer. I'm hoping I can save enough to come home in two years,' I say, in an attempt to lighten the mood. Everyone agrees that 'we won't feel it' till we're all together again. Soon the dinner conversation becomes more light-hearted and we make the most of the time we have together.

On the morning of departure we gather around the kitchen table for a traditional breakfast of bacon, eggs and sausages. Mammy turns sixty this year, but as a result of a lifetime of hard work she looks much older. Daddy still has a lot of energy and drive, but on this occasion he too looks old and tired. It strikes me that I'm seeing my parents as they really are, instead of through the eyes of a child.

After breakfast I collect a few remaining belongings. I walk around the house as if saying goodbye to each room. I look at my parents sitting together in our kitchen, tears rolling down their faces, and for a brief moment wonder if this grief isn't a bit excessive. Typically, I suppress my feelings. I've been dreading this moment and the plan is to get it over with as quickly as possible. The cases are already packed and loaded in the boot of the car.

We sit together for a while, not saying anything – listening to the ticking of the kitchen clock. And then I stand up, hug each of my parents, and walk quickly to the car that is waiting outside, engine already running. It's a beautiful, sunny August morning. My three brothers drive me to Dublin Airport to start the journey to Louisiana. Our farewells are brisk and as upbeat as we can make them: Irish boys don't hug or show emotion.

As the New York-bound Aer Lingus plane leaves the Irish coast, I take a last look at the green countryside below. I can see cattle and sheep grazing in the fields and cars driving on winding country roads. My head is still full of the tension and emotion of the last twenty-four hours. Though I am anxious about what lies ahead, it feels good to be finally on the way.

High in the skies over the Atlantic, the attractive thirty-something woman sitting beside me says I look too young to be a priest. (I am, of course, in clerical garb – the uniform of Father Edward Deevy.)

'What would motivate a good-looking young man like you to become a priest?' she says, sounding genuinely puzzled.

Nobody at home asked that question. It was considered an honour and a blessing to 'hear God's call' to serve as a priest, not something to be coolly evaluated and decided on in a rational way, like any other career option. As I formulate a response, I think of my admiration for the worker-priest movement and their efforts to bring about change on behalf of the poor and the disadvantaged, and their willingness to discard the Roman collar and get involved in the real world.

'I'm hoping that in some way I'll be able to promote social justice,' I tell her. 'Some of my motivation comes from the example of my mother, who works as a midwife around the area where we live.'

It's the best response I can come up with on the spot. I have a hunch about where she's really coming from with her question, but I don't want to get into a discussion of celibacy with a stranger on an airplane. Thankfully, she doesn't pursue it.

I go through customs at Idlewild Airport in New York and quickly find myself in the back seat of a spacious Chevrolet Impala, en route to my Aunt Irene's suburban home in Smithtown, Long Island. After a few days there, I move on for a brief stay with my mother's other sister, Aunt Helen, in Queens. It's the first time I have met my mother's younger sisters, who left Ireland as teenagers four decades earlier. They are both as warm and kind as my mother.

I then call to see various Deevy cousins in Jersey City. The family is active in Democratic Party politics and in my honour has organized a big dinner in an Italian restaurant. The dinner includes not only extended family but also a Who's Who of local politicians. I am introduced to some well-dressed types who tell me to get in touch with them if I ever have any trouble in Louisiana.

Back in Carlow College my professor and friend, Father P.J. Brophy, had spoken frequently about the vitality he experienced on visits to the USA. Immediately I feel this vitality and it gives me a much-needed boost of energy and enthusiasm. The few days of exploring and socializing in New York and New Jersey provide my first glimpse of American life, and everything seems so big – the buildings, the cars and the highways. The possibilities, too. I'm feeling excited about my new home and anxious to start my work within the community in Louisiana.

2.

A new home in the Bible Belt

As I relax on my New York–New Orleans flight, I'm thinking about how little I know about Louisiana. The choice of Louisiana as my destination was serendipitous. My sister Mary had a friend whose brother was a priest there. On one of his visits to Ireland, Father Gayer had encouraged me to consider his diocese as a possible choice. Most of what I've read is promotional material put out by the Louisiana Tourist Board. I've seen photos of the big white plantation homes, of course, but I realize they're mostly tourist attractions. I know that ordinary people don't live in these mansions. I've read about Creole food and the New Orleans Mardi Gras. I've read about Earl and Huey Long, famous politicians and both former Governors of Louisiana. And I've read *Miracle at Carville* – the tragic story of a young woman who was incarcerated in a leper colony in South Louisiana in 1929.

Despite my informal research I've little idea of what to expect as I land at New Orleans International Airport on 27 August 1962. Walking across the airport tarmac it feels as if I've stepped into a sauna. As I walk into the arrivals building, my woollen suit sticking to me with sweat, I'm thinking, 'This can't be America – this is the Tropics.' It's 105 degree heat and humidity. In Ireland, a temperature of 80 degrees would be considered a heat-wave. My welcome to sweltering Louisiana in the summertime feels almost literally like a baptism of fire.

My first stop is a junior seminary called Maryhill, located in the pine woods outside the City of Alexandria in central Louisiana. A cluster of relocated old military huts, it has no air conditioning. I feel like I'm in the jungle. The hungry mosquitoes and the suffocating heat and humidity make for a miserable and mostly sleepless experience. Within a week I get a call from the Bishop's office, advising me that my first assignment is St Matthew's Church in the city of Monroe in northeast Louisiana.

One of the Irish priests working in the diocese picks me up for the journey north. He can see that I'm struggling.

'You never get used to this heat and humidity,' he says, almost cheerfully.

Just what I need to hear!

'What about the winter?' I ask hopefully.

'There isn't really a winter. Just the odd storm and torrential rain from time to time. I hope you didn't bring an Irish topcoat. All you'll need around here is mosquito spray, suntan lotion and a raincoat!'

We travel north for almost three hours through flat, boring, wooded countryside. It is so far removed from the Irish landscape, I feel as if I've been transported to another planet. We pass through a couple of small towns, but the territory is mostly deserted. It doesn't look especially attractive.

I find it difficult to believe that people live in the small wooden shacks we pass along the way. It soon becomes evident that it's only 'coloured' people who live in these dilapidated shanty homes.

'My father wouldn't have cattle living in those conditions,' I say, eventually.

'Eddie, you have to remember that the people living in these shacks are descendants of slaves. They don't have the right to vote.' There is no condemnation in his tone; rather, he seems bemused by my naïveté.

11

Of course in Ireland we knew of the ongoing conflict surrounding the rights of blacks in America. I'd read about the economic conditions of poor blacks in the Deep South, but seeing the reality is stark and depressing. At the truck stop where we had lunch I had seen a sign saying 'For Coloreds Only' on the door of a toilet. Poverty like this is in sharp contrast to the values I'm here to preach and live.

Just a few months earlier, in Carlow College, I had read a book on the relationship between religion and public life by an American Jesuit and theologian, Father John Courtney Murray. The book outlined how the rights of the individual are enshrined in the American Constitution by the Founding Fathers. From that distance I imagined other priests would also be grappling with the contradictions of American life, particularly when it came to the way that poor and black people are treated. I make noises about America being held up as a land of opportunity for all.

'You'll find there's a big difference between talk and reality around here,' my driver says. 'All that stuff about equality is a lot of bullshit.' He adds that St Matthew's is a 'white parish' and he has some words of caution: 'Remember, you're an outsider – and be very careful that you don't get branded as "a nigger-lover".'

His response challenges my assumptions and makes me think that I'm in for a few surprises. I'm wondering just where I'll fit into this picture with my ideas on social justice.

THE FIRST PERSON I MEET AT St Matthew's rectory is a short, stocky, middle-aged man, Father Warren Larroque. He's an assistant pastor but devotes most of his time to serving as principal of the Catholic high school. My main job, he tells me, will be to 'babysit the Monsignor.'

'Don't worry – this is your apprenticeship, you will get out of here in one or two years.'

Providing companionship for the boss isn't exactly what I thought I'd be doing. So much for any notions of becoming a social activist! The wind has been taken out of my sails even before I have time to unpack.

Monroe is a fast-growing city with a mostly deserted centre. By 1962 St Matthew's Parish is in decline: a majority of the middle-class – white – Catholic families in the downtown area have moved to the suburbs. It's a case of 'white flight'. The parishioners left behind are those who can't afford to move – poor whites. The black and white communities in the city are separated on geographical lines. There is almost no interaction between them, apart from between middle class whites and the blacks who work for them. No black Catholics attend St Matthew's. The religious needs of black parishioners are the responsibility of a religious order, the Franciscans.

The two-storey rectory is a musty redbrick building with a gloomy interior that reeks of stale cigar smoke. The upstairs living room has a large colour television set, assorted stuffed chairs and a long table that I duly discover is mainly used for counting the weekly church collection.

I notice the absence of any greenery around the building. In a humid climate in which any plant on Earth would thrive, the rectory stands in a barren concrete space with not a blade of grass out front or at the back. It is also in the shadow of an old hotel long past its glory days, and adjacent to a bleak-looking high school campus. This bare and neglected environment is far removed from anything I've ever known.

It turns out that the pastor, Monsignor Marsh, a man in his sixties, is 'psychologically retired' and spends most of his time watching TV and worrying about parish finances. A short, plump, white-haired man with rimless spectacles, he has two major passions: golf and deep-sea fishing. His other obsession is a parish-owned mausoleum in a local cemetery. I learn that the mausoleum is a source of personal income for the pastor because he gets a kickback on each crypt sold.

A man of limited intellectual curiosity, Marsh shares the conservative views of his white Southern contemporaries. This is the heart of redneck Bible Belt country, where many white Baptists and other evangelicals interpret the Bible in such a way that racial segregation is part of God's plan. They believe God created blacks inferior to white people.

Just days after arriving in Monroe, the University of Mississippi, in the neighbouring state, becomes the stage for a bitter confrontation between Attorney General Robert Kennedy, brother of the President, and Mississippi Governor Ross Barnett. The attention of the nation is fixed on the town of Oxford as Kennedy threatens to use government troops to support a black student, James Meredith, in his efforts to gain admission to the university. One day over dinner I ask the Monsignor for his take on the confrontation.

'The Federal government should stay out,' he says dismissively.

It's a sentiment I'll hear from many others. It would take time to understand that the resentment of the Federal government had its roots in the Civil War, fought 100 years earlier. As a new arrival, I have no real appreciation of the historical significance of the Kennedy–Barnett showdown.

At St Matthew's I settle into a routine. Visits to parishioners in the local hospitals help pass a couple of hours each morning. This work brings me into contact with hospital staff, including a group of young nurses who adopt me as part of their social group. They regularly invite me to their parties and social events. There are more than a few dating invitations – all of which I decline. From my training I've learned to maintain a certain detachment to avoid becoming emotionally involved. Still, I'm deeply grateful for these young nurses occasionally rescuing me from a life with the sick, the dying and, in the case of the Monsignor, the uninspired.

The Monsignor regularly invites me to join him viewing *As the World Turns* and other TV soap operas after lunch. As often as I can, I find an excuse to decline. My excuses become increasingly fanciful and creative. Some even turn out to be genuinely good ideas. I come up with a proposal to carry out an opinion survey among parishioners. This provides an opportunity to get out of the stifling rectory and make friends. More importantly, I get an insight into the needs and concerns of the people we're supposed to be serving.

Soon, the rectory is attracting an increasing stream of visitors. This influx is partly a result of my getting out into the community to conduct the survey. A growing number come looking for counselling or information about the Catholic Church. I handle all of these requests and welcome every opportunity to stay busy.

As the weeks pass I become somewhat concerned about the way our maid is treated. Anabel is a young black woman who works at the rectory six days a week. Each day she walks to our downtown rectory from her home in one of the 'coloured' sections – a journey that takes almost an hour. At the rectory she cooks dinner for the household, cleans the house and does the laundry.

Sometimes after her day's work, if it's wet, Monsignor Marsh will give her a lift home. For these journeys, she sits in the back seat of the Ford Thunderbird. One day the Monsignor is away on a deep-sea fishing trip and I offer to drive Anabel home. She accepts. I insist that she takes the front seat.

'Anabel, why do you ride in the back seat of Monsignor's car?'

She seems surprised by my question. 'Because that's what's expected of coloured people.'

When I get to her home – a small wooden shack – I realize that this young woman lives in a world totally different from that of most white people.

As I consider Anabel's status, I think things haven't really moved on much since the times depicted in *Gone with the Wind*. That book and movie was about the Civil War and it's a century later, but so much of what it described is, unfortunately, still recognizable in Anabel's life today.

Father Larroque tells me that Anabel is paid five dollars a day. It strikes me as not much compensation for a hard-working woman trying to support her family. One day I suggest to the Monsignor that perhaps we could do a little better for her. He's not impressed.

'She's one of the best paid coloured maids in the city,' he says.

That is the end of the matter. He's the boss and there's to be no further discussion about it.

THE FIRST CHRISTMAS ARRIVES along with a bad case of home-sickness. By this time I've become friends with several families in the parish. A couple of them extend invitations to join them for Christmas dinner, but Father Larroque reminds me of my baby-sitting responsibilities.

'Eddie, I'm going home to New Orleans to be with family for Christmas. You should plan on having Christmas dinner with the Monsignor.'

The Monsignor gives no indication of his plans; he's come to assume that I am always available to join him for dinner. On Christmas morning I preach the sermon at all of the Masses. After the last one I return to the rectory to find the Monsignor already counting the collections. I join him counting money as the TV blares in the background. I think about how far away I am from a loving family and a true feeling of Christmas.

We complete our joyless task and the Monsignor decides we should go out for dinner. Downtown Monroe is a pretty dead place even during the week. On weekends and holidays it is a ghost town. We walk across the high school car park to one of the local hotels and into a mostly deserted restaurant. The Monsignor and I talk, but the conversation stays at a superficial level. I know little about his background or family. I assume most of his relatives have passed away, though I've heard mention of an elderly sister living in South Louisiana. He never asks me anything about my back-ground or family.

We each select the turkey dinner special. Not a memorable meal: bland hotel food on a day when I've always enjoyed a feast prepared by my mother. I'm thinking this must be how soldiers feel when they're away from home at Christmastime. My thoughts go back to the past, to all the excitement and anticipation that surrounded the Christmas celebrations in Drumagh. For this Christmas I'll have to be content with the memories.

The Monsignor and I walk back to the rectory and on the way he tells me there's a good movie on TV. I dutifully take a seat in front of the box. Afterwards, I excuse myself and retire to my bedroom. I lie on my bed, tears rolling down my face. Even though it's in the privacy of my bedroom and no one can see me, I am ashamed of this expression of emotion. It's cathartic nonetheless.

Lying on my bed and feeling homesick, I remember a quotation from scripture about leaving father and mother and brothers and sisters to preach the Gospel. On this Christmas afternoon these words offer little consolation. Now, I just want this Christmas 'celebration' to be over.

In the New Year, January 1963, I quickly get back into my stride and finally start to feel the energy of American life that I'd noticed when I'd arrived in New York. Most people I meet are upbeat and optimistic and, unlike what it felt like growing up in economically depressed Ireland, there is a real sense of possibility in the air. Each day I'm learning more about the American way of life and the stuff that really matters to people: sports and politics, just like Ireland. Most important of all is that parishioners have reached out and made me feel welcome. So after the initial months of loneliness and adjustment, I'm finally finding my niche. I'm on my way to becoming Americanized.

3.

A summons back to Ireland

At first I'm in denial, but just a few months after my arrival in Louisiana I can no longer ignore the dark hints about Mammy's health in the letters from home. I offer to return if the prognosis gets really bad. I know if a flight home becomes necessary, I can borrow an advance on my salary from the parish. The advice from Drumagh is to await further developments.

One morning in May I arrive downstairs and there's a telegram waiting on the breakfast table. The message is four stark words: 'Mammy dying – come home.'

Alone, I eat a breakfast of grits and eggs and try to take it in. Straight after, I book a flight to Dublin and within twenty-four hours I'm on my way. After a four-hour drive to New Orleans and the flight from New Orleans to New York, there's the red-eye flight to Dublin via Shannon Airport. I walk into the arrivals hall to find Andy waiting to drive me to Drumagh.

The early morning car journey is quiet. We were never good at talking about the personal stuff. We're both just absorbed in our grief and sadness. I know that Mammy is Andy's confidant. They had talked of him emigrating to Australia where Mammy's uncle, Pat Condren, had become a very successful rancher.

As we drive into the long, winding driveway leading to our house, Andy breaks the silence.

'Mammy's just holding on until you get home,' he says.

We're both in tears.

I'm jet-lagged, emotionally exhausted, and this whole experience seems like a nightmare. It has only been a little more than a day since I received that unexpected telegram and it hasn't really sunk in that Mammy's death is imminent.

Finally, after the marathon journey, I'm at Mammy's bedside. She'd asked to be sent home from a Dublin hospital once it became clear her time was limited. A bed has been set up in the parlour to make it more convenient for neighbours and relatives to pay their respects. I pull a chair close to her bedside, hold her hand and whisper to her that I appreciate all she's done for me. I've never said this before.

'Take care of yourself, Eddie,' she whispers, in a barely audible voice.

She seems so at peace with herself. Everyone is saying she held on to life just so she could say goodbye to me.

I walk outside and down through the fields. I want to be alone with my thoughts. It's a beautiful, sunny spring day and the countryside is bright and alive. I walk down the field in front of the house to the river I've crossed so many times on the way to the two-room primary school I'd attended with my brothers and sisters. Sitting on the riverbank, I stare at trout swimming in the clear water and recall spending Sunday afternoons fishing with my brothers. The technique we used was simple enough when compared to that of the well-equipped angler. We simply grabbed the unsuspecting trout with our bare hands and twisted their heads off. On a good outing we would return with a half-a-dozen fish – enough to convince Mammy to include them with the evening meal.

Here beside the river, there's not a sound except for the birdsong coming from the woods. I'm remembering my maternal grandfather's wake and how it affected Mammy. She was distraught as her father's body was removed from the small thatched house to be taken to the local parish church in Coon. I was just ten years old. She was devoted to him and we liked him too because of his gentlemanly ways. When he came to see us, my grandfather always brought us a generous supply of sweets and silver coins. We used to go visit him in a horse-drawn trap. On those visits we'd go picking *fraughans* (bilberries) in the boglands or blackberries on the country road. At night my Uncle Bernie's wife, Aunt Lizzie, would play music on the accordion while we played hopscotch on the kitchen floor. We'd ride home under the bright moonlight, travelling in silence save for the sound of the horse's hooves on the gravel road.

Mammy was the heart and soul of our home. Each evening, arriving home from school, my siblings and I would be greeted by the smell of freshly baked raisin buns or hot apple tart or some other treat. She had a magic touch in the kitchen. She also had a green thumb and the house was surrounded by roses, geraniums and other fragrant flowers.

A kind and gentle woman, Mammy's warmth and caring tempered my father's fierce driving ambition. On more than a few occasions she had rescued us when Daddy was in a rage and threatening dire consequences for some infraction; somehow she contrived to distract him from whatever was upsetting him. I picture her making the bed in my dormitory the first day she and Daddy left me in Knockbeg and how sad we were that day. On their visits to me at school, Mammy would usually slip me a few pounds to help with expenses. I presume she did the same with my brothers. It was money she managed to stash away from her tiny midwife's salary.

Unlike Daddy, Mammy never moralized and never tried to influence the decisions I'd made growing up. I always sensed that she knew I'd find my own way. Once, during my training, I told her I was considering leaving the seminary. 'Do whatever makes you happy,' she said. I wondered what her life might have been like if anyone had been as supportive of her as she was of her own children.

The walk down through the fields helps clear my head. I return to find family, relatives and neighbours quietly waiting for the end to come. Daddy leads everyone in the recitation of the rosary. And then all is quiet again.

A strange stillness comes over the house. Mammy breathes her last a few hours later. It is 21 May, the same date that her baby daughter, Brigid, had died nineteen years earlier. The official cause of Mammy's death: chronic nephritis. If someone had asked, I'd have said she simply wore out and died of exhaustion.

The next day neighbours and friends congregate at the house in Drumagh for the long walk to the church in Mayo. After the coffin is placed in the hearse we set out along the winding gravel driveway leading to the public road. This is the road Mammy travelled so often on her bicycle at all hours of the day and night in her role as a midwife. When we reach the blacktop road, we turn right and walk up the hill.

Walking slowly behind the hearse I can hear the rhythmic sound of footfall as hundreds of neighbours follow behind us. It's a quiet peaceful May evening and the crowd moves slowly, step-by-step. Coal-miners and factory workers mingle with farmers and labourers, Protestants with Catholics – she made no distinctions and delivered all their babies with care and efficiency. The obituary in the local paper later says as much: 'She lived a dedicated life of self-sacrifice. In her professional capacity she was loved by all her patients for her kindness and gentleness.'

It's customary in Ireland to speak well of the dead, but the comments I hear as we walk behind the hearse are generous and heartfelt. They tell me she was a 'great woman' and whisper about how she helped them in a time of need – they tell me I should be proud of her. And as we slowly work our way towards the small country church where Mammy had been a devout parishioner, I am proud that this unassuming woman's contribution to the community is so publicly honoured. But I'm sad that Mary and Rita are not part of this ritual. I feel a tinge of resentment towards the Church because of the rules that prevent these two young women from attending their beloved mother's funeral.

I say the funeral Mass the next morning. Still jet-lagged and attempting to come to terms with Mammy's death, I scarcely notice the large group of priests in attendance or the overflow crowd of mourners. It's as if I'm in another world, operating on auto-pilot. Church regulations do not permit me to eulogize my mother. Perhaps it would have been inappropriate to sing the praises of a woman who never sought recognition for her service to family and neighbours. Under the circumstances I simply weave into my homily the suggestion that she always put the interests of others before her own.

After the funeral Mass my mother is laid to rest in the graveyard beside the church and life in Drumagh is changed forever. I don't want to abandon my family at a time of need, but I know I have to get back to Louisiana. That is where my duty is now. After a few days I make a final visit to Mammy's graveside and then Andy drives me to Dublin Airport. The early-morning journey provides an opportunity for a private chat. Andy wants to know everything about life in Louisiana.

I feel sorry for Andy. The most academically inclined in the family, he had to give up formal education at age fourteen to work fulltime on the farm. As the first-born son, the unquestioned tradition dictated that he was the designated heir to my father's life. He is too loyal to ever bemoan his lot, but it's obvious that Andy isn't cut out for or all that interested in farming. He has a whole range of other interests that include drama, politics and travel. Daddy sees his involvement in the local dramatic society as particularly irksome, regarding it as frivolous. Ironically, Andy's social activities are good for the reputation of our family as he is well liked in the community; Daddy is not so popular. Andy is stuck in Drumagh for a career he didn't choose and from a young age

Daddy has been constantly on his back. Like our late mother, Andy is quiet and low-key – not one to assert his needs.

We arrive at the airport less than two hours after leaving Drumagh. After checking-in my luggage, Andy and I go upstairs to the cafeteria for breakfast and then walk downstairs to the customs area to say our goodbyes. As we part company, all that's on our minds is how we will come to terms with Mammy's loss and getting on with our lives. We are young and with our future ahead of us, so it's unimaginable that within the year there will be another family trauma, this time involving one of us.

As I sit back in my seat, waiting for the plane to taxi down the runway, I'm feeling overcome with sadness. I'm sad because Mammy has been snatched away before I was ready to give her up. I'm sad because I know Daddy will be lost without Mammy to take care of him. And I'm feeling concern for my brothers and sisters: the woman who'd provided the emotional glue to hold us together as a family is gone.

When I arrive in New Orleans airport it's night-time and I spend several hours searching the car park for my car – I hadn't taken note of where I parked it in the headlong rush to Ireland. The hopeless wandering in the dark fits my lost state of mind. I do my mourning privately. My isolated life in Monroe means I have no close friend or confidant, so I keep my thoughts and my grief to myself. Gradually, I get back into the day-to-day routine of attending to parish duties.

THE 1960S REVOLUTION IS UNDERWAY. Elvis Presley flicked a switched in young Americans in the late 1950s and they've discovered their own music and a world that's all about fun and liberation. Now we're hearing about a group from Liverpool called The Beatles who are reinventing music. There's optimism in the air. President John F. Kennedy promises that America will beat the Russians in the Space Race and be the first to land a man on the moon. We are contemplating the unthinkable in every sphere.

In the Church, Pope John XXIII is enjoying extraordinary popularity for his efforts to promote internal reform and understanding among various religions. I'm already thinking that this might lead to revolutionary changes, including a change in the requirement for priestly celibacy. So, I'm feeling energised. But I'm also restless. Babysitting the Monsignor is sapping my energy and I desperately need a change of direction and a new purpose.

4.

The winds of change in the South

A year after arrival in America I'm settled into my role as assistant pastor and getting more acclimatized. My day off each week is spent exploring north Louisiana in my Volkswagen Karmann Ghia convertible. Mostly I just visit the handful of Irish priests stationed in various parishes throughout our diocese.

'I love your Irish accent,' is a frequent comment. While Monroe has a significant number of individuals and families that claim Irish ancestry, I may be the only Irish-born person living in the city. The people in the parish make me feel very welcome. The people showing up at the rectory are from diverse backgrounds. Some are down on their luck and looking for hand-outs. My responsibility is to dole out meal vouchers for a local diner. Others who come to the front door are seeking advice or counselling on all kinds of personal issues.

One day I answer the front door to a young woman wanting to talk about a personal problem. Her name is Suzanne. She tells me she's not Catholic but understands that we offer counselling services. I listen, suggest several options for her consideration and set an appointment for a follow-up visit.

Suzanne is a senior at Northeast State College and just a few years younger than me. A stunningly beautiful young woman, she also has a warm outgoing southern personality. After a couple of visits she expresses interest in learning about the Catholic Church. As the weeks pass I wonder if the emotional bond developing between us puts us at risk of crossing some invisible line. One day our parish secretary, a gossipy lady, tells me that the Monsignor is concerned about my relationship with the 'cute young blonde'.

'Louise, you can expect me to elope any day now,' I say while keeping my face as neutral as I can.

The poor lady looks like she's about to have a heart attack. She obviously doesn't appreciate my Irish humour. After letting her suffer for a few moments I assure her my relationship with Suzanne is strictly professional. But I know this is an overstatement since the chemistry between us is real. Suzanne has become part of my fantasy life and the way I was raised, having lust in your heart is almost as great a sin as actually acting on your thoughts.

Suzanne becomes more and more interested in my personal life. She wants to know all about my family in Ireland. On one of her visits she asks if I'll take a trip with her to New Orleans to meet her family. For a moment I'm tempted to accept this invitation. I struggle to convince myself that it would be like any other visit to a friend's family. But I can't fool myself. I try to explain my situation.

'Suzanne, the rules don't allow me to date women.'

She's not discouraged. 'I was thinking we'd go as friends,' she says. 'We could check out the jazz scene and some good Creole food.'

'It's not a good idea. There's already strong chemistry between us.'

She can see that my objections are a bit half-hearted.

'What's the problem? There's no sin in going on a trip with someone.'

'Suzanne, I don't want to put myself in a compromising situation. My whole life as a Catholic priest is based on the assumption of celibacy.'

Again, Suzanne isn't impressed.

'I guess I just don't understand this idea of celibacy – seems strange that a young man like you can't have a girlfriend.'

We debate the wisdom of the proposed trip. Eventually, we arrive at an understanding that not only is the trip not a good idea but neither is the relationship.

Breaking off of the relationship with Suzanne leaves me wondering about the lifestyle I've chosen. Am I denying part of my own humanity? In truth, I know I'd like to feel free to be able to relate to women at a deeper level. It's been less than two years since I've been ordained and I'm already wondering if this way of living is more than I bargained for.

While I'm struggling with the requirement to be detached in personal relationships, I'm beginning to realize I'm somewhat disconnected at the civic level. As I go about the routine of hospital visits, confessions, weddings and funerals, I'm barely aware of the civil rights revolution underway throughout the Deep South. Although the living conditions of the black population and my fellow Irish priests' apparent unconcern had shocked me when I first arrived, I had quickly accepted the status quo. It took just a year for the newly arrived assistant pastor to embrace the conventional social norms of northeast Louisiana. If it wasn't for my distinctive accent, I could be mistaken for a Southerner.

Back in Carlow College, deep in the heart of mono-cultural rural Ireland, I'd argued passionately for racial integration. While I didn't have a real appreciation of how black people were degraded by segregation, I came to those discussions with the belief that all are created equal in the sight of God. Now, I'm unwilling to openly challenge the prevailing views of my colleagues and parishioners in the 'real' world. Racial segregation of all the Christian churches, including the Roman Catholic churches, is a fact of life in Monroe. Everyone around me accepts segregation, including the clergy. Each Saturday at noon I join other priests in Monroe for a dinner at one of the parish rectories. The group includes a couple of priests who take care of the 'coloured' parish. I never ask what we are doing to change things. When the Monsignor refers to an outspoken young black priest in our diocese as 'an uppity negro', I say nothing.

Slowly I learn about a growing movement to challenge institutional racism as it has existed in the Deep South. The movement hasn't yet arrived in northeast Louisiana. Most of the people I associate with consider the black civil rights leader Dr Martin Luther King nothing but a 'trouble-making coloured preacher'. They see the National Association for the Advancement of Colored People (NAACP) as a Communist organization.

Each evening at 6.30 pm I watch Walter Cronkite on *CBS Evening News* report the latest developments in the civil rights battle raging across the Southern states. One evening, in early June 1963, there's the story of the assassination of a young civil rights leader in the neighbouring city of Jackson, Mississippi. Medgar Evers, a peaceful man who had devoted his short life to improving the lot of his fellow blacks in Mississippi, becomes the victim of an assassin's bullet. As I go about my parish work, I hear few words of sympathy for the Evers family. (It will be more than three decades before a white supremacist, Byron De La Beckwith, is convicted of Evers' murder, a story told in the 1966 film *Ghosts of Mississippi*.)

On 28 August 1963, in the shadow of the Lincoln monument in Washington D.C., Martin Luther King is scheduled to deliver a speech. The March on Washington for Jobs and Freedom had attracted little press attention during the months preceding the event. Now there are 250,000 people gathered on the National Mall and some pundits are predicting a bloodbath.

Almost by accident I see King's speech. I'm reluctantly watching an afternoon show with the Monsignor when CBS interrupts regular programming to deliver a live report on the Washington protest. The young preacher offers a vision of an America free of racism and discrimination. I'd never before in my life seen a clergyman speak so directly and so eloquently on the issues of civil rights and social justice. It is electrifying.

Three years before King's speech, Harold Macmillan had delivered his 'winds of change' speech in South Africa, signalling the UK government's acceptance that Britain's colonial interest in Africa was coming to an end. As I watch King speak to that huge crowd in Washington, it's clear that the winds of change are blowing across the southern states of America, too. In a few short years these winds will become gale-force as thousands join the struggle for freedom and equality.

A few weeks later the racists deliver their response to King's visionary speech. The church in Birmingham, Alabama that is used for meetings by him and fellow civil rights leaders is bombed on a Sunday morning and four young girls attending Sunday school are killed. The nation is shocked. I am shocked. But still I'm a non-combatant in the struggle.

The months pass and I'm becoming more deeply engaged in the life of the Monroe parish. I've learned to balance the requirement to provide companionship for the Monsignor with my need to be closely involved with the parish. And I'm beginning, despite my silence on social issues, to get more satisfaction out of my work in ministering to the needs of parishioners. Of course, I still have no contact with Catholics in our community who are black.

It is once again thanks to the Monsignor's TV addiction that I witness another watershed moment in American history. We are watching a game show after lunch when programming is suddenly interrupted. The announcer tells us that President John F. Kennedy has been shot in Dallas, Texas – a city that's little more than a two-hour drive west of Monroe. Once I get over my sense of shock, my gut reaction is to blame the right-wing media for the vicious campaign carried on against the President. Some of the more outrageous op-ed pieces had gone so far as to suggest the President and his brother, the Attorney General, were Communists. Robert Kennedy's support for James Meredith's campaign to get into the University of Mississippi had clearly angered conservative white folks. I'd seen copies of the hate literature passed out during the

1960 presidential campaign, propaganda designed to influence the votes of uneducated rednecks. It went as far as predicting that the Pope would rule America if Kennedy was elected President. And the people who produced this trash considered themselves Christians. I'm feeling very emotional and I'm thinking, *Those hate-mongers killed my President.*

Still fresh in my mind is JFK's visit to Ireland just five months earlier, when he had captured the imagination of the nation, particularly during his trip to his ancestral home in New Ross, County Wexford. The Kennedy visit was clearly a boost in self-esteem for a people just emerging from the gloom of the 1950s. Family members had sent newspaper clippings describing the enthusiastic welcome he received at each stop on his journey. Growing up I'd heard Daddy boast about how, in 1928, he'd voted for Governor Al Smith, the first Catholic to run for the presidency. He was charmed that America's first Irish Catholic president had honoured the Irish people with a visit. The visit was also a powerful introduction to Ireland of the dynamism of the USA – the sort of dynamism I had felt when I arrived.

Now, America is in the process of laying its young president to rest. As in communities all over the country, there's an overwhelming sense of loss among our parishioners. Catholics make up a very small minority of the population in this Bible Belt town. Members of our congregation are deeply hurt over the assassination. Some believe Kennedy was shot because he was Catholic. I organize a Mass to give people an opportunity to express their grief. The church is packed with mourners for the dead president, many of them crying as if he is a family member who has been taken from them.

5.

Moving to Cajun country

In July 1964 I receive a letter from my boss, Bishop Greco, thanking me for my two years of service to the parishioners of St Matthew's and telling me that I'm to move to a town called Bunkie, to take up another post as an assistant pastor.

Bunkie, population 6,000, is in central Louisiana, over two hours south of Monroe and about 200 miles northwest of New Orleans. It sits on the dividing line between north Louisiana, which is primarily Baptist country, and south Louisiana, which has a predominantly French Catholic population. Bunkie represents a blend of these two very different cultures.

I drive into town on a warm August afternoon. On the way I notice a couple of cotton mills. This is sugar cane and cotton country. There's a railroad track running parallel to Main Street. I stop at a drugstore to ask for directions to St Anthony's Church.

'Father, you're welcome to Cajun Country!' says the woman behind the counter.

She takes the opportunity to introduce me to several customers and then provides directions. This initial encounter with Cajun hospitality leaves a favourable impression.

The first person I meet at St Anthony's rectory is the pastor, Monsignor Fred Lyons. This monsignor, a New Yorker, is youthful, attractive and highly personable. A Hollywood producer could have cast him for the role of a charismatic young priest. In addition to his responsibilities as pastor, he is also the right-hand man to Bishop Greco.

The rectory for St Anthony's Church is located in a normal residential neighbourhood. This is in sharp contrast to St Matthew's, where I'd felt isolated and disconnected from the community. A modern one-storey building, it has living accommodations for three priests and a guestroom. A short walkway joins the rectory with the Gothic-style parish church next door. This time I'll be living in a house surrounded by green vegetation – I can finally breathe again. My fellow assistant pastor, arriving just a few hours after me, is Father Bill Provosty. Bill is just a couple of years older than me. He is from Alexandria in central Louisiana, where his father is a lawyer.

Within a few days the Monsignor tells us he's travelling to Rome with Bishop Greco for a meeting of the Vatican Council.

'You have the green light to introduce the English liturgy,' he says. This is one of the innovations to come out of the Vatican Council. After centuries attending Mass celebrated in Latin, Catholics can now hear it in their own language. It seems like a sign that the Church is serious about modernizing.

The Monsignor is scarcely out of town when Bill and I go to work introducing the changes. Sunday Masses become high-energy celebrations, with people singing along to the sound of Bill's guitar. We're out to prove that a religious service doesn't have to be a boring experience. A few of the old-timers send word of their concerns to the Monsignor in Rome. Fortunately, there are no words of discouragement from Rome and we move full steam ahead.

Bill and I are treated as neighbours and invited to backyard barbecues and parties around our neighbourhood. I quickly blend into the informal social life of Bunkie and fall in love with the Cajun lifestyle. The hospitality reminds me of the neighbourliness found in rural Ireland. And with Bill as my colleague – still in his twenties, like me, and on the same wavelength – I feel like I'm finally hitting my stride. Bill is cut out of a different cloth than other priests I've met. He bubbles with energy and has a unique ability to connect with people irrespective of their background. He is just as comfortable hunting possum at night with town maintenance workers as attending a formal social function. Finally, a man with the common touch!

We discover it's easy to get things done in Bunkie. Parishioners jump in and help with whatever is happening. There's good civic spirit and all we have to do is tap into it. With the passage of time I become one of the locals. There's lots of opportunity to make a positive contribution. One program results from collaboration with the only other Irishman living in Bunkie. Fred Feeney, a native of County Roscommon, becomes my good friend and occasional golf partner. I tell him I'm considering developing a leadership program for young adults.

'Straight talk – that's what young people respond to,' says Fred, a veteran of the Korean conflict. Our Leadership Weekends are an immediate success. The word spreads on the grapevine and young people from different religions ask to participate. Highly dynamic, the weekends include a mix of music, discussions and motivational presentations. Fred plays a lead role. He has the stature and forceful personality of a Marine captain and a deep, resonant baritone voice to go with it. It's not surprising that Fred will become Mayor of Bunkie in later years.

In the process of facilitating weekend programs for young adults I discover hidden personal talents, including leadership and organizational skills. Soon, other parishes invite me to consult on programs to motivate their young people. It feels like I'm finally making a proper contribution to people's lives, which was the original focus of my vocation.

Of course, life isn't all about new initiatives and celebration. There are difficult tasks to perform, the kinds of heart-breaking human situations where priests are called to give comfort and explanation, however young and inexperienced they are. It's something I'm still getting used to: counselling people old enough to be my parents or grandparents. On one occasion I'm asked to preside at the funeral of a young soldier in a neighbouring parish. I learn he was just nineteen years old when he was shot dead in Vietnam. He's the only child of impoverished parents. His mother keeps asking me why he had to die.

'They're fighting the spread of Communism,' I say without conviction.

On another occasion, the teenage daughter of one of my best friends, a local optician, is killed in an automobile crash. One of only two children, she's killed by a train as she drives across a railroad track. Her parents are devastated and I'm at a loss to find words to console them.

In Bunkie, too, there is the shadow of segregation. The railway track that runs alongside the main street serves as a boundary, dividing the middle class white community with mostly comfortable homes from a black community where many live in old wooden shacks. The Catholic community is also segregated. Just one black person attends St Anthony's and then only rarely. He is the basketball coach at the local black high school and when he cannot get to Sunday morning Mass in his own church because of out-of-town games he comes to the evening Mass at St Anthony's.

As I am now in a parish where I feel I can make a difference and keep busy, my thoughts on what I should do to help the cause of civil rights are on the backburner.

The Monsignor comes and goes. We don't see him very much because he's often on the road with Bishop Greco. He has a private home built out in the woods, on the bayou, and this becomes his retreat where he entertains clergy and friends. I sometimes wonder about his lavish lifestyle. Despite, or perhaps because of, the lack of oversight, I thrive in my role as assistant pastor. And my social life is rewarding, too. I make regular trips with friends to Opelousas and Lafayette to eat Cajun food. And there are trips to the white sandy beaches on the Gulf Coast and to the French Quarter in New Orleans. There's the thrill of watching the Astros play baseball in the Houston Astrodome. I'm invited by friends to join them at Saints football games in Tulane Stadium in New Orleans. Watching Al Hirt on his trumpet lead 90,000 fans singing 'When the Saints Go Marching In' is worth the price of admission alone. Doesn't matter that the Saints rarely win a game.

A favourite hobby is playing a nine-hole golf course at a local state park on a course designed for duffers like myself. The best part of these outings is the Cajun cuisine dished up by the clubhouse 'pro'. At the end of nine holes there's a bowl of steaming gumbo or a plate of spiced crawfish or a generous helping of rice jambalaya.

Life in Cajun Country offers lots of opportunities to celebrate the good life. There are Roast Pig Festivals. There are Jambalaya Festivals. There are Catfish Festivals. There are Crawfish Festivals. And the Cajun music! I'm thinking, these people know how to enjoy life, not like those serious God-fearing Baptists up in northeast Louisiana.

6.

Tragedy on the home front

As I involve myself more deeply in the life of St Anthony's parish, I try to ignore what's happening back in Ireland. The bad news had started coming after my mother's death in 1963. One letter in early 1964 contains particularly distressing news: a bull on the farm attacked Andy, leaving him with a severe spinal injury. His future plans – and Daddy's – were crushed in that moment. There is some doubt as to whether he will walk again.

It gets to the point where I dread opening letters with the Irish postmark. Sometimes, fearing what's inside them, I leave the envelopes unopened for days or weeks. Some of this reluctance has to do with the knowledge that I'm so far away, there's nothing I can do to help. It's not that I don't care – it's that I feel helpless.

More recently the letters, when I finally brace myself to read them, offer some hope. I learn that Andy has left the rehabilitation hospital in Dún Laoghaire, County Dublin, and that despite the doctors' dire predictions he has stepped out of the wheelchair and begun the process of rebuilding his life. His courageous recovery makes the newspapers. Someone sends me a clipping from the *Sunday Press* with the headline, 'Andy Defied Doctors, Now Does Twist'.

Family tragedy is not limited to Andy's farm accident. In November 1964, 18 months after Mammy's death, Daddy marries

Elsie Ryan, a younger woman from Raheen, near Abbeyleix, about ten miles away from Drumagh. In December 1965 Elsie gives birth to a daughter, Patricia. This is the best news in a long while. But then there's another bad turn in Daddy's fortunes: just a few months later, in early 1966, Elsie is diagnosed with terminal cancer.

I decide to make a trip home to Ireland in the summer of 1966 for my brother Michael's wedding to his fiancé, Elsie McHugh. I'm shocked when I meet my new stepmother: it's obvious that cancer is already taking its deadly toll – she is skin and bone, a startling contrast to her bonny eight-month-old daughter. I'm particularly saddened as I discover what a warm, loving person Daddy has married. Elsie has the same personality traits I'd admired in my mother.

One morning I go with Daddy the half-mile up the road to an outlying bit of the farm to feed cattle. As we work side-by-side I tell him how sorry I am to learn of Elsie's illness.

'Tis the will of the Man Above,' he says. That's what he always says when bad things happen. The tears roll down his face. My seminary training hasn't prepared me for this kind of situation.

'I'll keep her in my prayers.'

My attempt at offering support sounds empty and insincere – even to my own ears. Inside, what I'm thinking is that Daddy is a victim of cruel bad luck. Two wives develop terminal illness within a few short years. And his firstborn son is involved in a life-altering accident. The Roman collar precludes me saying what I really feel about this tragic situation, which is that Daddy, as a devout Catholic, doesn't deserve to suffer all this misfortune.

I return to Louisiana knowing it will only be a short time until Elsie passes away. I'm wondering how Daddy will cope with another death and a tiny daughter to mind – and only four years after he buried Mammy.

Andy's accident has forced radical change at Drumagh. It is clear that he is no longer capable of the physical work required on a farm. As his mobility improves, Andy decides to leave Drumagh to start a new life in Dublin. Unable to confront Daddy directly, he leaves a note explaining his departure. His first job is in the city centre, delivering parts for an auto supply dealer. His injury prevents him from using his foot to shift gears so, with typical ingenuity, he invents a hand control for his car.

At sixty-two years of age, Daddy has to rethink all his ideas about the future. The new plan for the farm is for Michael and Elsie to take over running it. As part of this scheme Daddy builds a modest bungalow at the entrance to the driveway leading to the old homestead. It is to be a home for him, Elsie, on her rare releases from hospital, and their baby. In the meanwhile, Michael and Elsie move into the farmhouse.

Unfortunately, this is a short-lived plan. Daddy's need to direct and control everything happening on the farm is incompatible with my brother's pride and independent personality. Of all of us growing up, Michael was the most robust and wouldn't take guff from anyone, including Daddy. As a result, Michael and Elsie pack their bags and set out to build their own lives, free from the hassles of Drumagh

In 1967 Daddy sells the house and most of the farm that he had worked to transform for over three decades. He holds on to a small parcel of land to continue farming on a reduced scale. The farm and house were his pride and joy and it causes him great distress to part with the property.

As I try to get back into work in Louisiana, I cannot help but be preoccupied by the continual sense of crisis in the family in Ireland. And then the letter I've been dreading arrives: Elsie has died. She passed away in early October 1967, at the age of forty-two – less than five years after Mammy's death. Now Daddy, getting on in years, has an infant, not yet two years of age, as his sole responsibility. And I have a baby sister who has just lost her mother. A tragic situation, and I feel there's not a damn thing I can do about it.

My response to this latest tragedy is to turn inward.

I have good friends in Bunkie, but for this kind of thing there's nobody's shoulder to cry on – and there's nobody who would understand what I'm feeling. My religion tells me life is a 'vale of tears' and that personal tragedy must be accepted as God's will. That's what I've preached from the pulpit. But I'm having a difficult time coping with all this worry and anxiety – and religion doesn't seem to be of much help to me. There's too much trouble on my plate. I'm attempting to cope with my personal identity and choices as well as with family tragedies that are beyond my control.

I IMMERSE MYSELF ONCE AGAIN in my work as assistant pastor. This is my coping strategy. As time passes, my sense of disconnection from the important social changes going on around me starts to bother me again. It becomes more obvious from watching network evening news that there's a major social revolution underway throughout the Deep South. And I'm really not part of this revolution. I'm on the sidelines.

I could drive to Selma, Alabama, or Jackson, Mississippi, to join marches organized by the Southern Christian Leadership Conference, but somehow it doesn't occur to me that this is something I should do. Or maybe I'm afraid of what my white parishioners would think. Across the railroad track in Bunkie there's a whole other world that I know very little about. I'm disconnected from the black community locally, and I'm disconnected from the national movement in support of racial justice.

Locally, civil rights leaders are considered trouble-making agitators by most in the white community. Large highway signs depict Martin Luther King as a Communist. This view is widely accepted in the white community. My friends assume that as a white man I share these views – and I'm privy to many anxious, angry discussions about King and the civil rights movement. All the while, I'm a spokesman for a Church that accepts segregation as the norm. Just like in Monroe, in Bunkie I find myself dealing almost exclusively with white parishioners while a priest from a neighbouring parish ministers to the black families living across the railroad track. I'm on the wrong side of a very important issue.

My conscience is finally getting to me. I'm growing increasingly disturbed by the obvious contradictions between my personal convictions and the institutional Church's embrace of racial segregation. I begin to think the priests and nuns marching with Dr King have it right. And I start to seriously question my own assumptions and behaviour regarding race and social justice. For the first time I'm envisioning an activist role in support of human rights.

7.

A night from hell

Newspaper photos from the mid-1960s show a youthful, smiling priest not unlike the assistant pastor in *Going My Way*, the movie starring Bing Crosby. There are lots of cuttings. Whether it's speaking to the Rotary Club or at some event for the Catholic Youth Council or presenting gifts to the coaches of the high school football team or doing an event with the Catholic laymen's organization, the Knights of Columbus, or its junior wing, the Columban Squires – there I am. I'm among a handful of native-born Irish people in this part of Louisiana, so every St Patrick's Day there's some kind of cheesy feature about 'the wearing o' the green' in the local papers. One of them has me disabusing the reporter of the idea that St Patrick rid Ireland of snakes and quotes me as saying, 'From the Irish point of view he was a great man rather than a legendary leprechaun.' Clearly she had pushed one Oirish button too many.

The photos don't tell the whole story. They fail to reveal a personal struggle taking place on the inside. I'm living in a state of constant anxiety, wondering if I've outgrown the priesthood, scared about the consequences of what a change would mean.

I'm troubled on several fronts.

The assassination of Martin Luther King in April 1968 forces me to ask – yet again – what am I doing to promote civil rights and social justice? The record isn't impressive. I'm ministering to an all-white parish. And, by my silence, I appear to embrace the segregationist views of the people with whom I interact. Only once have I taken a stance that's unpopular with parishioners: when I support the use of the parochial school for the racially integrated summer Head Start program, an initiative for disadvantaged children that's part of President Lyndon Johnson's 'War on Poverty'.

I know the Catholic clergy are generally not part of the movement for social justice going on around us. There are exceptions, however, such as the Berrigan brothers, Father Daniel and Father Philip, priests who have taken a courageous and high-profile stand against the Vietnam War. Now, at this time of historic social unrest, I'm again questioning myself: am I, by my non-involvement, part of the problem?

Reading a book of Dr King's sermons leads me to more questions. King argues that the Christian message cannot be separated from the issue of social justice. I had argued this position almost a decade earlier in the seminary. I have to ask myself: what happened to the values I espoused as a student in Carlow College? My Sunday sermons stop well short of advocating racial justice and equality. In truth, I'm reluctant to say anything that might offend my white, middle class friends. Not exactly a role model for others to follow.

Although I feel like the Church impedes my evolution in some ways, it stimulates it in others. It's a time of historic change - a consequence of the Second Vatican Council – and I'm excited about what the future has to offer. A new spirit is creating major changes, including an exodus of priests from the ministry. Unfortunately, those leaving are some of the most progressive individuals. Though I'm becoming somewhat disillusioned with the Church as an institution, I still hope that positive change is possible.

By 1968 Bobby Kennedy is the man I most admire in American politics and I am excited about his run for the presidency. His book, *To Seek a Newer World* (1967), has made a deep impression.

His passionate demand that society do something about poverty hits a chord and appeals to those egalitarian aspirations I've simply chosen to ignore. Now I begin to understand that as a self-styled champion of the poor and disadvantaged, it's not so much that I'm missing in action when it comes to social justice, but that I'm more of a draft dodger. Kennedy's vision feels like something that I can be part of, something that will help me reactivate my best instincts.

For the first time, I'm taking an active interest in American politics and find myself inspired by Kennedy's message of justice and his presidential campaign. Alone in the living room of St Anthony's rectory late at night, I'm eagerly following the results of the Democratic Party's presidential primary in California as they are broadcast live. The pundits have already declared Kennedy a victor, and with a win in California it seems as if becoming the Democratic nominee for president is now within his grasp.

Then, suddenly, it's over. Kennedy is shot while making his way through the kitchen of the Ambassador Hotel in Los Angeles, shortly after making a victory speech to his supporters. Twenty-six hours later, he is dead.

I am bitterly disappointed, both for the future of the country and for my own nascent aspirations to be a part of making society better. I'd fancied that I might seek opportunities for public service if Kennedy was elected. Dreams of joining the Bobby Kennedy bandwagon disappear with the assassin's bullet.

Ironically, not long after the Kennedy assassination comes an opportunity for celebration. By 1968 I've completed the five years of residency needed to become a naturalized United States citizen. Although some other Irish priests pass on this opportunity, for me it makes sense. If I'm going to live my life in the USA, I might as well have the benefits of citizenship. Like my father before me, who also became a citizen, I want to engage with American life and gain the right to vote. And it's happening at a time when I'm becoming more and more politically and socially aware. Voting for Bobby Kennedy was going to be my first exercise of citizenship.

On the day of the swearing-in ceremony, my across-the-street neighbour, Harriet 'Booby' Reed, gives a surprise party – a backyard barbecue – and produces a flag-bedecked cake. The whole neighbourhood joins in the celebration. However, there are some mixed feelings as my American citizenship comes with a steep price: I've been led to believe I'll have to give up my Irish citizenship and I have decided to make that sacrifice. (Many years later I discover that I can hold dual citizenship and immediately I get a new Irish passport.)

Around the same time, on the family front, Daddy's life seems to take a positive turn. He writes to tell me of his plans to get married again, saying he needs to provide a mother for Patricia and asking for my 'blessing'. I write back to express full support. I'm thinking that after all he's been through, this might represent a change in his fortunes.

In October 1968, Daddy marries Maura Conroy, a woman in her mid-forties from near Portlaoise. Despite this there is ongoing anxiety in the family about the situation in Drumagh. The marriage is the result of match-making by a priest friend of my father's. The marriage to Elsie was arranged by the same priest. While Elsie was a lovely woman, we are not confident that this method of finding wives is a fail-safe recipe for living happily ever after.

As things seem more settled in Ireland, and I put years of family upheaval in the rear-view mirror, I should be feeling more settled myself. But I have this awful feeling that things will get worse before they get better. This is partly because I'm now very seriously considering what I'm doing in the priesthood.

It's not just the lack of social involvement that concerns me, of greater concern is the issue of celibacy and how it will affect me in the future. In the past, when I'd found myself attracted to a particular woman, I'd kept the relationships at a platonic level, as required. Recently, though, I've experienced a strong attraction to a young woman I met through youth work in Bunkie. I've been exceedingly careful not to engage in inappropriate behaviour because the idea of living a double life is not an option I'm ready to consider. Nonetheless, it has made me take a long, hard look at my situation and what I want in life.

I'm constantly questioning the basic values of clerical life and I've come to the conclusion that celibacy is psychologically damaging in the lives of some priests – and I don't want to be one of them. I've crossed an important threshold in my thinking. I'm finally willing and able to acknowledge to myself that I have a need for love and intimacy, and it will not be satisfied within the celibate lifestyle.

I'm still a young man – just thirty years of age. I look around and see older priests compensating for celibacy in various ways. For some, it's alcohol abuse. For others, it's unhealthy relationships. Our diocese has its share of 'problem' priests – though this issue is never discussed at meetings of clergy. Nor, unfortunately, will it be for decades to come.

Bishop Greco regularly imports priests who have gotten into trouble in other dioceses: some come down to Louisiana from French-speaking parts of Canada; a few are constantly on the move from one parish to another. Such moves in personnel are a response to any suggestion of 'scandal'. By definition, scandal is something the Church tries to avoid and it is not discussed. However, through the clerical grapevine I hear one of the migrants coming to Bunkie on a temporary assignment has had some problems resulting from his interactions with young boys. The rumour about our new colleague may be without foundation, but it causes Bill and me considerable anxiety. We tacitly agree to keep an eye on him and be alert to any suggestion of uneasiness about him. He remains in Bunkie for about a year before moving on.

It will be decades later before I hear the word 'paedophile' as a description of priests who abuse children. I come from a typically repressed and repressive Irish Catholic background where sexuality was referred to only vaguely, and then as something understood to be gravely sinful. We were not given a vocabulary to

45

discuss such things. As a heterosexual man, the concept of sexual attraction to children is outside my frame of reference. I don't link it to the idea I grew up with, of men 'interfering' with boys, the kind of adults you instinctively knew to avoid. In a world where we are aware of the importance of child protection, it is hard to grasp a time when the concept simply did not exist. So, in the Ireland I grew up in – certainly in my experience – men who might interfere with you were like the bogeyman, a hazy spectre whose path you might be unlucky enough to cross. You weren't quite sure what 'interfering' meant, but you guessed it was something 'dirty' (i.e. sexual). By definition, if you were interfered with it was something to be ashamed of. For example, a transient workman on our farm got me alone on a couple of occasions and played with my private parts. While I was pretty annoyed and repulsed, I didn't make much of it at the time, said nothing to anybody, and steered clear of him until the end of the season when he moved on. In the scheme of things that I would later feel were formative influences, this incident did not come particularly high in the rankings. I realise that other people would have had a different reaction. There were no sexual overtures from men in authority during my time in Knockbeg or Carlow College.

As a young priest, rape and systematic abuse of children are simply not on my radar. So, insofar as I give the nature of my new colleague's rumoured behaviour any thought, I presume he suffers from some kind of highly unusual personality disorder that the Church authorities are dealing with. In my short time in the priesthood I've become aware of lots of discontented men who bury themselves in everything from drink to golf, and this sounds like a particularly unusual version of a troublesome priest needing management. It never occurs to me to think of the issue in legal terms or as a systemic issue.

Now, I look back on my ignorance and naïvete with a sense of shame. I like to think that had I remained in the ministry I would have woken up to the nature of the problem sooner rather than later, asked the right questions and taken the correct action when required. But better men than me failed dismally in meeting that moral and legal obligation.

I'm beginning to wonder if celibacy may be contributing to some of the clergy problems I see around me and I'm concerned. How will celibacy impact my future – my mental health? How will I compensate for the lack of sexual fulfilment?

At first I try to banish stress-filled thoughts about the future. Simply re-evaluating my commitment to celibacy is enough to cause sleepless nights. This isn't an inconsequential matter. What if I decide I no longer want to be a priest? That would shock and disappoint many people, particularly my family in Ireland. I guess I am in a similar place to a married man considering the possibility that his marriage is on the rocks. But despite my concerns, I'm not yet ready to take the radical step of asking the Church for a 'divorce'.

And then, something happens that brings the issue of celibacy front and centre.

In the neighbouring city of Alexandria, a big celebration is planned to mark the fiftieth anniversary of Bishop's Greco's ordination to the priesthood. The bishop enjoys a well-deserved national reputation for his outstanding work in providing services for individuals with mental disabilities. Monsignor Fred tells me about the reception and suggests it would be appropriate to make an appearance. I make the thirty-five-mile trip north to join my colleagues. When I arrive, the room is already crowded with priests. I order a scotch and water. And then I have another. As the alcohol takes over I'm feeling I don't belong here. These clerical gatherings are not my thing. But I'm not quite sure what it is about them that make me so uncomfortable.

The evening wears on and I'm becoming inebriated. This is a totally new sensation. I'd never even had a drink of alcohol until my late twenties, and my experience handling liquor is very limited. The drinks take their toll.

Mercifully, I find an excuse to escape the party while I can still walk. As I amble to the parking lot I take off my collar and the fresh air revives me a bit. It takes some work to find my Pontiac, but soon I'm driving down south towards Bunkie on the main winding two-lane highway, with the window open and country tunes blasting from the radio.

Before too long, as if on autopilot, I wheel my car into the pebbled parking lot of a tavern about ten miles south of Alexandria. The neon beer signs in the windows are blazing, the honky-tonk music is blaring from the jukebox and another drink or two seems in order. Any local would have recognized this joint as a house of ill repute from the conveniently attached motel advertising rooms by the hour. But this lamb wanders unsteadily but willingly into the briar patch.

After a couple of drinks at the bar I'm feeling no pain and an attractive girl, who hasn't wasted money on excessive clothing, hitches up onto the stool next to me.

'Would you like to come back to my room? We can have fun.'

I hear a voice that sounds just like mine only somewhat slurred say, 'Yes, yes I would.' She puts her arm through mine and off we go.

She smiles, quickly undresses and I fumble nervously with my clothes. I didn't know what I thought I was buying for $50, but it sure wasn't lovemaking, warmth or emotion. Just sex. Totally impersonal. Though certainly noteworthy for a complete novice, the event leaves me empty and eager to get out of there.

Rolling out onto the highway I wish I could say I feel this way or that way after the fact but, frankly, I am too busy trying to navigate my way home. I seem to be managing okay until suddenly there's a major confrontation between my car and an electricity pole.

Soon a patrol car appears and a young policeman helps me get out of my totalled car. He offers me a ride home to Bunkie. Tells me I've succeeded in knocking out the power for the entire town of Cheneyville.

'What part of Ireland are you from?' the policeman asks.

'I grew up in County Laois, about sixty miles from Dublin.'

'I'm told my great grandmother was from Cork,' he says.

As we drive through the total darkness, I'm thinking how this has become the night from hell.

The next morning I'm a little sore, have a headache, but feel better than I have any right to. Looking in the mirror, however, isn't such a good idea. I look like something out of a cheesy horror movie. The dark circles under my eyes are complemented by the big gash on my lower lip. A long, hot shower helps a little. There's a serious effort to clean up the scars before presenting myself as celebrant of the seven o'clock morning Mass. Inside I am burning up with shame and embarrassment. I have flashbacks of the night before, but nothing's that's a source of pleasure. Though I know it's impossible I can't help thinking that people must be able to see that I'm a fallen man. And if they can't, God certainly can. It is probably the most excruciating situation I have been in as a priest. And it's all of my own making.

Over the next few days I ease back into my routine, hoping that I can put that shameful night behind me. But it's not to be, not yet anyway. While I don't typically believe that God directly intervenes in the affairs of ordinary humans like myself, I'm beginning to believe that this time He has a message for me. This message – perhaps I should say this burning message – arrives a few days later when it becomes clear that my encounter with that young lady has left me with more than just a guilty conscience.

Guilty and embarrassed, I trudge off to see one of two local doctors in Bunkie. We don't know each other. He is not a Catholic and so not a member of our congregation. Awkwardly, I tell him the details of my encounter in the motel.

'Reverend, you're not the first to walk out of that gin mill with a reminder of the visit – you got what you paid for!' the doctor says with a trace of a smile.

I appreciate his attempt at humour, but it doesn't help as much as the shot that soon clears everything up.

I feel deeply ashamed. I'm shocked at what I've allowed to happen. What kind of priest – what kind of man – am I? Clearly, the time for serious reflection is long overdue.

I enter a period of intense introspection. I have endless conversations with myself and experience a deep sense of aloneness. Though I share my encounter in the road-house in confession, to seek absolution, I feel I can't talk to other priests about my uneasiness in the priesthood. Gradually, I come to the conclusion that the celibate lifestyle is becoming destructive. The encounter in the motel begins to look more and more like a career-defining experience.

Six years after ordination I've come to a serious fork in the road. Should I ignore what happened, or should I face up to the fact that I'm not cut out for the celibate lifestyle? These life-changing questions weigh heavily.

My gut is telling me that my days in the priesthood are numbered.

8.

Deciding to bail out of the ministry

In Carlow College I'd read stories about men who left the priesthood and women who left the convent. The title of one of these books, *I Leap Over the Wall* (1949), seemed to suggest that leaving religious life was analogous to getting out of prison. Actually, the author of this book, Monica Baldwin, wrote eloquently about the difficulties of adjusting to life on the outside after living 28 years behind the walls of an enclosed convent.

It's clear a decision on my part to leave the ministry will add to Daddy's troubles. In Ireland there's still considerable stigma associated with being an ex-priest. There was even a stigma associated with leaving the seminary; those who opted out were called 'spoiled priests'. When I was growing up, neighbours talked in hushed tones about a young man who had studied in Rome for several years and had then returned home to our parish. The way they talked about him, it was as if he had contracted some fatal disease. But I'm beginning to see my situation as a matter of self-preservation – no matter what the burden of guilt might be.

I consider my career options and write a letter to the Attorney General of Louisiana, asking for information about the requirements for working as a counsellor or psychotherapist. I guess I'm assuming the AG's office is the best place to go for guidance on the regulations governing any professional position in the state.

I indicate in my letter that the inquiry is confidential and that I'm merely considering the possibility of a career change.

I receive no response from the AG's office. However, I soon discover that the request for my letter to be treated as confidential has been ignored. As I sit reading the newspaper late on a Sunday afternoon, I receive a telephone call from one of the Bishop's assistants. He expresses an urgent need to meet with me. I've no idea what it's about. Am I about to be transferred to another parish? Has my recent activity in support of the local Head Start program resulted in parishioner complaints? One hour after the telephone call the Bishop's emissary is standing in my office. It turns out that the Attorney General, a loyal member of the Knights of Columbus, has shared my letter with Bishop Greco.

'Father Deevy, please don't leave us,' my visitor pleads. 'You're one of our best men in the diocese.'

I'm momentarily speechless. My secret is no longer a secret?

'Look Father, I appreciate your concern – but I just don't want to talk about this right now ... I'm planning to go see the Bishop.'

'The bishop wants you to stay – we all want you to stay.'

'Well, I haven't made a final decision to leave ... I need some more time.'

My visitor doesn't get the message.

'Father, if you would like a break from parish work, we have a number of chaplaincies you might consider.'

Again, I tell him I'll discuss my situation personally with Bishop Greco.

Deep down, I'm feeling violated. I have no desire to engage with the Bishop's emissary. I hardly know this priest – and how can I explain myself to someone whose mission is to convince me to stay? The conversation goes nowhere and after a short time my visitor leaves. I'm too agitated to go back to reading the newspaper.

Initially I'm feeling betrayed by the Attorney General and more than a bit stupid. It hadn't occurred to me that in America this kind of collusion would go on between Church and civil authorities. And then I realize that this isn't all bad. I'm forced to make a decision: leave the ministry or get on with life. It's beginning to look like an easy choice.

Feeling stressed out, I decide it's time to go away for a few days for a conversation with myself. It will be time-out in a place where I don't have to wear a Roman collar or be identified as a clergyman.

I drive east from Bunkie, through Mississippi and Alabama and on to Pensacola on the Gulf Coast. Friends in Bunkie have loaned me their beach house on Santa Rosa Island. This is the most beautiful beach I've ever seen – miles and miles of fine sand that's almost the colour of snow. No crowds – just the occasional couple spread out on beach towels, soaking up the sun. The warm Gulf water splashing on my feet has a soothing effect. It's the perfect place to figure out what I'm going to do.

I HAVE TO ADMIT TO MYSELF that I don't really know what made me decide to seek the priesthood in the first place. As children and teenagers, all aspects of our lives were dominated by religion. Devotion was in the air we breathed. Daddy blessed the horses with holy water before going to work in the fields. In the early years of our childhood, when he was still using a horse and cart to bring milk to the creamery, Daddy would bring us along on summer mornings and we would manage to fit in a rosary on the way. Later, when we got a van, he'd say 'In the name of God' as he turned the ignition key when setting out on a journey of any distance. There was always Grace before meals, of course, and work came to a halt when the Angelus bell rang out at midday. We never ate meat on Fridays, and fasting during Lent was a serious business.

Every night there was the family rosary, with each of us taking turns to lead one of the decades. Daddy would often interrupt me, demanding that I enunciate the prayers louder and more clearly. Maybe he was trying to train me for preaching in later life. I always felt embarrassed by his admonitions. When we got the 'trimmings' after the rosary, we prayed for all kinds of good causes. We prayed for fine weather. We prayed for the conversion of Russia. We prayed for the pagans in Africa. We prayed for vocations to the priesthood. When some of the animals were sick, we prayed for their recovery. If one of the babies Mammy had delivered was sick, we prayed for the baby.

At Mass on Sunday, while Mammy was lost in prayer, her rosary beads in her hand, Daddy kept a watchful eye on all of us to make sure that we were concentrating and there was no fidgeting or looking around. Daddy saw himself as having direct responsibility from God as head of the family – an assumption strongly supported from the pulpit. On the way home from Mass, Daddy would give a ringing endorsement to the parish priest if he had condemned any evidence of moral decay in the parish. He was a big fan of 'fire and brimstone' sermons. Thankfully, Daddy took seriously the admonition about not working on the Sabbath, so on that day we did only the work necessary for sustaining the farm operation – milking cows, feeding calves and taking care of the needs of other animals. (If the weather was very bad and there was danger of losing the harvest, the priest would give farmers 'permission' to harvest crops on Sunday.)

At school in Knockbeg the day began with morning Mass and ended with night prayer. A vocation to the priesthood was described as the highest calling, higher than marriage. I knew this from home, where a visit by a priest was considered a big event and it was obvious that having a member of the family ordained a priest was a great honour and a special blessing. As students we were constantly reminded that a decision to go forward for the priesthood had to be voluntary and free of any coercion. The calling to the priesthood came directly from God. It was assumed all students would be open to the call. I knew my parents had sent me to Knockbeg in the hope I might discover a vocation. However, they too understood that vocations came from God.

I began senior year feeling the pressure to come up with a career decision. The months passed and I was still agonizing. A number of classmates declared their intention of going on to study for the priesthood, an option I was still considering. The popular slogan 'once a priest, always a priest' suggested there was no going back once you joined. That caused me considerable anxiety.

One afternoon a classmate dropped dead on the football field. He was a close friend and his sudden death left me thinking about mortality and the afterlife. A few weeks later the Rector died, also suddenly. On the day of the Rector's funeral, Daddy turned up with a cousin of his from New York. She worked as a magazine journalist for the Hearst Corporation and was particularly interested in the rituals surrounding an Irish wake and funeral. She wanted to photograph everything. Daddy was very proud, showing her off and showing everything off to her, introducing her to the priests, demonstrating the strength of the faith in the old country. I was glad to excuse myself to join the funeral procession.

These two deaths, both resulting from heart conditions, left me thinking that life was fragile and uncertain. I decided priesthood was the right option for me. There was a certain amount of youthful idealism in the decision. I had visions of myself as a pastor who would be on the side of the less advantaged in society.

Almost one-third of my Leaving Certificate class entered the seminary, which was about average at the time. Seminary life resembled army boot camp. It was designed to be a tough experience that would separate the weak from the strong. A substantial percentage of any entering class wouldn't be expected to survive the experience.

On the day of arrival we trooped into the Senior Chapel for the solemn Reading of the Rules. 'Silence will be observed at all times except ...' were the opening words of one of the rules. The rules were very detailed. No secular newspapers. No food to be obtained from the outside. No visiting of other students' rooms. No leaving campus without express permission of the Dean. For some rule violations the consequence was automatic expulsion. The main gate leading out on to the street remained closed at all times. The gatekeeper made sure that nobody left and that no un-authorized individuals came in. The high stone walls surrounding the college gave the campus a claustrophobic feeling.

We were told this experience would prepare us for the tempta-tions that would confront us when we went abroad. We were led to believe that if we survived the rigours of life at Carlow College, we would have the character to withstand whatever challenges we might encounter.

From the beginning I decided I would conform to all the ex-pectations. It was at a time in my life when I rarely questioned any-thing I was told by a person in authority. I adapted quickly to this regimented life. Fellow students called me 'the professor' because of my studious behaviour. At the end of first year I was awarded first prize in English, and as a reward received books by G.K. Ches-terton, Hillaire Belloc and Evelyn Waugh – all Catholic writers, of course. For the first time I felt comfortable in my academic abilities and I enjoyed that side of seminary life.

My least favourite activity in the seminary was the mandatory walk on Wednesday afternoons. We would march, two by two, down Carlow's main street and then out into the countryside for several miles. On these walks we wore black suits and hats and, for reasons unknown, carried a cane. One day I had the perverse thought that the canes were intended to provide defence in case we were attacked by a group of beautiful women. The experience of parading down the main street in town was particularly uncom-fortable. I kept hoping no neighbours from home would recognize me on one of these walks. Of course that wasn't likely to happen since, like soldiers in an army unit, we all looked alike.

I also dreaded the Saturday evening talk by the Junior Dean, a humourless man who delivered stern warnings about rule viola-tions. There were common themes in talks by the Dean and in ser-mons at retreats: the priesthood was a special vocation and priests were set apart from the rest of men. Celibacy was a superior way of life. To live the celibate life it was necessary to avoid relationships with the opposite sex. The best way to avoid getting into trouble after ordination was to cultivate relationships with priests rather than getting involved with laypeople.

After completing two years devoted to the study of philosophy and the liberal arts, I moved on to the School of Theology. I read everything I could find on the role of religion in the modern world. At times I would get bored and for escape would bury myself in detective novels. My other form of escape was walking the pathway that went around the edges of the football field. I would have numerous talks with myself on these solitary walks. Many of these conversations focused on whether I'd be able to live up to a vow of celibacy after I got to the United States.

I found the rules to be more irritating as the years passed. We were young men getting ready to go abroad but were still being treated like adolescents. Obedience and conformity were the most important virtues. Once I had a visit from family friends who, not knowing the rules, brought me a bag of fruit. I didn't want to be discourteous so I took the contraband goods. As I brought the bag back into the building the Senior Dean made a big song and dance about confiscating it. I wanted to tell him where to go, but I knew that would have resulted in my becoming an ex-seminarian by nightfall. I did what always did – I accepted his rebuke and said nothing.

As I think about all this now, on the white sandy beaches of Santa Rosa Island, I come to realize that my decision to join the priesthood was driven by the culture in which I grew up, and particularly by my father's influence. And I have to admit that it was driven by these at least as much, if not more, than any deep personal convictions.

As I leave Santa Rosa, I'm almost certain that I am about to reverse the decision I'd made as a teenager in Knockbeg twelve years earlier. On the long drive back from Florida the phrase that keeps going through my mind is simply, 'I'm outta here'.

I stop in Hattiesburg, Mississippi, for an overnight visit with a former Carlow College classmate. Peter is one of those I most admire from seminary days. He's a quiet, down-to-earth man from the west of Ireland. In his low-key way he's earned the admiration of Mississippi blacks because of his strong support of the NAACP. Ironically, most of his classmates back in Carlow College would not have considered him likely to take a strong stand in support of civil rights. But here he is, living proof that the Church can foster social engagement. Over drinks and a steak we talk late into the night.

I tell him that back when we were ordained, I would never have thought I'd be one of the first of our class to leave the priesthood. Though he's the same age as me, Peter is wise and philosophical and reminds me that our lives back in Carlow were very cocooned and that our circumstances have changed utterly since then. He states the obvious: change is a part of life and inevitably I've changed, as has he. As one of those working towards a more progressive Church, he's just sorry to be losing a friend and colleague who shares his vision for a Church that is socially engaged.

Peter is very patient as I go back and forth, thrashing it all out. It is the toughest decision I've ever had to make and he is the first person to whom I've revealed the turmoil I've been experiencing. I keep reiterating that I'm not expecting him to give me any answers, that I know it's a very personal decision, one I have to make on my own.

He asks if I can pin down what finally triggered the decision I appear to be reaching.

I say that there's lots of stuff – I've been so let down by so many of the Church's pastoral shortcomings since I arrived in Louisiana – but that if I'm being really honest, I would probably stay and try to make things better if it wasn't for celibacy.

THE PROSPECT OF LIFELONG CELIBACY was an ongoing issue when I was in the seminary. At times it looked overwhelming and

I'd make plans to leave. But each time that happened I'd reconsider after discussion with a spiritual director. At the end of third year, realizing that mine had been a mostly sheltered life up to that point, I decided I had to get a taste of the 'real' world. I planned to spend the summer working in London, a decision that was not greeted with enthusiasm by my father, but I stood my ground. In my mind the time away would help me decide if I really wanted to commit myself to a life in the ministry.

Within a couple of days I had a job as a barman in a pub in Camden Town and a small room in a rundown tenement house. My living conditions were primitive, with just a mattress on the floor, a sink and a gas stove. Camden had become a Mecca for the thousands of Irishmen who, for decades, had fled the poverty of rural Ireland and felt like outcasts in London. I saw many drinking late into the night to bury their loneliness and sense of isolation. I wondered if an education system that stressed the historic injustices of British rule in Ireland might not be having an unfortunate consequence: these Irishmen felt like aliens in a foreign land.

I made friends with a young Dubliner called Bill, who wasn't like the regular customers. He was interested in debate. Sometimes after closing Bill and I would go to a Wimpy bar and chat for hours. He was a member of the Communist Party and was surprised when I told him I was a student for the priesthood. 'How do you know you want to live as a priest if you haven't been with a woman?' he asked.

One night Bill asked me to accompany him to Soho. When we got there I discovered our destination was a brothel staffed with young Irish girls. We were ushered into a small waiting room. Bill departed with one of the girls into a back room. A young woman asked if this was my first visit. I nodded. After a moment of nervous silence I told her I needed to step outside and that I'd be back in a minute. I started walking down the street and continued walking until I was back in Camden Town. I assumed Bill thought he was doing me a favour. I considered the encounter in Soho to be a test of my commitment to celibacy. I had passed. I could go back to the seminary secure in the knowledge that I had overcome temptation.

That autumn I found the winds of change were beginning to blow through Carlow College. Some of the more archaic rules were changed and the Wednesday afternoon walks were abolished. There was excitement about the election of Pope John XXIII, and optimism that the upcoming Second Vatican Council would go a long way towards modernizing the Church. I began to see 'light at the end of the tunnel' and started to think about what life would be like when I got to Louisiana.

At the end of my fifth year, in 1961, we were ordained as deacons, a ceremony in which I pledged myself to a life of celibacy. The ceremony was preceded by a week of silent retreat. I had agonized many times over this step. While I had the normal sex drive of any young man of my age, I somehow accepted the centuries-old premise that celibacy was a viable alternative to the married state. In the end I had decided that I couldn't realistically say I'd observe a lifelong vow of celibacy. What I could do was make a commitment to a genuine effort and to take the responsibility 'one day at a time'.

On the morning of the ceremony, robed in long white vestments, I walked into the sanctuary of Carlow Cathedral. There were thirty of us lined up in a semicircle, lying prostrate on the hard floor. Somewhere in the back of my mind flashed an image of us as lambs being led to the slaughter. I quickly banished the thought. As we recited the Litany of the Saints in Latin, I felt the perspiration dripping down my back. The ceremony was over in two hours and then we walked out to accept the congratulations of fellow students. The whole experience was draining. I accepted the fact I was now 'married' to the Church. There could be no turning back.

As I go through it all with Peter, I know I simply cannot imagine living a celibate life for the rest of my life. I think about a number of the priests I'd known who had fallen in love and left the priesthood to get married. For these men the choice was between the priesthood and the love of a woman. In my case there are no marriage plans – though I'm hoping this is something that may happen in the future. Right now my primary concern is regarding the appropriateness of celibacy as a lifestyle. After all the soul-searching, I know I want to be free to live life as I see fit – and this includes the possibility of sexual relationships.

We continue to chat late into the night. Next morning, as I get ready for the final leg of my journey back to Bunkie, Peter and I say our goodbyes and promise to stay in touch.

The months of soul-searching finally lead to a definite decision to make a career change. Apart from celibacy, I've outgrown the priesthood as a lifestyle. My decision isn't much different from that of a nurse or a teacher deciding to give up on hospital or classroom work and change direction. I'm ready to leave a life that offers long-term security for a future full of uncertainty. I'm hoping I will be able to find a new life that allows me to continue to be of service to people.

Back in Bunkie I craft a long letter to Bishop Greco, outlining the reasons for seeking a leave of absence from the ministry. I say that there are two reasons why I'm making the request. First, my conviction that celibacy is 'an impossible way of life' for me. I write:

> It is clear that some priests reach the Pauline ideal and for them celibacy is a beautiful creative way of life. For me it is a destructive way of living for which I am emotionally and psychologically unsuited. Seven years ago I freely accepted this vow, knowing what it involved in the way of personal sacrifice. At that time I had reservations about the value of celibacy, but I willingly accepted it as a sine qua non for the priesthood I sought. The doubts I had then have increased to the point where my life has become a misery.

Second, I invoke my concerns regarding the teaching of the Church on birth control. In the wake of Pope Paul VI's encyclical letter, *Humanae Vitae*, rejecting all forms of artificial birth control, this is a hot-button topic that is causing massive upset and debate throughout the Catholic world, so it's a plausible line of argument:

> Pope Paul's encyclical, *Humanae Vitae*, created a spiritual crisis for me as it has created a crisis for many Catholic couples and priests. I have studied the Letter, prayed about it and tried to convince myself to follow its teaching. Yet, in the matter of birth control, I find myself using double-talk and all sorts of casuistry in counselling to be true to the deep convictions of my own mind ... Today people will not accept confusing and evasive answers to their problems. It would be neither Christian nor humane for me to guide couples with principles that run contrary to my deepest convictions. It would be dishonest and indecent for me to continue using my privileged position as an ordained priest to teach morality formally rejected by the Church's magisterium. Because of this conflict between Church teaching and conscience, I have chosen silence. To turn a blind eye to this encyclical demands a total lack of integrity.

In truth, I know that referring to qualms of conscience is a smokescreen since I'm already comfortable telling people to follow their conscience on moral issues. I think of a family where the mother experiences severe psychotic post-partum depression after each birth. The couple are devout Catholics and take church teaching on artificial birth control seriously. The husband is deeply concerned about his wife's psychotic episodes and worried for the safety of his young children.

One day he asks me if I'd approve some form of artificial prevention for them, given his wife's serious mental condition. He wants my 'permission'. As a spokesperson for the Church, I'm expected to tell them that artificial birth control is morally wrong.

'Follow your conscience,' I say. 'Do what you think is right.'

Hypocritically, I sidestep the issue and secretly hope they'll have the good sense to avoid a new pregnancy. Just as I don't want people telling me how to live my life, I don't want to be in a position of telling others how to live theirs. I'm developing a growing distaste for any kind of moralizing. I've evolved to the point where I'm increasingly uncomfortable defining 'good' and 'bad' behaviour.

When the Pope made it official that Catholic women may not use contraceptives, he opposed the recommendation of his own advisory group. His stance in *Humanae Vitae* is a global news event and many – both inside and outside the Church – seem surprised by it. I don't take much notice. I've already concluded that I shouldn't be telling people how to behave in the bedroom.

My letter to Bishop Greco is followed by a visit to his residence in Alexandria on a Sunday night in July 1969. The Bishop expresses sadness at my decision to leave. I thank him for courtesies extended during my years with the diocese of Alexandria and then I walk out, knowing I've crossed another difficult threshold, another point of no return.

9.

A giant leap into the unknown

On Sunday, 20 July 1969, Neil Armstrong lands on the moon. He utters the historic words, 'That's one small step for man, one giant leap for mankind.' The following Sunday, 27 July, I am making a giant leap in my life's journey. After seven years in the priesthood I am moving into a new life as a layman.

It's time to make my 'divorce' public, but I don't want to disappear into the sunset without saying a proper goodbye to parishioners. The congregation in St Anthony's Church listen in stunned silence as I announce at Sunday Masses that I'm taking a 'leave of absence' from the ministry. Understandably, many friends are disappointed. Over the years in Bunkie I've developed a warm bond of friendship with the people I'm leaving.

I keep my message from the pulpit brief. No apologies. No excuses. No moralizing. Just a heartfelt 'thank you' for all the kindness I've received. After each Mass parishioners gather outside the sacristy to wish me well. It feels like leaving 'family', and this makes it all the more difficult.

My last day in the ministry ends with the six o'clock evening Mass. Having completed my final official duty, I return to the empty rectory and remove the Roman collar and cassock. Then I pick up a few remaining belongings and walk out of this building that has been my home for five years. The car with all my possessions is already packed and ready for the road.

As the red sun goes down over the western Texan sky, I drive out of Bunkie and head south on Highway 71. I've chosen Baton Rouge, the capital of Louisiana, to be my provisional home. As I travel south I'm aware this is more than a two-hour trip. What's involved is a profound change in my approach to life. Up to this time I've been concerned with meeting the expectations of others. I've listened to external voices. Now, I'll have to listen to the voices within. There will be no script to follow or institution to tell me what to do. I'm entering a new world.

It seems as if I've lived all of my life in some kind of psycho-logical 'prison', always trying to please other people and never feel-ing I'm completely my own person. Maybe this is my own doing. Growing up in a patriarchal home, I'd experienced the control of an authoritarian father. The years in seminary, with its rigid rules, were destructive of personal freedom, as they were designed to be. In a variety of ways the institutional Church conditioned me to think and to act in a certain way – but not to think for myself. Now I'm hoping that's all behind me. This evening, as I drive down the highway, I'm feeling liberated. The words of Martin Luther King's 'I have a Dream' speech come to mind: 'Thank God almighty ... free at last!'

I can't help thinking back to the celebrations at home the day after my ordination. That was part of the tradition: the day after the ordination ceremony the newly ordained young men went to their respective towns and villages to celebrate a First Mass. I said my First Mass in Mayo Parish church on 10 June 1962. On that June morning a hundred neighbours and friends joined the family on the lawn in Drumagh for an outdoor reception. It was a beautiful sunny day and the roses and other flowers were in full bloom; you could smell the sweet aroma from the meadow in front of the house. The tables were dressed with white Irish linen and sparkling silverware. It had all the trappings of a wedding celebration.

That had been a proud moment for the family and the culmination of Daddy's ambitions – a son a priest, a massive source of status in a rural Irish parish. Not only that, but two daughters had entered religious life. Daddy had conservative ideas about women and in consecrating their lives to God, Daddy no doubt believed his daughters would lead lives of great virtue, piety and hard work, preserve their purity and bring blessings on the family. For a man of humble beginnings, with such a staunch devotion to the Church, he must have considered himself truly blessed by God at that moment. He seemed to be surrounded by proof that his was the embodiment of an upstanding, prosperous Catholic family. The troubles that assailed him in the years that followed seemed almost Old Testament in their cruelty, designed to cut him back down to size.

Seven years since my ordination and so much has changed, both in our family and in the world. I'm hoping my father and my siblings will understand what I have chosen to do. I decide not to think about them any more today. I sit back, begin to relax and start enjoying the twilight and the Cajun music on the car radio. I'd developed an appreciation of this music during the years in Bunkie. Like much traditional Irish music, this music was born out of a history of struggle. This evening the music of a Cajun fiddler suits my reflective mood.

I'm wondering what the future has in store. The immediate concern is survival. Will I be able to find a job? Have I got enough money to get by until I find employment? My bank account is rather small and I've no idea of what tomorrow will bring. How am I going to take care of myself? Will I settle in Baton Rouge or move on to some other place? I tell myself I'll worry about these things tomorrow. Despite the circumstances, I'm already looking forward to getting started on something new.

When I reach Krotz Springs, halfway to Baton Rouge, I pull into a truck stop to get a hamburger and gather my thoughts. I'd come to like big sprawling truck stops for the anonymity they provide. People come and go and no one takes notice.

I unwind in the privacy of a corner booth. All the stress that has built up over months seems to drain out of my body. A Tammy Wynette song of heartbreak coming from the jukebox captures my melancholy mood. I'm just another lonely soul looking to find love.

Once again, I find myself looking back to seminary days in Carlow – needing to revisit the years invested in preparing for the priesthood. And once again I compare myself to a man who is newly divorced, looking back over the years invested in his failed marriage. Now, I'm asking if these were 'wasted' years. Is there something I can salvage from student days at Carlow College that will be useful in the future?

I recall Monica Baldwin's story, and how she had faced the challenge of adjusting to life on the outside after more than two decades in an enclosed religious community. Coming out of the convent in 1941 she found the chaos and turmoil of war-ravaged England to be to her advantage. I also have the advantage of coming out into a society experiencing social turmoil. My plan is to just blend into whatever is happening around me.

My solitude is broken by a visit from a friendly and attractive waitress. And she seems to have a perky personality to go with her voluptuous looks.

'Hi! I'm Wendy. What's the matter young man – you get jilted?' she asks as she cleans off my table.

'No – just taking a break in my journey.'

'If you're looking for some action, there's a private club just down the road.'

'Thanks, Wendy. I've other things on my mind.'

I'm not going to make that mistake again!

Wendy moves on and leaves me alone with my thoughts and my Marlboros. After an hour I decide I've done enough reminiscing. This isn't the time to be analysing my past life. I need to start focusing on the future. I need to get on the road and find a place to sleep for the night.

Arriving in Baton Rouge, I check into a cheap motel – after all, this may be my home for a couple of weeks while I explore future options and I don't want to squander my money. The motel room, with its strong smell of stale cigarette smoke, is sparsely furnished with just a bed, small side table, green plastic deck chair and table lamp. There's a black-and-white TV that doesn't work. A noisy air conditioner does little to reduce the sweltering heat and humidity. At least it drowns out the noise of the highway traffic.

I throw myself on the bed fully dressed and stare at the ceiling. I'm relieved this day is over. I've worried for so long about how parishioners would respond to the news of my departure. Would they feel betrayed? Would they see me as ungrateful for the support they'd extended over five years? These concerns turned out to be unfounded. Even the most disappointed, including my immediate neighbours in Bunkie, have offered expressions of support.

I may have told parishioners I was taking a 'leave of absence', but in truth I know there will be no going back. In my mind, I've made a final decision.

'Thank you, Eddie', I say, as if congratulating myself. There's nobody else around to give me a pat on the back. For better or worse – better, I'm hoping – I've put aside the Roman collar for a new life as a layman.

As I unwind I'm feeling good about having had the guts to 'leap over the wall'. This is definitely the most courageous thing I've done in my life. And then, in this moment of self-congratulation, I remind myself not to get too carried away. What if I suffer the same fate as some of those ex-priests I'd read about back in Carlow College? I hadn't read about any men who had left the ministry and then moved on to a successful second career.

There is just one more job to do – to tell my family and friends in Ireland that I have left the ministry. While I've earlier dropped hints to some family members about what I am thinking, I expect this news will still be a shock.

In my letter to Bishop Greco I had written:

> For seven years I have sought to bring hope and consolation to God's people. I can only hope that I have not spared myself in this task. I can only pray that this decision will cause a minimum of scandal to the many people that I know and love.

The avoidance of 'scandal' is always a key concern and it is uppermost on my mind when I draft a letter that will accompany a copy of my letter to Bishop Greco, which I plan to send to those who need to know. I commence the letter:

> This is the most difficult letter that I have ever had to write. I hope that you will understand what I have to say. This letter may disappoint some of my family and friends, but I sincerely pray that it will in no way affect the faith of anyone.

I explain the state of constant mental conflict I have been feeling about 'certain matters relating to my priestly life', and tell them I feel I have no other option but to take a leave of absence from the ministry.

As well as these two letters, I send a more personal note to close family members. To Michael and Elsie I write:

> The enclosed letters will probably surprise and disappoint you. Anyway, I have reached a clear decision and I am relieved and happy with it…. I will rest for a few weeks as I have been very nervous and need to relax. Don't worry about me as I will be fine. I will have a lot of adjustments to make … I told Aunt Helen about my move and she was most understanding and encouraging. She is a lot like

Mammy.... When I told the congregation there were a few tears but they were very understanding of my position. I guess people have more kindness than we sometimes expect.

The letter to them is probably the most real expression of my state of mind: nervous and fragile.

After an hour of daydreaming I decide to undress and go to bed. Tomorrow will be a new beginning and I'll need to be rested. I kneel beside the bed, bless myself and whisper a silent prayer of thanks for having gotten through this difficult experience. 'Thanks be to Jesus, Mary and Joseph, it's all over.'

This has been the most traumatic day of my young life. I turn off the bedside lamp and sleep soundly until long after the sun has come up the next morning.

Part 2

THE LONG VOYAGE

10.

Signing up for the 'War on Poverty'

I crawl out of the bed in my cheap motel room on Monday morning, 28 July. It's the first day of my new life as a layman. I'm slightly disoriented. And I'm thinking this has to be the most depressing room in Baton Rouge. The air conditioner has been on all night but has done nothing to cool down the room. The sun has already come up and it looks like it might be 110 degrees outside. I pull back the flimsy window curtain and can see the busy traffic. I walk into the tiny bathroom, where I'm confronted by what looks like the largest cockroach in the world. I make a mental note that I'll not stay in this hellhole one more night.

'Time to get to work,' I say to myself as I grab a bite of breakfast in a nearby cafe. I don't have time to indulge in deep reflection this morning – second-guessing will only drain my energy. Besides, I have more than a few good memories from my years in the priesthood and an appreciation of the skills I've gained. On this first morning of my new life, I'm hoping I'll quickly find a way to put these skills to work.

I begin the search for a new career in the classified pages of the Baton Rouge *Advocate*. My preference is to find a job in human services or a related field. I'm thinking I might be able to get a job as a counsellor or social worker. An advertisement for the position of supervisor with VISTA, working with the local anti-

73

poverty agency, Community Advancement, looks interesting. A call to Community Advancement results in an invitation to come in for an interview with Executive Director Charlie Tapp.

I wonder if my background in the ministry will be a problem. What will I say if asked about my work experience? These concerns are short-lived as Tapp says my background isn't an issue and that one of his managers is an ordained Baptist minister.

'Any hang-ups about working in the black community?' he asks.

'None – I'll welcome the opportunity to get involved.'

Tapp offers me the job and we agree I'll start the following Monday. That same day I also receive an offer to work as a recruiter for a private women's college. Given my background and desire to make a contribution to society, it's an easy decision.

My next step is to rent a place to live. I settle on an apartment in a modern suburban complex with a swimming pool and other amenities. Life goes on almost uninterrupted. Within two weeks of leaving the ministry I'm relocated in Baton Rouge and gainfully employed. I've discarded the black suit and Roman collar in favour of casual business attire.

And now, as a thirty-one-year-old, I'm finally feeling as if I'm a mostly liberated person. I'm anxious but excited about the future.

The first challenge after starting my new job is to find out what VISTA is all about. The letters stand for 'Volunteers in Service to America'. Conceived in the Kennedy administration years, and introduced by President Lyndon B. Johnson, the program is the domestic version of the Peace Corps. Most volunteers are young college graduates committed to working in low-income communities for one or two years. They're expected to live in the communities where they work. Each volunteer receives a small stipend from the Federal government to cover living expenses.

The Baton Rouge project includes over twenty young people, most in their twenties, from throughout the USA. Several of the male volunteers are of draft age but have convinced local draft boards to let them serve in VISTA in lieu of service in Vietnam. The group includes nurses, educators, lawyers, urban planners and generalists. They're assigned to indigenous community groups to provide technical support.

Only three days after joining the staff of Community Advancement I get my introduction to Charlie Tapp's view of the 'war on poverty' and the issue of racial discrimination.

Tapp, tall and youthful-looking, has a dynamic take-no-prisoners leadership style. Although a Southern white man, there's no doubt about his commitment to civil rights. Charlie's second-in-command, Percy Simms, a veteran of the civil rights struggles of the 1950s, has a more laid-back leadership style. A black man, he grew up in the segregated Deep South with its Jim Crow laws.

Together, Charlie and Percy form an impressive team. I get an insight into their leadership style at the first management meeting I attend in my new role as manager of the VISTA project.

We assemble around a long conference table for the weekly meeting of project managers. Charlie and Percy sit at the head of the table. The meeting begins with each programme manager giving a brief progress report. Rosemary, a black woman and director of the Head Start program, mentions that she was refused service at a nearby restaurant during the previous week. The reports continue. The meeting ends at noon and we get ready to disband. Then Charlie makes an announcement.

'Percy and I are going down the street to have lunch at the restaurant that refused our friend Rosemary. I understand they have good barbecue chicken. Y'all are welcome to join us.'

We all walk down the street and file into the almost empty restaurant.

The tension is as real as the smell of the barbecued chicken. My knees are shaking. We wait and wait, but nobody comes over to our tables. Finally, Tapp asks to see the manager.

'We don't have all day to sit around here,' says Tapp. 'We want to be served now.'

'Yes, sir,' says the manager as he disappears into the kitchen.

I'm nervous and more than a little fearful. What if some crazy redneck produces a gun! After all, this is Ku Klux Klan country. After another long wait a waitress comes over. I notice her hand is shaking as she writes down our orders. The southern fried chicken is tasty, but it isn't my idea of a relaxing meal. The stress is palpable. For the first time, blacks have been served in what had previously been an all-white restaurant. It's a small step forward.

I leave the restaurant having finally experienced the fear associated with a racially charged encounter. It leaves me wondering how civil rights leaders cope with this kind of nerve-wrecking stress on a daily basis.

Soon there's another learning opportunity. At a meeting with members of our VISTA group I learn there's considerable disagreement about where to focus our resources. Some want members of the team involved in providing social services, while others believe we should be working to address the root causes of poverty. It's partly a question of priorities. Eventually a consensus emerges that fighting racism and discrimination should be our major priority. I suggest we do a survey of attitudes and concerns in low-income black communities.

Two members of the group volunteer to take the lead in managing the survey project. We receive technical support on designing the survey instrument from a sociology professor at Louisiana State University. Community residents are recruited and trained to do the interviews.

The results of the survey reveal police brutality as the number one concern of low-income blacks; to my colleagues in the anti-poverty agency this isn't a major surprise. A summary of survey results is sent to all local media outlets. One TV station reports on its evening news that survey data indicate *positive* relationships between the police and the community. It's an outrageous distortion of our survey results. I'm dumbfounded at this blatant misrepresentation. The next day, after consulting with Charlie Tapp, I issue a news release demanding a correction by the TV station.

That same day I appear on John Camp's popular noontime radio program to reaffirm the findings of the survey.

'What's an Irishman doing in this part of the world?' Camp asks, putting me somewhat on the defensive.

'Well, some might consider me an outside agitator, but I'm a naturalized America citizen.'

We discuss the survey results. It turns out Camp is very supportive of VISTA's effort to measure attitudes in the black community.

We get more mileage out of the survey than we could ever have expected. The TV station that had broadcast the distorted version of the survey results asks for on-camera comments. Reluctantly, I find myself drawn into a public role. I'm quickly learning about institutional racism and getting intensive on-the-job training.

Over a period of several months our VISTA group becomes more cohesive and organized in its work. We take on the most pressing social issues in the community. A couple of members are at the forefront of an effort to pressure local government into greater responsiveness to the needs of people living in the city's ghettos. Volunteers succeed in mobilizing students from local universities in support of their community projects. One volunteer persuades medical doctors to support a clinic in a low-income black section of the city.

I take on my new responsibilities as VISTA supervisor with an abundance of self-confidence, despite the fact that I've little experience as a manager. The job includes taking care of administrative details as well as maintaining liaison with Federal program officials in Washington and Austin, Texas. Beyond the supervisory responsibilities, I have the freedom to work with individual volunteers on their various projects.

I quickly come to see myself as a mentor and collaborator to members of our VISTA group. Luckily, few require hands-on supervision. They're self-motivated and generous in their commitment of time and energy. I feel like I'm making a useful contribution rather than just directing the behaviour of others.

As I settle into my new role I grow a beard, adopt a casual lifestyle and enjoy the challenges associated with my job. The hours are long but the work is energizing. Our VISTA group becomes an extended family. The arrival of new volunteers and the departure of old ones is celebrated. Birthdays are celebrated. Our frequent parties include generous amounts of cheap Boone's Farm Apple Wine and loud Motown music. We mix work and pleasure.

Several months after leaving St Anthony's parish in Bunkie, I'm hitting my stride. The transition from clergyman to layman has been much smoother than I could have imagined.

And there's an interesting development in my personal life, too. I find myself, after work, regularly joining colleagues at our favourite watering hole, the Press Club in downtown Baton Rouge. Located on the top floor of the White House Inn, the Press Club is a hangout for politicians and media people. Our group usually includes Charlie Tapp, Percy Simms and two women co-workers, Diana Williams and Joan Vincent.

Diana, a professional social worker by background, is responsible for research within the agency. An attractive woman with a slim figure, she has deep brown eyes and a warm engaging smile. Still in her twenties, Diana is full of youthful, high-spirited energy and loves to joke and tease. She somehow manages to be fun-loving and serious at the same time. I'm attracted by her outgoing personality as well as her passion for effecting social change.

Over dinner one evening Diana mentions that she'd been married several years earlier to a young man from New Orleans. She mentions he'd been drafted and sent to Vietnam. It's not clear what the status of the relationship is and I don't ask questions.

Diana and I become good friends. And then the relationship becomes more intimate. This is something that happens spontaneously. Up to this time all my relationships with women have been platonic. The relationship with Diana is different. Unlike the unfortunate encounter on the night of the Bishop's anniversary celebration, this relationship is based on warm feelings. Sometimes Diana calls late at night and asks to be invited over to my apartment. There are no hang-ups and no guilt.

Diana mentions one day that she'd like me to come over for a meal at her place on Friday evening. I walk into a house packed with co-workers and friends. A birthday to remember! My first ever birthday party turns into an all-night affair. I came to appreciate the fun-loving side of Diana's personality.

One Sunday afternoon, as I relax in my apartment, I get a call from Diana. I assume she wants to get together for the evening. And then I realize something is wrong. She is hesitant, not like her usual self.

'I just got a call – my husband is on the way back from Vietnam.'

This is an unexpected development, though I don't know why I'm surprised. Somehow, I'd conveniently blocked her husband out of my mind.

We'd been acting as if the relationship would go on forever. Diana comes over to my place and we sit on the couch and talk. I sense Diana would say 'yes' if I ask her to stay with me. My Irish Catholic conscience tells me I shouldn't contribute to the break-up of a marriage. We're both conflicted about what to do. I wonder if I could commit to this relationship even if Diana was not already involved in a committed relationship. This is clearly the kind of dilemma I've never faced before.

I don't want Diana to feel rejected, as I'm grateful for the support she's provided during my transition from the ministry to a new life as a layman. She's helped bring laughter back into my life. In our relationship I'd discovered a capacity to truly enjoy the company of a woman. The relationship had helped me get in touch with my own humanity and sexuality. For the first time, I'm feeling like a normal man.

After some discussion we agree that the right thing to do is for Diana to rejoin her husband.

I'm not feeling very good about myself as a result of this whole situation and I'm wondering if I've used Diana, or if we've both used each other. Diana leaves Baton Rouge to start a new life in New Orleans with her husband. We never see each other again.

During the days that follow her departure there's a feeling of emptiness. Someone who was an important part of my life is gone away. And I keep thinking I haven't said a proper goodbye – it all happened so fast. The whole experience brings home how inexperienced and clumsy I am in handling personal relationships with women.

With the passage of time I come to view the relationship with Diana as much more than an 'affair'. After the seminary experience and the celibate years in the priesthood, I was unsure of my ability to relate to women. Without a lot of serious talk, Diana and I seemed to acknowledge that we were meeting each other's needs and that was okay. We acted like young lovers. I conclude neither of us had in mind a lifelong partnership.

After the break-up with Diana I live the life of a regular unattached guy. Relationships are free and easy. On weekends there are late-night parties – mostly in the black community. There are trips to the French Quarter in New Orleans. And there are occasional trips with friends to the beaches on the Mississippi Gulf Coast. Life becomes a combination of hard work and a fair amount of partying. Sometimes I think about how removed this life is from the sexually repressed environment of 1950s Ireland, with the constant scrutiny and fear of 'giving scandal'. And it's also removed from my more recent life in a fishbowl as a Catholic priest. The freedom suits me.

It doesn't seem to matter to new friends that I've spent several years working in the ministry – it's really no big deal. Sometimes on Sunday mornings I worship at the Newman Centre at Louisiana State University. At other times I join a friend to worship at the

Unitarian Church. This is where most of the human rights advocates – black and white – congregate on Sunday mornings. These gatherings are always energizing, if not exactly religious experiences in the traditional sense.

Within a few months I've graduated from the ministry to a more relevant and meaningful role as social activist. I'm now an active player in the revolutionary changes going on around me – no longer sitting on the sidelines. And I'm learning how to enjoy life. Nearly eight years after leaving Carlow College, I've found a new identity.

11.

Police entrapment, Louisiana-style

It's Friday evening, 20 March 1970, and I'm getting ready to take off for a weekend visit to a girlfriend at Northeast State College in Monroe. Just as I'm leaving my apartment the phone rings. It's Dennis Swinehart, one of the VISTA volunteers.

'Ed, Frank Stewart has been arrested, and there's a warrant out for the arrest of Wade Hudson.'

Dennis tells me the District Attorney has appeared on a local television station, alleging that law enforcement have foiled a conspiracy to murder the Mayor, Woody Dumas, and Police Chief Songy of Plaquemines Parish. I'm having difficulty believing what Swinehart has just told me.

'Dennis, you've got to be kidding, not these guys, no way.'

I'm wondering what the hell is going on. Frank Stewart and Wade Hudson conspiring to commit murder? It has to be a mistake.

Stewart and Hudson, both African-Americans, are members of our VISTA group. They're also members of an indigenous community organization called SOUL (Society for Opportunity, Unity, and Leadership) that operates a free breakfast program for children and provides other social services in a low-income black community.

Frank, a graduate of Southern University, is head of SOUL. He has served in Africa with the Peace Corps. A slight, soft-spoken man in his mid-twenties, his major preoccupation is in improving living conditions in his local community. Wade, the number two person at SOUL, is an aspiring poet and also a Southern University graduate. I'd recruited both Frank and Wade into VISTA as a way of providing financial support for their community work.

Minutes after receiving the call from Dennis and cancelling the planned trip to Monroe, I'm in my car racing downtown to the courthouse. 'This shit can't be true,' I keep saying to myself. Two of 'my' people accused of conspiring to commit a very serious crime. Knocking off public officials is definitely not part of our VISTA work plan.

Within fifteen minutes I'm at the courthouse. This downtown building is mostly deserted as employees have already left for the weekend. There are a couple of sheriff's deputies around, but they can't shed light on the fate of the arrested 'conspirators'.

Wade Hudson wanders into the courthouse to turn himself in. He's quickly ushered away and locked up in a jail cell.

I learn that TV stations have made the alleged conspiracy the lead story on the evening news. They've broadcast dramatic pictures of the District Attorney leading Frank and another alleged conspirator, Alphonse Snedecor, into the courthouse. I'm already thinking this smells like a staged media event, designed to benefit local elected officials.

Within an hour VISTA volunteers and their friends are congregating at the courthouse. A member of our group is on the phone to get representatives of the legal community over to visit the jail cells. At nine o'clock two attorneys emerge from the jail to reveal the inside story. We adjourn to an all-night coffee shop.

In the coffee shop the lawyers share their conclusions from their interviews. The story they tell sounds like the plotline from a Hollywood movie. Bottom line, they believe Stewart and Hudson are innocent, unsuspecting victims. According to the attorneys, it's a classic case of police entrapment.

It emerges that the key figure behind the arrest is a police snitch known in the local black community as 'Tiny Tim'. Rumoured to make his living by supplying information to the police, Tiny Tim is a disreputable character who has been accused of serious crimes on several occasions. It's widely believed that the District Attorney had gotten him off the rap each time because of services rendered. The District Attorney himself has an unsavoury reputation in the black community. He's regarded as a racist and in the past has publicly referred to blacks as 'niggers'.

As we huddle in the coffee shop, the story of what happened begins to take shape. According to the lawyers, Tim had been used to infiltrate SOUL as an undercover agent. It's the era of the Black Panthers, the radical black rights group, though Baton Rouge has no Black Panther Party chapter. Local law enforcement is paranoid about any black organization, even one that focuses its energies on a free breakfast program. According to our attorney, James 'Tiny Tim' Moore, the informant, had befriended Alphonse Snedecor. Snedecor hung out at SOUL and was known to be psychologically challenged. He was AWOL from the US Army and the word on the street was that the Army wasn't too interested in finding him. He had talked constantly about revolution and about leading black people out of bondage. A revolutionary in his own mind.

While Tiny Tim and Snedecor discuss bumping off the Mayor, the District Attorney and other public officials, a tape recorder in Tiny Tim's car records these conversations as 'incriminating evidence'. Guns had been purchased with Tiny Tim's money, presumably money that came out of law enforcement funds.

One day Tiny Tim and Snedecor stop at Frank and Wade's apartment to invite them to go for a ride to the country. Wade declines, but the unsuspecting Frank goes along. He hears them talk about the murder plot but dismisses them as a couple of delusional fools. He's heard this kind of talk before in the ghetto and knows it's just a way for young blacks to blow off steam and express anger against the white establishment.

A few miles outside Baton Rouge, on a quiet country road, they stop the car near a railroad track to go target shooting with their newly purchased weapons. This is the road the Mayor travels each morning on his way into the city. Frank stands beside the car, bored, waiting for the ride back to town. Little does he know that police cameras are recording his presence. It's a case of a taxpayer-funded law enforcement effort to set up alleged black 'conspirators' for arrest. A classic sting operation.

In the coffee shop on this Friday night we talk for hours. I want to deny what's really happening. There are lots of unanswered questions. Why would the police want to sabotage an organization trying to help disadvantaged people in the community? Why go after Stewart and Hudson? These young men can in no way be considered violent revolutionaries. This elaborate effort to entrap black leaders seems beyond belief, even for a racist city like Baton Rouge.

Our coffee shop post mortem breaks up and I find myself sitting alone in my apartment replaying, over and over, the strange events of this evening. It doesn't make sense – unless you believe bigoted white politicians are willing to exploit the race issue for political advantage. None of my experiences growing up in rural Ireland has prepared me for this kind of situation.

On Saturday morning my apartment is crowded with VISTA volunteers and community leaders searching for a strategy to liberate the 'conspirators'. VISTA attorney George Kurr is on the phone in search of a civil rights lawyer to take the case. Frank's brother expresses the concerns of the Stewart family: he's worried about Frank's asthmatic condition and wants him out of jail as soon as possible. Jody Bibbins, the most radical black leader to emerge since H. Rap Brown's recent departure from Baton Rouge, has a different view.

'The most important thing is not getting the dudes out of jail,' says Bibbins. 'We need to expose the whole white racist fuckin' system.'

My concern is that Bibbins and his followers will sacrifice my two VISTA volunteers in order to push their own agenda. I have a more immediate agenda – to get them out of jail. I pull Bibbins aside to express my concerns. He's having none of it.

'Look, brother, no disrespect but you're a honkey – you don't understand. The community needs to know what's going down – this is a problem for the brothers and the sisters.'

This is familiar rhetoric.

Bibbins proclaims himself the new head of SOUL and sets out to tell the TV stations and newspapers his views on the alleged murder plot.

I'm in telephone contact with Charlie Tapp to discuss the idea of a press release defending our VISTA volunteers. Tapp enthusiastically supports this idea. The hastily drafted statement indicates in clear and unambiguous language that our two co-workers won't be suspended and will continue to receive VISTA stipends. The statement receives front page coverage in the local Sunday morning Baton Rouge newspaper, and has the desired effect of planting questions about the motivation behind the arrests.

By Saturday evening George Kurr has succeeded in lining up an outstanding constitutional lawyer, Benjamin Smith. In the 1950s, before it became popular to represent black civil rights leaders, Smith had defended many of them throughout the Deep South. At one time his activities led to arrest on the charge of being a Communist.

Our initial strategy session in my apartment is followed by a period of frenzied activity.

Smith's petition to get the $100,000 bond reduced is refused. A few days later, however, Wade Hudson is released for lack of evidence. From the prison cell, a few days before his release, Hudson pens a message to his co-workers that I've saved these many years:

To VISTA:

From the depths of my heart I thank you all for what you have done! I know words most of the time fall short of expressing the true meaning one desires to express concerning a feeling. For lack of another way, I warmly thank you. I am sure I speak for Frank.

You know, it's quite pitiful the way this city is, this state, this country. Several times, as I lay in bed here, I am hoping that a bomb or something would just blow it off the map – even me and the things and people I hold dear. I guess I was drowning in a sea of negatism and fatalism at the time.

What's the answer? What's the answer to all this shit? I'll be damned if I know!

There is something about the innocent that makes them vulnerable. I don't know if it's their trust of people, or their belief in righteousness. Anyway, we fell victim.

Again, I thank you. And I assure you of our innocence.

Let's hope for a brief moment, humanness, love and truth walk into this city. And let their entrance ring out the beginning of a new era. Right on! More power to the People!

Yours in the struggle,

Wade Hudson.

We get a letter in a similar vein from Frank Stewart, still in his prison cell. In it he expresses the hope that 'justice will open her eyes to reveal to Baton Rouge true justice, honesty, and truth.'

The 'Free Frank Stewart' movement is formed and a legal defence fund is started. A New Orleans newspaper writes an exposé of the case. Hundreds of copies of the story are mimeographed and mailed out to friends. I use every opportunity to mobilize support.

The months pass and despite the legal manoeuvres Frank remains in jail. The local politicians use the alleged murder plot to full advantage. The Mayor receives extra police protection. The District Attorney gets bulletproof windows for his office.

The case becomes my obsession. I can't sleep easy, feeling a member of my team is depending on me to help win his freedom. The effort is exhausting and I'm beginning to suffer from fatigue. It seems as if it's an impossible battle – we're up against a powerful local political establishment.

Just when feelings of desperation are about to take over an unexpected opportunity presents itself. A letter of invitation to a national meeting in Washington D.C. arrives from a group calling itself the National VISTA Alliance. This group, organized to fight efforts by the Nixon administration to water down the VISTA program, has convened a Washington meeting to rally VISTA volunteers across the country. I spot the opportunity to raise Frank's case on a national level.

On Sunday, 26 July 1970, accompanied by Ken Baker, a member of our VISTA group, I fly to Washington D.C. to mobilize support for Frank. On the eve of the meeting, Ken and I meet with the organizers at a rundown D.C. hotel. They tell us they've studied the material we sent and are prepared to offer a resolution expressing support for our efforts to free Frank Stewart.

I explode.

'Offer a resolution! Have we come all the way to Washington to hear this bullshit? Shove your resolution!'

They're surprised – shocked – at the intensity of my response. They get a glimpse of how an Irishman can behave when he loses his temper.

'We're trying to get a brother out of a god-forsaken jail in Louisiana and all you have to offer is a fuckin' resolution.'

Ken and I storm out of the meeting and go in search of a cheap hotel room for the night.

When we arrive at the conference hotel the next morning it's clear something has changed since our initial encounter. We're quickly ushered into a back room for a private meeting with top organizers. For whatever reason, they've decided to mobilize around the Frank Stewart case.

This time the organizers ask our ideas on how to move forward. I advocate that the group invade the Capitol and lobby representatives and senators on behalf of Frank. There are no dissenters. We hold a rally and send conference participants to lobby the politicians on Capitol Hill.

That evening I call Charlie Tapp to give him an update. He tells me that political pressure is already flowing to Baton Rouge. His advice: keep up the pressure.

Next morning I lead a group of several hundred VISTA volunteers in a march to the headquarters of the Office of Economic Opportunity (OEO). Marching down the streets of Washington we look more like a band of hippies than government-paid community workers. At OEO headquarters we demand a meeting with OEO chief Donald Rumsfeld. A former Republican Congressman from Illinois, Rumsfeld is widely considered to be hostile to the interests of the low-income people his agency is supposed to assist. (And yes, this is the same Rumsfeld who, decades later, will help lead America into an ill-conceived and morally dubious war in Iraq.)

We're told Rumsfeld is out of town, visiting with Nixon at the Western White House in San Clemente, California. A meeting with mid-level Federal bureaucrats is quickly arranged. There's lots of shouting and swearing. It's clear we're being stonewalled.

In utter frustration several women in the back of the room start chanting, 'Racist chauvinist fuckin' pigs! Racist chauvinist fuckin' pigs!'

Their oratory melts few hearts. The government bureaucrats get confirmation of their worst fears, however: the VISTA experience is having a radicalizing effect on these young Americans.

Before leaving Washington we're treated to a rousing speech by Sargent Shriver, the first Director of the OEO and brother-in-law of the late President John F. Kennedy. Shriver dishes out blame to the Republican administration for a 'creeping euthanasia ... moving the entire body politic'. He adds: 'The politics of death is name-calling, resentment, rage.... The politics of life is helping the poor to dream to become strong.' It's a much-needed boost as we get ready to head back to Louisiana.

As we had hoped, the meeting in Washington puts a national spotlight on the Stewart case. The *Washington Post* and the *New York Times* carry stories highlighting our protest. Ken and I fly back to Louisiana hopeful that the end might be in sight. A few days after the conference, the *St. Louis Post-Dispatch* publishes a detailed expose of the case under the headline, 'Jailing of VISTA Worker Called Police Hoax and "Southern Justice".'

A few weeks later a Federal judge in Baton Rouge orders that Frank be released. All the charges against him are dropped. There's a loud cheer in the courtroom, causing the bailiff to call for order. Outside, after the judge's decision, there's hugging and celebrating. I look at Frank's aging parents and think about how much they've suffered through this ordeal. I wonder how I would have responded if I'd been the victim of this kind of 'justice'. I am happy that, along with many others, I have played a role in Frank's vindication. It had taken way too long, though. All the time that we were fighting, I was aware that an innocent man, an individual who had given distinguished service to his country, including work with the Peace Corps in Africa, was wrongly being held in jail. Now, though, we have to focus on the fact that he is free, and we have won a small but decisive victory over those who seek to preserve inequality.

That evening I host a celebration at my apartment. It turns into an all-night bash with the usual large quantities of cheap wine and loud soul music.

The week following the release, Frank, Dennis Swinehart and I drive to Florida for a short holiday. One afternoon, on a boat ride down Key Biscayne, we're stopped and searched by the Coast Guard as a result of getting too close to Nixon's Florida home (known as the Winter White House). It's enough to generate a high level of paranoia given all we've been through during the previous months. The Coast Guard officials confiscate the film from Swinehart's camera and let us go with a warning.

After a few days relaxing on Miami Beach we're ready to head back to Louisiana. The return trip is marked by a brief encounter with a couple of rednecks at a truck stop in the Florida Panhandle. They obviously don't approve of a black man eating at a white man's restaurant. We quietly make our exit and continue on our homeward journey.

The Frank Stewart case has the effect of opening my eyes to institutional racism in the Deep South. It's a transformative experience. I learn that politicians are willing to exploit vulnerable people for their own advantage. And I lose some of my innocence about the people who are paid to uphold the law. (I caught up with Frank in Santa Barbara in May 2014. He told me that Alphonse Snedecor is still in Louisiana State Prison, having got into trouble with some prison guards.)

After barely a year in Baton Rouge I've had my 'Road to Damascus' experience. I've certainly travelled a long way in the eight years since leaving Ireland with a bag of idealistic views about the 'promised land'.

12.

Billy Graham comes to town

In late October 1970 the Reverend Billy Graham and I have a memorable encounter, triggered by the issue of racial segregation. My showdown with the famous evangelist earns me the enmity of important people in high places – and, for a brief moment, puts me in the national spotlight. I come to think of it as my 'David versus Goliath' moment: the idea that a soft-spoken Irish ex-priest would challenge the most high profile and influential preacher in America will still surprise me years later.

In 1970 Billy Graham was on the polling company Gallup's list of most admired and influential Americans. Born in 1918, Graham is a Christian Evangelist who speaks to the hearts and minds of middle class conservative America. For over twenty years his 'Crusades' – rousing revivalist events – have been filling venues such as football stadia not only in the USA but all over the world. His influence has grown with his national profile and he has been the spiritual advisor to a number of American presidents, including Eisenhower, Lyndon Johnson and Nixon. This makes him the unofficial chaplain to the White House, John F. Kennedy being the notable exception. Graham's actions in 1960 – when he worked behind the scenes to campaign against a Catholic getting into the White House – fed into the paranoia of Bible-thumping preachers who believed, or pretended to believe, that the Pope would rule America if Kennedy was elected president.

I don't actually set out to have a confrontation with Graham. I see his rallies as stage-managed made-for-television productions that have nothing to do with me. Despite the high-powered media campaign preceding his upcoming visit to Baton Rouge, I'm taking little notice.

One evening in late October Frank Stewart and his friend, Barbara Favorite, stop by my apartment. A black student at predominantly white Louisiana State University (LSU), Barbara, like Frank, grew up in a religious family. Our conversation turns to the upcoming visit by Billy Graham to conduct his Crusade at LSU's football stadium. Huge billboards and a Madison Avenue-style media blitz are part of the build-up for the Baton Rouge Crusade. The choice of LSU isn't accidental. The university is low on protest and high on football – the antithesis to Kent State and other universities in turmoil. It's a safe place to stage a religious revival crusade.

Graham is not a racist and from early in his career he has made progressive moves on racial integration. He was close to Martin Luther King, inviting King to share the pulpit at his crusades in the late 1950s and bailing him out of jail on occasion. However, his willingness to be the uncritical guest of segregationist politicians and church leaders – thereby giving them and their beliefs an apparent endorsement and putting his considerable moral weight behind them – is impossible to ignore.

Frank, Barbara and I tease out our concerns about Graham's silence on the civil rights struggle underway throughout the South – not to mention the segregationist policies of the local churches sponsoring his Crusade. We wonder why these churches are unwilling to provide moral leadership on critical social problems such as racism and discrimination. Apparently, Graham and other evangelical preachers do not consider raising social issues as part of their remit. Perhaps I should not be surprised, given my own underperformance when a member of the Catholic clergy.

We talk late into the night and reach a conclusion: we'll use the Graham visit to highlight the issue of institutional racism in the churches. We conclude the time is right to address the issue. The winds of change are blowing across the Deep South, so why not challenge the churches to play a role in breaking down racial barriers? The Gospel, we conclude, should be about more than accepting Jesus and being 'saved', which appears to the be the evangelists' sole focus and the limit of their vision. If the message of the Gospel is to mean anything, surely it is about its social implications.

Our plan is to invite a small group to my apartment to map out a strategy. The group of twelve that show up includes several VISTA volunteers and a number of professional people, both white and black. We develop a simple plan. The first step will be to test a select number of local 'white' Baptist churches to see if they still practice racial segregation. These churches generally preach a fundamentalist form of Christianity. Two volunteers – one white and one black – are assigned to each of five churches. Dressed in their Sunday best, the volunteers will visit these churches on the Sunday preceding Graham's arrival in Baton Rouge. My job is to coordinate the effort and be available in case of an emergency.

The 'Sunday best' couples gather at my apartment on Sunday morning, 18 October, for coffee and last-minute strategizing. The instructions are to be extremely polite and not to attempt to gain entry if the usher indicates they're not welcome.

By noon the results are in. All five selected churches, including the prestigious downtown First Baptist Church, refuse entrance to the blacks. I had thought maybe one of the churches might challenge blacks that attempted to enter. The fact that all five churches refuse admission is a bit of a shock. After all, this is 1970 – racial barriers are already disappearing in many areas of public life in the Deep South. And these blacks are all respectable, well-dressed, middle class professionals, not fearsome Black Panther-type revolutionaries.

On Sunday afternoon our newly formed group, calling ourselves 'Citizens Concerned with Social Responsibilities of the Church in Baton Rouge,' put out a press release deploring the segregationist policies of the sponsoring churches and publicly asking Graham to address the issue during the upcoming Crusade. The press release is picked up by the wire services and becomes an instant national story.

We've dropped a bombshell on the Graham Crusade. His high-powered media team is caught by surprise. The Graham people are not used to deviations from their carefully scripted events. Things move quickly. We learn that Graham will be flying into Baton Rouge and holding a press conference on Monday at one of the local hotels. Our plan is simple. Barbara Favorite and I will crash the press conference and I'll ask that Barbara be allowed to read our 'Statement of Concern' – a one-page manifesto calling on Graham to address the issue of racial discrimination at the Baton Rouge Crusade.

We arrive for Graham's press conference with a small group of friends and supporters. A Graham staff member asks if we have press credentials and I say 'yes' and continue walking. We sit nervously and wait. After a while the evangelist arrives with an entourage comprised of fresh-faced young white men. Graham himself is immaculately groomed and with his bronze tan looks more like a member of the professional golf circuit than a man of God. He gives a short speech about preserving the moral fibre of America and then opens the conference for questions.

After a few soft-ball questions from local media I grab the floor and Graham's attention. My knees are shaking.

'Are you the fellow that used to be a priest?' Graham asks.

What an asshole, I'm thinking, *trying to put me down in front of all these media people.* I wonder how he knows about my background. Obviously, members of his advance team have done their homework.

I tell Graham that I know something about Christian theology and that I'm here to have an associate present him with our 'Statement of Concern'.

He asks if she is a member of the press. I say that she's not, but she has a message that he will find relevant.

Graham says the press conference is only for press people.

I tell him that's fine and announce to the roomful of reporters that Barbara and I will be holding our own press conference in the lobby of the hotel immediately after the conclusion of Graham's conference. We somehow manage to hijack his staged media event. (At which, the coverage notes the next morning, he goes on to accept questions from non-reporters.)

In the hotel lobby Barbara, a petite, articulate young woman with an impressive Afro hairstyle, stands on a chair as reporters clamour around. She calmly reads the 'Statement of Concern' addressed to Dr Graham:

> We appeal to you to address yourself to the urgent problems of exploitation and discrimination in our area during the Baton Rouge Crusade. We know that these problems cannot be solved by government action. The solution lies in the hands of ministers, priests and preachers who have the courage to teach the implications of the Gospel message. We urge you, Dr Graham, to devote one full evening of the Crusade to teaching the clergy of the area the social doctrine of Christ ... Emotional pious platitudes may make people feel good or 'saved' but they will not uplift the quality of life in Baton Rouge ... Dr Graham, we had addressed this message to you on the eve of the Crusade because we want religion to be more than 'a good show'. We want it to be a reality in the lives of the people.

Barbara not only reads the statement but adds her own off-the-cuff remarks: 'Why do churches in Baton Rouge collect money for missionaries in Africa but refuse to help poor blacks in their own city?' she asks. 'They're a bunch of hypocrites!'

Barbara tells the assembled reporters that members of our Ad Hoc Committee will be attending the Crusade each evening to see if Graham responds to our challenge. Meanwhile, Graham's people look on helplessly.

After the press conference our group adjourns to my apartment to plan the next move. Our major goal has already been accomplished. The Associated Press and United Press International wire services have picked up the story. We've put a national spotlight on what we consider a serious social problem.

That night I receive several threatening phone calls. In sadness I reflect that each caller would probably call himself a good Christian. One caller is particularly intimidating: 'Look nigger lover, watch out – you could find yourself floating down the Mississippi River.'

This warning makes me nervous. I'm not naïve enough to ignore these kinds of threats. The Ku Klux Klan is still a force to be reckoned with in east Baton Rouge.

Meanwhile Charlie Tapp sends a telegram to Graham, asking him to dissociate himself from churches with racist policies.

The next day the *State-Times* reports Graham's response to our interruption of his press conference:

> During the press conference, Graham told the audience social concern is a part of religion, but we must not lose sight of teaching the gospel. He said he cares about social problems, the poor and minority groups, 'but the main thrust of my message is to be converted and born again ... I think we ought to get back to the gospel'.

As expected, the Graham machine fills LSU's Tiger Stadium each night of the Crusade. The organizers are experts at staging an event of this magnitude. With the music and star performers, the nightly crowd of 30,000 is treated to a spectacle. Dr Graham is spell-binding. While he doesn't have much of a theological background, that doesn't matter. Many of those attending 'find Jesus'. But while there's a lot of talk about 'finding Jesus', nothing is said about racial intolerance.

A major surprise is Graham's total refusal to respond to our challenge. We speculate this may have something to do with fear of a backlash from the churches that provide the logistical and financial support for his Crusades. Of course, it may be that he honestly doesn't believe that churches should be involved in promoting social justice. We're not privy to his motives.

One member of the Ad Hoc Committee suggests we sponsor a mini-crusade on 'Religion and Social Justice' on the grounds of LSU to coincide with the second-last day of the Crusade. We all agree it's a good idea. There's no difficulty finding local clergy to participate. More than two hundred attend our hastily organized event on a sunny Saturday afternoon. It's like one big picnic, with the crowd sitting on the grass. One speaker, the Reverend Edgar T. 'Toby' Van Buren, a Unitarian minister, accuses the Baptist churches supporting the Crusade of 'outright hypocrisy'. He has some tough words for the evangelist.

'Billy Graham follows public opinion but does not lead it,' said Van Buren. 'He espouses easy answers to complex questions.'

Our efforts inspire students and faculty at the university. The LSU student newspaper joins in the challenge to Graham.

'It is not that the people are not listening Mr Graham, it is that you are not saying anything,' proclaims one editorial.

As I sit in LSU's Tiger Stadium with Barbara Favorite and other members of our group on the last night of the Crusade, it feels as if we're part of the supporting cast for one of Graham's television productions. I'm thinking this definitely is not about promoting racial tolerance and brotherhood. And it's not, in my mind, a resurrection experience. Maybe I've become too cynical about religious fundamentalism to be inspired by this kind of gathering. Graham would probably say that I need to confess my sins and be 'born again'.

By late Sunday evening, at the end of the week-long Crusade, I'm relieved the whole episode is behind us and I'm feeling positive about what we've accomplished. We've demonstrated that a handful of committed people can take on one of the most powerful men in America. We manage, with relatively little effort, to draw national media attention to institutionalized racism.

With the conclusion of the Crusade I'm happy to get back to my regular routine on Monday morning. Charlie Tapp informs me that Mayor Dumas has been called by a member of the Crusade team with a complaint of 'harassment'. Then I get a call from Washington D.C. It's an official of the Federal government, letting me know that an investigator is en route to Baton Rouge to investigate the activities of the VISTA volunteers during the Graham Crusade. So much for getting back into my routine: there's obviously trouble in the works.

My grey polyester visitor is a staff member from the OEO office in Atlanta. I suspect his visit is prompted by a complaint made either by Billy Graham or by one of Graham's people. He confirms that somebody in the Graham organization had lodged a complaint.

The investigator turns out to be a stereotypical government bureaucrat who knows very little about the VISTA program. He asks about my involvement in Crusade activities and I provide all the details. After his brief visit the investigator returns to Washington.

Charlie Tapp, Percy Sims and I meet one morning to discuss a possible response.

'Do you think the media might see this as a human interest story – Nixon and Graham ganging up on a group of young Americans fighting for social justice?' Charlie asks.

Percy and I recognize immediately that Charlie is on to something.

'Let's call their bluff,' says Percy.

I put in a telephone call to local UPI reporter Mike Miller and he's in Charlie's office within thirty minutes. The story is on the news wires by mid-afternoon.

The UPI news release includes the information that the investigation 'was apparently ordered by OEO director Donald Rumsfeld on Monday after Graham or an official of the crusade complained of Deevy's activity'. The OEO investigator is Fred Mosley from Atlanta and the UPI story continues by quoting Charlie Tapp saying that Mosley has told him that 'Rumsfield himself had ordered that an investigator be sent to Baton Rouge'. Like Graham, Rumsfeld enjoys a special relationship with Nixon.

Within twenty-four hours I get a call from Washington saying the investigation is merely a routine response to a complaint from a concerned citizen. I'm led to believe the case is closed. In the spirit of fair play I think we may have an unfair advantage because of our friends in the local media. Then I reflect on wheels within wheels, turning behind closed doors, unseen hands doing the bidding of unseen forces. I have a gut feeling that my challenge to Dr Graham may have consequences down the road.

As usual, Charlie Tapp provides unqualified support. On 30 October 1970, he's quoted as telling the *Times-Picayune* in New Orleans: 'If we dodge this issue, we ought to close our doors.'

The encounter with America's most celebrated clergyman leaves me pondering my motivations. Why get involved in this protest, which was sure to be unpopular with many devout southern Christians? It was also unpopular with some of my former clerical colleagues in the Diocese of Alexandria. I know from my experience in the ministry how difficult and unpopular it is to take a public stand on racial segregation. Perhaps that is why it was important for me to put myself out there on this occiasion: in my days as the public face of the Catholic Church in two white parishes, I had done nothing to advance racial integration. Whatever the motivation, the whole experience has taken me well outside my comfort zone. I'm happy that the Crusade, and the fall-out from it, is over and I can move on.

13.

'Shut up, nigger lover!'

By early 1971, after less than two years as VISTA superior, I've already been involved in two significant confrontations with the Establishment. It's time to cool it, I tell myself. It's not that my bosses at Community Advancement have any issues with my advocacy work, but I realise myself it could become a distraction and a problem for them.

I'm relieved to find myself back into everyday routine work. There are, however, ongoing anxieties, nestled at the back of my mind, about facing the family back home in Ireland. I know at some time the prodigal son – the ex-priest – will have to return to make peace with his father. But the thought of such a visit is extremely stressful. Truthfully, I'm not yet psychologically ready for it. And I'm wondering if Daddy or other family members might not want to see me, though I'm hoping this is not the situation.

In the meantime I'm encouraged that news from the family is ever more positive. Andy is now firmly anchored in Dublin. He has a job as a night telephonist and in September 1971 he married Mary Ann Fitzpatrick, from Kilronan on the Aran Islands. As I did not yet feel ready to face the family as a layman, I did not go to his wedding. With proceeds from the sale of Drumagh, Andy bought a house near Dublin city centre, just off the South Circular Road, and he and Mary Ann have started married life there.

They have also acquired the house next door and keep lodgers in both properties. And now they are expecting a baby, a first niece or nephew. Michael and Elsie are also well settled into the home and farm they bought near Portlaoise. Michael combines nursing with his first love, farming. Tom is enjoying life in London where he is a nurse in a busy general hospital, while Mary, Rita and Lena (now a religious sister and doing community work in north Dublin) are each absorbed in their work and seem fulfilled. And nobody has anything much to report from Drumagh, definitely a case of no news being good news!

Still, though, there is the lingering worry about what's going to happen when I eventually go home – and I'm going to have to face Ireland sometime. I simply put family concerns into the background as I become more involved in my emerging social advocacy role. My experiences are transforming my views on social justice.

One of my responsibilities is to debrief VISTA volunteers as they get ready to leave Baton Rouge after one or two years working in the community. The departing volunteers always talk about how their involvement has transformed their lives. One member of the group, on the eve of returning to California, verbalizes a sentiment regularly expressed by departing volunteers: 'This experience has radically influenced my thinking. I've learned more in one year working in the Scotlandville community than I learned in four years of college.'

My involvement in community work is having a similar impact on me. I'm undergoing a transformation in consciousness. The most profound change has to do with my growing understanding of the experiences of black people in Southern society, an understanding born out of real world encounters in the streets and neighbourhoods of Baton Rouge. During the years in the priesthood I'd lived in white ghettos. Now I'm finding out, albeit vicariously, what it's like to be a black person in the Deep South.

An encounter that brings home the depth of racism in this capital city happens only a few months after moving into my suburban apartment. One day the apartment manager tells me I can't have visitors who are black.

'Look friend, you've been a good tenant. It's just that I've had complaints from other tenants – you understand?'

'No, I don't really understand. Why can't I entertain co-workers – I pay my rent.'

My protest falls on deaf ears. Unfortunately, the apartment manager doesn't share my views about my rights as a tenant. It becomes clear I've only one option. Within weeks I relocate. I rent an upstairs apartment in a large house on Park Boulevard. Located in a college community just a few blocks from the LSU campus, there's less possibility of hassles from racist neighbours.

A more dramatic consciousness-raising experience happens as a result of an encounter in a Baton Rouge nightclub. This is a case of innocently stumbling into trouble. I'm a guest at a party at a local hotel for a Legal Services attorney, a black woman, who's leaving town to take up a position in Washington D.C. We celebrate for a couple of hours and then, after the party, a black friend and I adjourn to the hotel lounge to have a chat, listen to music and have a drink. We're having a relaxing conversation at the bar when a white guy with a small mind and a big fist walks up and just sucker punches my companion in the face.

The attack is totally unprovoked. I'm outraged. What a racist jerk, I say to myself. A young, white Baton Rouge cop soon arrives on the scene and I attempt to protest about what happened.

'Shut up, or you'll find yourself in jail, nigger lover,' he says.

'But look at what's happened to my friend,' I say. 'He was just minding his own business.'

'I said shut up or you'll be on your way downtown. Don't you understand English?'

'Officer, I want to file a complaint.'

'Shut up!' he snarls.

The cop has hate in his eyes. I'm thinking, if I were black, having these kinds of encounters on a regular basis, it would be enough to turn me into a gun-toting radical.

As time passes, there are other experiences that provide insight into the racism experienced by blacks in Baton Rouge. During my years in the priesthood I was totally oblivious to the fact that many blacks experience all kinds of abuse at the hands of racist law officers. The trumped-up charges against Frank Stewart had brought home to me the vulnerability of blacks in the face of abuses by law enforcement. Now, as I venture beyond the racial divide, I'm beginning to understand the anger of Malcolm X and H. Rap Brown and other young black leaders. I'm thinking, why should blacks allow themselves to be abused by white bigots, even if they wear law enforcement badges?

My evolving consciousness begins affecting my attitudes and behaviour. I'm becoming radicalized. I want to stand up and be counted. Opportunities to take a stand are not hard to find. One of these opportunities happens almost serendipitously.

One night in March of 1972, I'm having a drink with Charlie Tapp, Percy Simms and Charlie's friend Joan at the Baton Rouge Press Club. The discussion turns to the impending eviction of an elderly black woman who's the victim of a loan shark scam. The eviction is scheduled for the following morning. It has become a major story in the local Baton Rouge media. At the same time, the Louisiana legislature is debating a law that would tighten the loopholes used by loan sharks.

'Guys, what do you think about making a stand in this situation – anyone up for a little civil disobedience?' asks Tapp.

We all agree the impending eviction offers a unique opportunity and we decide to stage a protest. Next morning, 7 March, Charlie, Percy, Joan and I sit on the steps of the doorway of the house and block the sheriff's deputies from entering. We're arrested and taken away in a police van, with the cameras clicking. Charlie, Percy and I are in one jail cell and Joan is in the next cell.

Later in the day we're released on our own signatures. Charges are dropped. We succeed in making an important statement and we're hoping the Louisiana legislature will take note.

Legislation does, indeed, get passed, but too late for the elderly lady.

On a noontime visit to the LSU campus I learn that a student named David Duke is using a forum at the Free Speech Wall to spout his particular brand of race hatred. I step forward and challenge Duke in front of hundreds of students. Our debates become a regular noontime feature for several weeks. Duke has a slick presentation – he quotes the Bible in support of his thesis about the superiority of white people. The truth is, I'm no match for this demagogue. My appearances at the Free Speech Wall have little impact on Duke's diatribes, but they provide some personal satisfaction. Duke becomes a Grand Wizard of the Ku Klux Klan a few years later and gains national and international notoriety for his white supremacist views.

My evolution in consciousness is not limited to the issue of racial discrimination. I'm also becoming more aware of the women's movement. This happens as a result of a friendship that developed after moving to Park Boulevard, near the LSU campus, back in the autumn of 1969. I become friends with David Madden, writer-in-residence at LSU, and his wife Roberta, a feminist and president of the local chapter of the National Organization for Women (NOW). The Maddens live directly across the boulevard in a beautiful old Southern mansion with their son, Blake, and David's novel, *Cassandra Singing* is receiving great acclaim. He's the first widely published writer I've ever met and he fits my stereotype that writers are naturally progressive.

Roberta is not just into promoting the rights of women. She's also passionately interested in social and civil rights for all groups. Occasionally, I'd walk over to the Madden home for the monthly NOW meeting. David and I are sometimes the only men in attendance. I like that ratio. Roberta jokes that I might find a partner by attending meetings regularly. I come to think Roberta is on my side in more ways than one! Certainly the NOW meetings offer the opportunity to meet some of the brightest and most dynamic women in Baton Rouge, and I develop several rewarding friendships. But I assure Roberta that I'm not just interested in the meetings to hit on attractive, clever women.

On another front, our Baton Rouge VISTA project is a refuge for several young men who don't want to go to Vietnam, so-called 'draft dodgers'. As time goes on I become more involved in the anti-war movement – and in supporting VISTA volunteers who are opposed to the war. Several members of our group organize protest meetings and stage all-night vigils at LSU. Some are waging their own personal wars with their draft boards. A law professor at LSU provides free advice to these individuals.

One day my boss in the OEO expresses concern about our anti-war activities: 'Ed, you know about the Hatch Act – your VISTA volunteers, as employees of the Federal government, are not supposed to be involved in anti-war protests.'

The Hatch Act of 1939 stipulates that Federal employees may not take 'any active part' in political campaigns. I advise members of the group to exercise discretion in their anti-war activity. They understand where I'm coming from. The reality is I don't really care that much about the Hatch Act. As a pacifist, I don't believe we should be sending our young men to fight in Southeast Asia.

With the evolution in consciousness resulting from in-the-trenches experiences, I'm no longer the same person who drove into Baton Rouge in July 1969. The extent of the transformation comes home to me during a visit with old friends in north Louisiana.

One day I get a call from an Irish priest in Shreveport, telling me he's having a small St Patrick's Day dinner party at his rectory for a few fellow Irishmen. He extends an invitation and I accept. It's nice to spend St Patrick's Day with people from home.

It's a relaxing evening. Several of the guests are priests I'd gotten to know well during the years in the ministry. After a few drinks and an enjoyable dinner we adjourn to the living room to continue the chat. And then one of my old friends says, 'Eddie, what's this about you getting involved with those coloured folks in Baton Rouge?'

He's not the only one with concerns.

'Eddie, I read a story in the *Morning Advocate* about you getting arrested,' says another of my former colleagues. 'Not good for your reputation – people will start thinking you're a troublemaker.'

Suddenly, I realize I'm on a different wavelength from my former colleagues. I respond defensively: 'You all might be surprised to hear me say this, but I consider what I'm doing to be the Lord's work.'

They could see the old 'Father Deevy' they'd known had been radicalized, that my agenda now had more to do with effecting social change than saving souls. Perhaps there was also an implied criticism in my response. Either way, it introduces a note of tension.

The party breaks up at midnight and I set out on the long drive home to Baton Rouge. Cruising down the almost deserted highway, I've time to reflect back on the journey travelled since first setting foot in the USA. I'm feeling positive about the direction my life has taken since leaving the ministry. As I drive through the pine woods of northeast Louisiana, I'm thinking how lucky I am to have successfully made the transition to a new life as a social activist. My 'leap over the wall' has resulted in a soft landing.

14.

My first ever rock concert

In the middle of all the advocacy there's an interesting weekend interlude in June 1971. On a Friday evening I am at home, looking forward to a quiet weekend, when I get a call from my friend Sondra.

'Eddie, would you like to go to the Celebration of Life?'

The controversial music festival, billed as the southern version of Woodstock, has been all over the local media for a couple of weeks. The organizers had been having trouble getting a location. Originally scheduled to be held on an island on the Mississippi River, it had been postponed several times because of injunctions filed by local communities. It's now to be held in McCrea, a small hamlet on the banks of the Atchafalaya River, about an hour's drive from Baton Rouge.

Sondra tells me she has a spare ticket because the friend that was supposed to accompany her has had to drop out.

'I'll pick you up at your place in an hour. Bring some wine and soda and I'll bring food. And bring a blanket or a sleeping bag.'

One hour later I'm on my way to my first ever rock concert. Sondra had come into my life as one of the many young professionals I've met while campaigning for Frank. We would run into each other occasionally at gatherings of progressives, for instance at the local Unitarian Fellowship. She is a thirty-something divorcee and though she normally looks appropriately sober, when she picks me up wearing skimpy cut-off shorts and a light summer shirt she appears to have turned into a hippie. She looks great.

I tease her about being dressed for the weather.

'Eddie, we're going to swamp country ... it's going to get hot and sticky.'

The concert site is several miles off the main road and in the middle of nowhere. A New Orleans motorcycle gang is handling security at the entrance. There's a one-handed biker, with brass-knuckles, threatening anyone trying to get in without a ticket. That's not us, so we have no trouble getting in.

Inside we find thousands have already set up in the vast open space. We eventually find ourselves a clear patch near the main stage, just a couple of hundred yards from the Atchafalaya River. We stake out our territory.

As the evening passes we welcome several young couples into our space until we're a mini-community of eight. Sondra and I are the only locals. The rest have come from faraway places like Chicago, Miami, Ohio and San Francisco.

By nightfall the crowd has swelled. To the naked eye there seems to be tens of thousands of people. The music starts. Nobody knows who's playing but that doesn't seem to matter. We've been told that the list of performers includes Chuck Berry, the Chambers Brothers, Melanie, It's a Beautiful Day and Stephen Stills, but that the line-up is going to change – because the dates of the festival had been changed several times, performers have had to drop out.

One of the bands is still playing at two o'clock in the morning when I drift off to sleep. By noon on Saturday the temperature is over 100 degrees and, as Sondra predicted, it's hot and sticky. I wander about to take in the scene. The air reeks of marijuana smoke. The guys are all shirtless. So are many of the girls. I'm still far too much of a repressed Irish Catholic to take the sight of so many bare-breasted women for granted. I'm certainly not in Kansas anymore!

In the middle of the afternoon the heavens open. The torrential rain is heavier than any I've ever experienced in my life and there's mud everywhere.

After the rains the sun comes out and again goes down in a red ball of fire. We share food and Boone's Farm Apple Wine. A girl from San Francisco suggests that we get ourselves into the right mind-set before the fireworks display and produces some Mexican weed. This certainly enhances the experience. The ugly delay tower carrying the sound around the venue is transformed into a beautiful piece of art surrounded by a rainbow of colour. The crowd, spread out as far as the eye can see, becomes a community celebrating life. It's an out-of-body experience. Happily, when it ends a few hours later, there are no bad side-effects from my trip.

On Sunday the heat and humidity are again unbearable. There's no escaping the blazing sun. Hundreds go skinny-dipping in the Atchafalaya, oblivious of the danger posed by this fast-rushing river. And again the torrential rains come in the afternoon. Mudsliding becomes a diversion. We hear rumours of violence. From time to time there's an announcement from the stage warning people to watch out for undercover cops busting people for their drugs. These announcements are greeted with cheers.

Conditions are rapidly going downhill. It's just the second day of the festival and it's difficult to find basic supplies. The portable toilets are inadequate for a crowd that's swelled to well over 100,000. Many are upset because several of the big-name rock bands are no-shows. Food becomes the most precious commodity. Occasionally someone comes up to us offering drugs in exchange for food. We hear a rumour that the concert might be shut down by the authorities because of public outrage. We understand that there's growing concern in the outside community about the drugs, sex, nudity and violence. I can well imagine that: this is the heart of the Deep South after all.

On Sunday evening I start looking forward to getting back to Baton Rouge. We've run out of food and drink. The downpours have turned the place into a muddy swamp. Sondra and I plan to leave at sunrise on Monday morning.

In the meantime, I become aware of tension in our group. An older guy named Bud, who is from Texas, has been trying to make a move on Sondra. The girl he came with disapproves. And I'm not happy about his pursuit of my friend. At four o'clock on Monday morning I wake up to the sounds of an argument. Bud's girlfriend is pissed off and she collects her few belongings and disappears into the night.

Sondra suggests we pack up our stuff and leave. It's not yet sunrise as we start making our way to the main exit. By five o'clock, after a slow, tedious walk through the sleeping bodies, we reach the car.

'Eddie, it was pretty obvious you didn't like Bud. Were you upset with me?' Sondra says as we drive south.

'I didn't like the fact that he was so aggressive. The guy was a jerk. The way he treated his girlfriend and, I know we're not lovers, but I didn't like him messing around with you. I wasn't upset with you, but I was pissed-off with him.'

There follows a conversation about whether or not I find Sondra attractive (I do) and why I didn't make a move on her (the conditioning of a repressive Irish Catholic boyhood probably, but I don't burden her with that stuff). Back at my apartment we end up sharing a shower. She suggests it will save hot water. She obviously doesn't have my hang-ups.

Afterwards I'm grateful to Sondra for inviting me to share in the festival. Already I know it's going to be an experience I'll always remember. At the VISTA office, I decide not to say anything about my weekend.

Next day I hear that the police pulled the plug on the concert on Monday night. The planned eight-day event comes to a halt after four days. The lack of sanitary facilities is a factor in this decision.

Time magazine sums up the Celebration of Life festival as 'a bleak experience of mud, sweat and tears'. I could not describe my weekend as bleak. It had been liberating.

Later I learn that two people died in the fast-rushing Atchafalaya River and that undercover agents made more than 100 drug busts. I'm thinking that what had started at Woodstock two years earlier may have ended in that vast open field in the middle of nowhere.

15.

Surviving a Texas hold-up

In the ghettos of Baton Rouge I continue to discover a whole new world that I'd never before experienced. Baton Rouge has three main low-income areas: Eden Park – the most blighted area with poor housing, poverty and high rates of drug-related crime; Scotlandville – a mostly low-income black community that also includes middle class black areas; South Baton Rouge – a predominantly black area, though again more of a mix of low-income and middle class housing. Apart from these, the City of Baton Rouge and the Parish of East Baton Rouge (a consolidated administrative area) also has pockets of white poverty and several VISTA volunteers work in these areas.

Sociologists use labels such as 'the inner city' or 'the underclass' to describe this world. However, these labels don't begin to describe the poverty, crime, hopelessness, violence and drug addiction that are an integral part of this experience. In the impoverished areas of Baton Rouge I see these conditions first-hand. I get to know young black girls who drop out of school, have babies and become dependent on welfare payments. I get to know 'dudes' who rob and steal and who would kill for a fix. Regularly on Monday mornings, when I get to my office, I ask one of the VISTA volunteers if any of the people we are working with in the low-income black neighbourhoods had been shot during the weekend. Too often the answer is in the affirmative. Life is cheap in the ghetto.

But it's only when I have a violent encounter with young men from one of those neighbourhoods that I gain a truly meaningful appreciation of living with fear of crime and violence. One dark winter night my car breaks down on the way home from a community meeting. I decide to park and walk the short distance home. Within a few hundred yards of my apartment I'm ambushed by several young blacks and robbed. Since I am ambushed from behind, I don't know how many of them there are, and it's probably no more than two, but it feels like more. They knock me down, steal my wallet and leave me lying on the street with a bruised, bleeding head and a broken right arm. Dazed and confused, I stumble down the street to my apartment and up the stairs to my second-floor apartment. 'Jesus, look at my bloody face,' I say to myself as I look into my bathroom mirror. There's blood everywhere. My face, in my hair and all over my clothes. I manage to call VISTA volunteer Sandy Bagley, a nurse who lives just a few blocks away. Sandy comes over and cleans the cuts and patches me up. I'm getting angrier by the minute.

'Sandy, these fuckers didn't have to slam my head against the pavement to get my wallet.'

'Ed, there's no point in getting angry. You need to get that arm checked out tomorrow. What you need now is a good night's sleep.'

I'm too shaken-up to go to sleep.

Next morning, word about my mugging spreads at Community Advancement. Betty Williams, a black community leader and a co-worker, comes over to my apartment to commiserate.

'Ed, I'm sorry the brothers did this to you. You're out there helping and this has to happen. This is bad shit.'

By this time my head no longer hurts, but I'm nursing a sore arm. I've cooled off and have become more philosophical about the whole thing.

'Don't feel sorry for me,' I say to her. 'The thing is, what can we do about the conditions that contribute to making these dudes feel alienated and hopeless?'

The mugging in Baton Rouge turns out to be a rehearsal for a much more frightening encounter in Austin, Texas shortly after. I'm in Austin to attend a meeting for VISTA supervisors. After attending a kick-off event on the first evening, I lose my way on the way back to my motel. I'm driving in circles, so I stop at a red light and roll down the window to ask for directions. A young man walks up to the car, apparently offering directions. Within seconds I have company in the back seat. The fellow giving directions jumps into the front seat. A hard object that feels like the barrel of a gun touches the back of my head.

'Okay man, just keep your fuckin' mouth shut and do what you're told.'

'Where are we going?'

'I said keep your fuckin' mouth shut.'

We arrive at an open, deserted place high above the city of Austin. I have no idea where we are. It's pitch dark and I'm thinking this might be the place they bring the city garbage. Below, the lights of the city stretch out for miles. I'm alone with these two fearsome strangers. They ask for my wristwatch. It has special sentimental meaning – a friend in Bunkie had given it to me – but this isn't something to think about at this moment. Then I hand over my wallet. It has a couple of hundred dollars in $20 bills. The young man in the back seat becomes agitated and wants to know where the rest of the money is hidden.

'Give us the fuckin' money you've hidden,' he demands.

'I've given you everything I have,' I say.

'Don't give us that jive – is it under your seat?'

The back-seat passenger taps me on the back of the head with the gun. 'Look man, if you value your life, you'll tell us where the fuckin' money is hidden.'

115

I realize a false move could be fatal. I'm thinking they could just shoot me, dump my body and nobody would ever know what happened. As I sit in the driver's seat – terrified – the thought flashes through my mind that my family in Ireland might never find out what had happened to me. The argument in the car goes on for what seems like a lifetime. They finally accept my word that there's no money hidden in the car.

I breathe a sigh of relief.

One of my captors – the young man in the front seat – says he's a heroin addict and would steal from his mother for a fix. He's almost apologetic about what has just happened. I tell them I have acquaintances in Baton Rouge who are heroin addicts, including a friend who stole my stereo equipment. We begin talking about the problems that causes dudes to turn to drugs. It's a strange conversation to be having under the circumstances.

The back-seat passenger gets agitated, says it's time to get back to town. He insists they're going to have to leave me behind.

'Let me drive back, I'll drop you guys off and then I'll be on my way.'

The back-seat passenger objects. He's concerned I'll go to the police.

'Look man, what's happened is between us – going to the police to turn in two brothers is the last thing I'd want to do. The pigs will never know about this.'

At first they argue among themselves. Finally, they agree to let me drive the car back into the city of Austin.

We continue to talk on the way back. I'm telling them how I grew up in Ireland and ended up working for the anti-poverty agency in Baton Rouge.

'And how are black folk treated by the police in Ireland?' one of them asks.

'As a matter of fact, there are no black people living in Ireland, except maybe a few university students.'

This bit of information surprises them. They talk about how little opportunity there is growing up as a young black man in America. We're sharing anecdotes about the similarities between conditions in Baton Rouge and Austin. I'm thinking about how surreal this is. They have robbed me and the drugs have robbed them of any sense of appropriate or inappropriate behaviour, so now we're talking like old friends.

As I'm about to drop my two 'passengers' at a rundown housing project the young man in the front seat hands me a $20 bill.

'This will get you back to Louisiana,' he says.

A godsend! I know it will be enough for a tank of gasoline and some breakfast. They give me directions on how to get back to my motel. It's about two o'clock in the morning and the streets are deserted. I walk into the motel room and begin to think about what's happened – and what could have happened – on this fateful night. I'm shaking all over.

Exhausted, I kneel beside the bed and bury my head in my hands. 'Thanks be to Jesus, Mary and Joseph,' I say to myself.

I'm grateful for having survived the ordeal. I try to forget about my near-death experience – it's too frightening to contemplate what might have happened. I can hear myself breathe as I attempt to regain composure.

My thoughts drift back to childhood, to Drumagh. It's a world far removed from the kind of violence I've just encountered. As a child growing up I'd heard Daddy talk about the one murder in recent memory that had occurred in the entire countryside. The 'Smyth Murder,' as it was known, had been a national sensation in the late 1930s and became part of the local lore. (A butter buyer, Cornelius Dennehy, who was living in Abbeyleix, was robbed in his car on a quiet road just a few miles from Drumagh. The thief shot Dennehy in the head at close range. After an eight-day trial that held the country in thrall, local man James Dermot Smyth was convicted of the robbery and murder and was hanged in January 1939.)

Kneeling beside this bed, almost five thousand miles from home, I'm asking myself if this is the life I really want. Has my life moved too close to the edge? Should I give up crusading for social justice and live like other middle class men of my age? Should I pack up and find myself a quiet place in my native Ireland?

The tap of a gun on the back of my head has forced me to consider some serious existential questions.

Now, in this gloomy motel room, my mind is racing and I realize I'm getting into an agitated state. It's time to get myself together and start moving. Daydreaming is getting me nowhere.

There's no use trying to go to sleep – I just want to be on my way. I take a shower and pack my belongings. The sun comes up and I go in search of a cup of coffee. It's only six o'clock but I'm ready to hit the road. I call the conference hotel and leave a message for my boss, the Regional Director of VISTA, to say I have to return to Baton Rouge for personal reasons. I'm too shattered to participate in management workshops.

On the long drive back to Louisiana, I reflect on how large sections of American cities are becoming human wastelands. It's a world unknown to public officials and media pundits. All these communities have to offer is fear, poverty, crime and rat-infested living conditions. This is the 'other America', that which the socialist intellectual Michael Harrington had written about in his ground-breaking 1962 book, *The Other America: Poverty in the United States*.

What's the answer, I keep asking myself. Maybe some kind of Marshall Plan for the underclass; if America could provide funds to rebuild post-World War II Europe, surely it could do the same for its own people? I'm thinking the prospect that society will address the issue of poverty in America isn't good – not in the Nixon era anyway. Besides, so long as the problem is hidden away, why should the politicians be concerned?

The near-death experience on that hilltop outside Austin leaves me with nightmares for weeks and months. Sometimes I wake up

scared and frightened. And then I realize it's just a nightmare –
and I thank God that I'm still alive.

With the passage of time, memories of what happened on that
fearful night in Texas fade into the past. It becomes just another
incident on a wayward Irishman's unlikely journey.

16.

The prodigal son returns to the homeland

My work in Baton Rouge begins to take its toll. I'm feeling stressed-out, suffering from battle fatigue. And as I become increasingly involved in civil rights activity, I'm becoming more aware of the emotional price I'm paying for my work as social activist.

My mind and body whisper that it's time to go home. This farm boy needs to be surrounded by green and needs to replace the Southern drawl with an Irish brogue. While I tell friends I'm planning a trip to the 'auld sod' to get away from the stresses of Baton Rouge, I know deep down there's a more fundamental reason for making this trip to Ireland. I'm beginning to feel like a fugitive and I need to reconnect with family and homeland and to make peace with my father, who I haven't seen for six years.

As I describe the planned itinerary, I discover that I'm not the only one longing for some R'n'R. Soon, I have three travelling companions signed up for the trip – VISTA volunteers Sandy Bagley and Mike McCarthy, and Mike's wife, Joan. Sandy and Mike are coming to the end of their tenure in Baton Rouge.

I am experiencing considerable anxiety about my first trip home since leaving the priesthood. While I know it's becoming more commonplace in Ireland for men to leave the priesthood, there's still a stigma attached to this decision. Such men are perceived as having failed on two fronts: having the audacity to think they had it in them to be priests in the first place, and then not being up to it. In addition, if there's any hint that a woman is the reason for a man leaving the ministry, this suggests weakness or a selfish surrender to base human instincts. Daddy has dropped a few lines occasionally – mostly just to say hello. My letters to him have been somewhat impersonal – 'hope you're keeping well' and that kind of stuff. I wonder what kind of reception I'll receive when I arrive in Dublin. And how will Daddy's wife of nearly four years, Maura, respond to me? At least I know I can count on Michael and Elsie's hospitality. They've already assured me I'll always be very welcome at their home.

My stomach is churning as I step off the plane at Dublin Airport in the late summer of 1972. I have no idea what to expect. I'm not even sure if any family members will be there to meet me. Mike, Joan and Sandy are not aware that this is my first trip back to Ireland without the Roman collar and I haven't told them how I'm feeling.

We collect luggage and walk through customs. I'm surprised – relieved - to be greeted by a large welcoming party that includes my father.

There are the stiff hugs – hugging is not something that happens much in our family – and handshakes. While members of my family greet my travelling companions, Daddy says he'd like to talk to me privately. I go off to the side with Daddy and Mary. But there is no speech or significant declarations. It's a bit strained but as I get into the detail of our travel plans, we both start to relax. Obviously he just needs one-on-one time to get the measure of this new incarnation of his son, this shaggy-haired guy in jeans who is so far removed from the clean-cut boy and young cleric he used to know. He needs to take in and register the changes and to make whatever internal recalibrations are needed. Come to think of it, I need that too. He asks when I'm going to come to Drumagh.

I can now relax - the most traumatic part of this visit is behind me. The ice is broken.

Mike, Joan, Sandy and I set out on a tour that first takes us south to County Wicklow and then up to Northern Ireland. We approach the border full of curiosity and apprehension. We know that security is a deadly serious business and we act accordingly. It turns out to be a rather intimidating experience – British soldiers surround us with guns at-the-ready. Every inch of our rented car is searched. All this security speaks volumes about the strife crippling Northern Ireland. As I watch the young soldier prodding through our personal belongings with the barrel of his gun, I have a sudden sense of connection with my father and his brother as young men, imagining how they must have felt being subjected to this kind of harassment and intimidation on a regular basis.

After the border experience we arrive in Belfast to find a city that looks like an armed camp. There's bombed-out buildings everywhere. Lots of barbed wire and sectarian graffiti. 'Brits Get Out!' competes with slogans demanding 'No Pope Here!'

'Don't stop – keep moving!' says Sandy, as we crawl over speed-bumps and move slowly through streets lined with armed soldiers. We have white knuckles and white faces by the time we get through the city.

Mike and Joan tease me about bringing them to a war zone and not providing flak jackets. We all laugh nervously and are very glad to leave Belfast in the rear-view mirror and find ourselves travelling through the beautiful countryside of County Antrim. We motor on through Donegal in the Northwest, and down through Sligo and along the west coast. From Galway we take a boat to the island of Inishmore.

Inishmore is the highlight of our trip. Though I'm Irish, I'm as much of a tourist as my American friends. This is a wild western world that feels quite removed from my sober south Laois upbringing. The grey, sparse, uncluttered island is perched out in the Atlantic waves, far away from the hassles of the modern world.

Island natives earn a living from fishing and tourism. Most speak Irish as their first language. The preferred mode of transport is the bicycle. A visit to the local parish hall helps us discover the aerobic value of traditional Irish dancing. At a pub in Kilronan, the main settlement on the island, we sit and listen to stories of the past. One night Tim Pat Coogan, editor of the *Irish Press* and author of a recent book, *The IRA: A History*, is holding his own, telling stories with the islanders. He may be a celebrity of sorts on the mainland, but here he is just another customer.

One evening at sunset I find myself sitting on a high cliff over the sea, looking south towards the Cliffs of Moher. It's a quiet place to commune with nature. All of the battles back in Louisiana take on a different perspective as I listen to the sound of the waves pounding against the island. I feel the stress draining from my body.

Sitting alone on this rock, I'm feeling like a pilgrim who's been on a journey. I remember a story I'd first read as a student in Knockbeg College. It's the story of Odysseus, told in Homer's epic poem, *The Odyssey*. I'm remembering how Odysseus, on his return journey from Troy, visited various islands.

Mine, too, has been a turbulent journey, and as I gaze on the ocean waves, I'm moved to consider the winding road already travelled. There are no regrets. But for a moment I wonder if, like Odysseus, I might be tempted to settle in to island life and grow roots. This thought passes. Soon, I know, I'll be ready to resume my American Odyssey.

After the retreat to Inishmore my travelling companions and I spend a day at the Oyster Festival in Clarinbridge, outside Galway City. We're supposed to be celebrating the oyster harvest but it seems more like a Guinness festival. Getting in the spirit of the day, Mike McCarthy and I demonstrate our ability to put away pints of the black stuff to the accompaniment of traditional music, dancing in the streets and unbridled celebrating. It's a mini-version of the New Orleans Mardi Gras.

'We're a long way from Eden Park,' says Sandy, referring to the impoverished neighbourhood where she works back in Baton Rouge. We are indeed culturally in a very different world.

Towards the end of the trip we spend several days on Michael's farm. One evening Mike McCarthy, Michael and I go on a visit to a pub in the local village of Timahoe. A competition has sprung up between 'our' Timahoe and Timahoe in County Kildare, both claiming to be the ancestral home of Richard Nixon. Each community is motivated by a desire to attract tourists.

'We're here in Timahoe on behalf of President Nixon to determine if this is his ancestral home,' says Mike with his midwestern accent. 'You know our president is very proud of his Irish roots.'

The people in the bar appear to buy the story and make appropriate efforts to influence our decision. We enjoy an evening of fellowship and good fun. As we get ready to take our leave, I propose a toast: 'Let's drink to a famous descendent of Timahoe, President Richard Nixon!'

The locals have no idea of the cynicism behind this toast. I know that this shifty-eyed politician is planning to destroy the programs established by President Johnson to combat poverty in the United States. On the way home we take delight in the fantasy of 'Tricky Dick' finding out we had a couple of drinks at his expense.

My final stop is Drumagh. Sandy and the McCarthys go their own way and I head for home. I know from our airport conversation how important it is to Daddy that I spend time with him, Patricia and Maura. This will be my first opportunity to meet Maura.

I arrive late in the evening. Maura is a sturdy looking woman with a plump handsome face and dark curly hair. She is also, undoubtedly, nervous about our meeting, realising how fraught the situation is for Daddy – my first visit since leaving the priesthood, my first stay in the new house, my first meeting with her. She is less socially at ease than Elsie was, but is nonetheless very pleasant and welcoming. The hot tea she brews is very welcome; not the see-through iced tea of Louisiana. This cuppa seems to carry healing qualities. After tea, Daddy and I are left to chat in the sitting room. I'm a little apprehensive. It's obvious he has something on his mind, so I clutch my tea and wait.

'Is it true?' he asks, almost as soon as the door closes behind Maura.

'Is what true, Daddy?'

'Eddie, are you married to a black woman back in the States?'

For a moment I think Daddy is putting me on. He's definitely gotten my attention. I respond with humour.

'Yes Daddy, I have her hidden outside in the boot of the car. I want you to be the first to meet her.'

His relief at my joking response is surprising to me. How little he knows me if he believes I would have married anyone, no matter her race, skin colour or culture, without telling the family. I tell him I have a circle of close women friends, including several black women, but that I haven't seriously considered marriage with anyone.

'Daddy, where did this story come from?' I ask.

'I'm not sure ... someone told me they heard it from someone else.' There are lots of extended family and neighbours with relatives in America. Perhaps someone spotted the story about my encounter with Billy Graham and jumped to conclusions: *If he has left the priesthood and now he's speaking up for blacks, he must be in a relationship with a black woman.*

That Daddy would put credence in gossip speaks volumes about the power of the grapevine in rural Ireland. I assure him he'll be the first to know if I make wedding plans.

The conversation continues. At times it's awkward and uncomfortable. Daddy talks about himself and his misfortunes. He sounds like the biblical Job. I'm thinking, I don't want to be made to feel guilty for any of my life decisions, including the decision to leave the priesthood. I decide to be firm but diplomatic.

'Daddy, I left the priesthood because I believed it was the right thing to do. I followed my conscience. It's really that simple.'

He listens, but I'm not sure he fully understands. I have the realization that he's more concerned about himself than about me – there's something self-protective in his rambling monologue. Perhaps I should be grateful he isn't focusing on my shortcomings. I suggest we continue the conversation at another time. I'm feeling emotionally and physically drained. I sense that I'm coming down with the 'flu.

Daddy gets up and fixes me a large hot whiskey. That night I sweat buckets and the 'flu symptoms disappear. Next morning, after a big traditional fry-up, I go out with Daddy to help feed the cattle. This token effort is bringing back all kinds of memories of the early years on the farm in Drumagh. And it brings back memories of a visit six years earlier. At that time I was commiserating with him about Elsie's illness and he was in tears. Now, as we hand bales of hay to the animals, we both seem to be in better places. The process of healing has begun.

The visit to Drumagh goes better than I could have expected. Maura has welcomed me with open arms. And Patricia, just six years old, is delighted that one of her big brothers has come home. Now that we've all adjusted to the new realities, I'm thinking that I won't leave it so long to come home again and I'll spend more time on my next visit.

Our family c. 1948: Michael, Tom (on Mammy's knee), Mammy, me, Mary, Andy, Daddy, Rita, and Lena in front.

Mammy and Daddy's wedding picture in the mid-1930s. They are in their early thirties, both from rural north County Kilkenny. She is a midwife and he is developing the farm he has recently acquired at Drumagh, Crettyard in County Laois.

Giving Daddy my first priestly blessing in the grounds of Carlow Cathedral after my ordination in June 1962. A proud moment for such a staunch Catholic father. He holds rosary beads in his clasped hands.

Lined up in front of the porch at Drumagh for the reception after my First Mass in our parish church are: Lena, Tom, Mary, Mammy, me, Daddy, Rita, Andy and Michael. Mary and Rita are not usually allowed out of the convent, but a brother being ordained is a special occasion. (Mammy's funeral eleven months later – sadly, not an occasion that they are permitted to attend.)

By the early1960s the broken down house and poor farm that Daddy had bought in the 1930s is a handsome property and his pride and joy. Within a few years he will have to sell it and by the early 1990s the house, the gardens and the out-buildings no longer exist, and the landscape we grew up with is unrecognisable.

Sure and 'tis Time for

By Verdis Dowdy
(Town Talk Feature Editor)

Sure and it'll be a great day for the Irish tomorrow, when anyone with even a remote connection with the Ould Country will be wearing a touch of green. St. Patrick's Day is here again!

St. Patrick's Day is a holiday of tremendous importance in Ireland, when homage is paid to the saint and much emphasis is placed on the Irish heritage. And because the Irish people have migrated to all parts of the globe, St. Patrick's Day is now an almost world-wide celebration.

A Wee Bit o' Green

A little bit of Ireland makes its way to Central Louisiana every year around this time when a box of shamrocks is received by Rev. Edward Deevy, assistant pastor of the Church of St. Anthony of

An example of the kind of Paddywhackery that goes on in the local papers in Louisiana every St Patrick's Day. As one of the few native Irishmen in either of the places I minister – Monroe and later Bunkie – I am usually featured. Even being hospitalised for a minor procedure in March 1969 doesn't get me off the hook.

At work in Bunkie in the mid-1960s. Looking the part of the busy and thoughtful young cleric writing some inspirational words for my Sunday sermon.

Summer 1968. On the day I am sworn in as an American citizen my Bunkie neighbour, Harriet 'Booby' Reed, throws me a surprise party and produces a flag-bedecked cake. The whole neighbourhood joins in the celebration.

Partying with co-workers from the anti-poverty VISTA programme in Baton Rouge in 1970. In some ways the transition from priest to layman is surprisingly smooth.

July 1973. Leaving Baton Rouge after four tumultuous and transformative years as a civil rights activist. This picture accompanies a feature in the local paper titled 'Goodbye Mr VISTA'.

With my friend, VISTA volunteer, Frank Stewart, on the water in Key Biscayne, Florida in late summer 1970. Frank has just been released from jail after five months behind bars on a trumped up charge of conspiring to murder the mayor of Baton Rouge. It is only when we get national attention for his case that the bogus charges are dropped.

Church Mix Statement Is Refused

Evangelist Billy Graham refused to accept a statement Monday from a young black woman about the reported refusal of certain Baton Rouge churches to admit her to worship services Sunday morning.

Graham refused to allow Barbara Favorite, an LSU student, to present him with the written statement at a press conference Monday afternoon.

"Only press people would be asking questions," during the gathering, the evangelist said.

The written statement was from the Citizens Concerned with Social Responsibilities of the Church in Baton Rouge. The group identifies itself as an ad hoc group whose membership includes people of different

RAPS WITH GRAHAM—Edward Deevy, right, requests permission from Bill Graham to allow Barbara Favorite, left, to present him with a statement during a press conference Monday afternoon. Graham said the newsmen came "to hear what I have to say." The statement concerned the refusal by several churches in Baton Rouge Sunday to admit blacks to worship in their services.

Coverage in a Louisiana newspaper, the *Advocate*, for the campaign to have the Reverend Billy Graham speak out against segregationist churchmen in Baton Rouge when he brings one of his Crusades to Louisiana State University in October 1970. Confronting the world famous evangelist is pretty nerve-wracking for a soft-spoken ex-priest from rural Ireland.

Billy Graham speaks at the LSU Crusade. He has a lot to say about 'finding Jesus' but little to say about social justice.

A 1974 team picture from Maple House, the psychiatric half-way house in Holyoke, Massachusetts that I manage in the mid-1970s. A short-lived romance with my co-worker, Carol (bottom left), proves ill-advised.

Patricia and Daddy in 1973.

Mid-flow in the late 1970s. By now I am a doctoral student at the University of Massachusetts and loving academic life.

Gathering to celebrate Mary's twenty-five years in religious life in the summer of 1984. Me, Andy and Michael at the back. Mary, Lena and Rita at the front. Tom could not travel.

In the early 1980s Tom is ready to give up nursing and pursues a science degree.

With Ted Kennedy in spring 1980 when he is on the campaign trail, seeking the Democratic nomination for President. A gang of us put together a memorable fundraiser for his campaign.

With Patrick Sullivan, owner of New England Patriots, at a 1987 symposium for business leaders in my local town, North Andover. I am relishing my new life as an organizational psychologist.

I am honoured and humbled that Dick Goodwin and Doris Kearns Goodwin host the launch of my book in June 1995. They are both distinguished writers, historians and intellectuals, and significant figures in American public life.

Revisiting Carlow College in summer 2008, forty-six years after I had left it as a newly minted Catholic priest. The former seminary is now a co-ed third level institution specializing in the humanities and social studies.

Escorting my niece, Ann, up the aisle at her wedding in August 2011. Ann is the sixth of Andy's seven children.

After a heart by-pass operation in late 2006, I realize that it's time to wind down my work and focus on relaxation. Here I am in the boat of my long-time sailing partner, Steve Shea, in summer 2007.

17.

A gathering storm

We arrive back in the USA in late August, and Sandy and I stop in Washington D.C. to visit the campaign headquarters of the Democratic Party's presidential candidate, George McGovern. We find a group of dedicated young people working in crowded conditions and trying to be optimistic. Phones ringing. Copy machines churning out materials. There's a sense of extreme urgency, bordering on panic. The prospects are not good. The pundits have already written off McGovern's chances of defeating Nixon in the 1972 campaign. A Nixon victory will be bad news for all of President Johnson's Great Society anti-poverty programs, including our VISTA project in Baton Rouge.

Back in Louisiana, I realize that big changes are underway. There are increasing signs – though as yet not very clear – that my days as a social activist may be coming to an end. Apart from anything else, it's obvious that the administration's support for advocacy work is diminishing and that, as Nixon looks sure to get re-elected, things can only get worse. I try to come to terms with that political reality: time is running out and it's time to execute what American football coaches call 'the two minute drill' – to, so to speak, make as many plays as I can before my allotted time in Baton Rouge ends. With my energy restored from the successful trip home, I am ready to throw myself back into advocacy work in the community.

By this time I've come to see my role as supervisor of VISTA volunteers as secondary to work as a freelance community organizer. One day I'm organizing anti-war protests. Another day I'm protesting police brutality. Community activists see me as a resource to be called upon no matter what the issue.

One afternoon two young black friends come around. Jim Marshall is a Vietnam veteran and a proven team leader whom I've known for a couple of years. His friend, Tim Dent, also has effective natural leadership skills but, sadly, is a heroin addict. Jim and Tim want to organize a protest against Community Advancement as a way of highlighting the problems of unemployed, black Vietnam veterans.

'Ed, young black dudes go to Vietnam and put their lives on the line. They come back home and can't get a fuckin' job. What kind of a fuckin' country is this?'

I understand their frustration.

'Look guys, this agency is not where you need to focus attention,' I suggest. 'You need to go after the people who have the resources to help.'

I convince them to redirect their energies towards Baton Rouge city government. That afternoon we tease out the issues for hours. We end up forming a new organization called Grassroots. Our strategy is simple. We'll mobilize a large group of community people to attend a public hearing of the City Council. We'll use the fact that Council members will be discussing salaries paid to city workers to raise the issue of unemployed Vietnam veterans.

On the night before the Council meeting, Sandy Bagley and I attend a community meeting to go over the final details. I underscore the importance of pursuing a non-violent strategy. The Vietnam veterans decide they'll wear their old military uniforms. The fear I keep to myself is that they might also bring weapons.

I arrive early for the four o'clock meeting and sit at the back of the Council chamber. City Hall resembles an armed camp. A friendly reporter gives me a tip I'd rather not hear.

'Ed, the police know about your meeting with the Grassroots people last night.'

My knees are shaking. What if the whole affair turns violent and things get out of control? I'll be accused of inciting a riot. As I sit quietly alone in a back seat I can hear my heart beating, and I'm wondering how I'll muster up bail if needed.

As the meeting gets underway the tension is palpable. The Grassroots people don't show up at four o'clock as expected. I wonder what might have happened. Maybe the police blocked their entry into the building. Or maybe they got high on drugs and copped out. And then I hear the commotion. I walk out into the lobby and find Jim lining up the veterans for their grand entrance. He tells me everything is under control.

'We'll create some shit if they don't listen,' says Jim with the self-assurance of a general leading his troops into battle.

I'm not sure what he means, but I'm scared.

'Jim, let's not have any trouble,' I say.

Tim pulls me aside to tell me the group has the resources to take care of any problems that might arise – as if this is good news! I start praying that nothing bad will happen – I'm a nervous wreck.

Within minutes, representatives of the group are in the Council chamber and on their feet complaining about the plight of unemployed veterans. There's a lot of shouting back and forth. The confrontation ends with the intervention of a black City Council member. It's agreed that the Grassroots group will develop a proposal to operate a small, city-funded job referral agency for Vietnam veterans.

After the meeting I go into the first bar I can find. It doesn't matter that it's a redneck honky-tonk dive. A couple of stiff drinks help calm my shattered nerves.

'Those niggers are always protesting these days,' says the waitress matter-of-factly as she gives me another bourbon-and-coke. She's commenting on a story that has just come across on a local TV station about the Grassroots demonstration at City Hall. I say nothing, but nod my head in approval. Wouldn't want it known around this place that I had a role in staging the City Council protest.

A few nights later several members of Grassroots meet to write their proposal. Tim lays stretched out on the floor, strung out on heroin. Occasionally someone takes a towel and wipes the sweat and saliva from his face.

Driving home from the meeting, I'm again thinking about how lives are wasted in the ghetto. And I wonder if it's a lost cause – much like the war in Vietnam, still dragging on after nearly seventeen years with no end in sight.

One day a co-worker and friend at Community Advancement tells me I should start thinking about another job.

'But this work isn't finished,' I say.

'Wake up, Ed!' she says. 'The Great Society is ready for the Last Rites. Can't you see the writing on the wall?'

I guess I can see it, but I don't want to. In a changing political climate, advocacy has become a dirty word. The idea of organizing the poor to advocate on their own behalf has become passé. Yet I'm still holding out hope that politicians won't want to abolish programs that are helping poor people. I'm operating as if Lyndon Johnson still occupies the White House. And I'm still harbouring the belief that those in Washington D.C. who are paid to represent the interests of 'We The People' are really interested in addressing the issue of poverty. After all, why would the people paid to represent us not care about the welfare of the most vulnerable in society?

Nixon is re-elected in a landslide victory. The Republicans interpret this as a mandate to get rid of Lyndon Johnson's programs to assist low-income people. The new administration has a mandate to do whatever it wants. Locally, the situation also looks discouraging. My supporters at Community Advancement are moving on. I look around and don't see much political support from the new agency administrators.

After Nixon's re-election another friend, Etta Kay, tries to talk sense into me. Etta Kay is a young civil rights lawyer who grew up in rural Mississippi. At first I'm somewhat intimidated by her forceful personality. She speaks the kind of militant language I'd expect from a Black Panther. It's taken her a while to concede that I'm not just another 'honkey' like the racist whites she encountered growing up in Mississippi.

One January afternoon in early 1973, Etta shows up at my apartment unannounced.

'What's happening, Ed?' she asks.

It just so happens I'm not in a good place. I've completed more than three years as a VISTA leader in Baton Rouge but with Nixon about to be inaugurated, I'm worried about the future.

'I just think that while we're winning a few battles here in Baton Rouge, we're losing the war. My boss from Texas told me several months ago that I should be looking for a new job – that the Nixon administration will make its move after the election.'

'That may be good advice, Ed.'

I'm wondering if she knows something I don't. 'Etta, they are not going to wipe out the anti-poverty program, are they?'

'Let me tell you a basic fact – Republicans have no interest in doing anything for poor blacks in Baton Rouge. You need to get that into your head.'

Intellectually, I know what Etta is saying may be true. It is clear Lyndon Johnson's Great Society initiative, and all of the anti-poverty programmes – not just VISTA – are in serious trouble.

The changing political terrain leaves me confused. I'm baffled and depressed by the political manoeuvring and wonder why the Republicans are so hell-bent on undermining programs designed to empower low-income black people. Wasn't Abraham Lincoln, the president who fought slavery, a Republican? I'm confused. After more than a decade living in the USA I still don't understand American politics.

I'd registered as a Democrat after becoming a US citizen – hardly significant since that's just about what everyone in Louisiana did at that time. Also, I was Irish and in the era when two progressive Irish-Americans were at the heart of the Democratic Party, there was no other choice. However, in the intervening years I hadn't really engaged with party politics. Now, I'm being confronted by political realities. I'm beginning to think of the Republican Party as the party with little concern for the have-nots in society, especially people of colour. But I'm not impressed with the Democrats either. The Democratic Party in the Deep South has its share of segregationists, including several governors and, closer to home, a US congressman, John Rarick, who represents the people of East Baton Rouge Parish in Washington D.C. and is rumoured to be affiliated with the Ku Klux Klan. His supremacist views certainly seem to support the rumour.

I understand the realpolitik of my situation when I learn of a proposed Presidential Reorganization Order (PRO) that will move the VISTA volunteers out of OEO, the anti-poverty agency, and into a new organization called ACTION. I've been around long enough to know that when an administration wants to kill a particular program they 'reorganize' it into something different. It's no surprise that the PRO will effectively take the volunteers out of the business of advocacy on behalf of the poor.

It's obvious the Nixon people want to turn back the clock, to castrate anti-poverty programs by prohibiting them from mobilizing the poor in support of their own interests. The understandable fear is that if the poor become politically empowered, they will vote for the Democrats.

Our group in Baton Rouge joins a national letter-writing campaign mounted to block the move to reorganize the VISTA program. I write a letter to Senator Walter Mondale, a strong supporter of the anti-poverty program, asking for his support. As a matter of protocol I send a copy of the Mondale letter to John Rarick. I'm definitely not expecting help from my ultra-conservative congressman; a reporter for the *St. Louis Post-Dispatch* has described Rarick as a man whose 'career has been distinguished primarily by his long inserts in the Congressional Record from various radical right wing publications attacking civil rights groups and similar organizations'. It seems like a good summary of our congressman's career in Washington. A few days later I get a response from my Congressman:

Dear Mr Deevy:

I acknowledge receipt of a copy of your letter to Senator Mondale regarding the President's Reorganization Order to merge VISTA into ACTION.

Your activities in the Baton Rouge area are well known to all Louisiana taxpayers and citizens. You have an invincible record of hurting the chances of the poor and agitating to worsen race relations.

I think that I speak plainly for the overwhelming majority of the people of my district when I advise you that I will do nothing to defeat the President's Reorganization Order.

Sincerely,

John Rarick, Member of Congress

I feel truly honoured that Rarick has taken the trouble to draft such a letter. This is something to attach to my resumé: if a man such as John Rarick feels the need to let me know how much he despises me, I've been doing something right. Colleagues at the anti-poverty agency suggest I have it framed.

But the Congressman is not my only critic. I am in the sights of the Baton Rouge branch of the White Citizens' Council. The council is a more mainstream expression of white supremacism but totally in line with Ku Klux Klan beliefs; essentially, it is a vehicle for business people and professionals to get around racial desegregation. The local Council puts me as Number Two on its list of the sixteen most subversive people in Baton Rouge. My friend Roberta Madden, head of the local chapter of the National Organization for Women, is number six on its list, so I'm in good company. I think the radical right-wing folk have an inflated view of my influence. I hardly qualify as a person with 'an invincible record' of doing anything.

It's not just Congressman Rarick and the White Citizens' Council who are concerned about my activities. I've also fallen out of favour with Federal bureaucrats in Washington and Dallas. For the first time in my tenure as supervisor, the top administrators send us two clearly unhappy middle-aged volunteers instead of the well-motivated young graduates we normally get. One is a disbarred lawyer, and the other has a serious drink problem. When it quickly becomes obvious that they're not suitable for our project, I request that they be removed. My request is refused without explanation. Requests for additional volunteers are denied.

I'm hanging in the wind, and I'm beginning to believe that politically motivated government administrators are out to kill off the Baton Rouge project by attrition. And as I see it, there's nothing I can do about it. I ask my immediate boss in Texas what is happening.

'Ed, I've told you before – times have changed.'

It appears to me that as well as destroying the project from within, plans are afoot to take me out. The alcohol-dependent volunteer, seemingly unhappy with my efforts as his supervisor, takes his complaints to the regional office in Dallas, substantiating them in a fourteen-page letter. One day I get a call from a staff person in the regional office, a friend, giving me her take on his diatribe.

'You won't believe what's in this letter – it's mostly incoherent. He was obviously drunk when he wrote it.'

Despite myself, I ask what's in it.

'He accuses you of cohabitating with VISTA volunteers, stealing government money, holding pot parties and various other illegalities – anyone who didn't know you would think you're a real party animal!'

I ask if there's nothing about my activities as a Communist agitator!

'Not a word, Ed. Just the personal stuff.'

I'm almost disappointed.

I'm summoned to a conference of VISTA managers to be held in Little Rock, Arkansas. I'm told the purpose of the conference is to instruct project managers on how to write grant proposals. I soon discover the real reason for the meeting is to brainwash me and my colleagues. We're informed that VISTA volunteers are no longer to be involved in advocacy work. Effectively, we're going to be about as politically engaged as boy scouts or girl guides. There's no room for dissent at this meeting.

Having a cup of coffee in the hotel restaurant one morning, I read in the *Arkansas Gazette* that President Nixon has appointed Howard Phillips to phase out the anti-poverty programs. The editor of the *Gazette* describes Phillips's appointment as 'the ultimate expression of Nixon's contempt for the poor of America'. This is in a newspaper in conservative Little Rock, Arkansas, so the editor is not a flag-waving liberal.

The news of Phillips' appointment only adds to my sense of foreboding. I request a private meeting with Mr Ortego, the newly appointed Regional Administrator of ACTION. The job is a reward for electioneering work on behalf of the Republican Party in Texas. We meet in his hotel room and get down to business without any chit-chat.

'Mr Ortego, am I the cause of the problems with the Baton Rouge project?'

There's a short pause. Then he surprises me with a straightforward answer.

'Yes, Mr Deevy, you are the problem. There are some questions about your loyalties.'

'What do you mean – questions about my loyalties? I consider myself a patriotic American.'

'Well, there's some question about your loyalty to the administration – your commitment to our policies.'

I realise there's not much more to talk about. He confirms what I already suspect. I leave the conference and head home. It's a long car journey back to Baton Rouge, which gives me plenty of time to think. With every mile that passes my sense of foreboding grows. But I'm betting it will be at least a year before I'm sent packing. The Federal bureaucracy isn't known for its efficiency in carrying out change.

18.

Nixon's hatchet-men get down to business

Back in Baton Rouge after the encounter in Little Rock, I'm immediately confronted with the reality of the changing political climate. Howard Phillips has sent a memo to community action agencies, including Community Advancement, announcing his intention to begin the process of phasing out anti-poverty programs. Phillips is taking his job as hatchet man seriously.

Despite all the warning signs, I'm still surprised at how quickly the axe falls. I get a message that Lee Wesley, the newly appointed Executive Director of Community Advancement, wants to see me. I assume it's about routine administrative business.

In his usual friendly manner, Wesley tells me my services will no longer be needed. Not what I'm expecting to hear. It takes a few seconds for it to sink in that I've been fired.

'You know you're *persona non grata* with some people in Washington?' Wesley says somewhat apologetically. He tells me the request that I be terminated has come from the upper levels of management within the Federal government.

'Lee, these guys, whoever they are, simply don't give a shit about the poor or about anti-poverty programs.'

'Well Ed, don't blame me. With Nixon back, it's a whole new political environment.'

I'm angry, disappointed and somewhat baffled. It's clear that my problem goes right to the top – anonymous senior administrators in Washington. I wonder why my job would be of concern to anyone in the national government. Don't they have more important concerns than some $8,000-a-year community worker in Louisiana? Maybe I should feel flattered.

After returning to my office, I try to make sense of what's just happened. Perhaps I should not have been surprised. One month earlier I had a conversation with my immediate supervisor in which he expressed concern about my 'free-wheeling management style'. He pointed out that I had allowed VISTA volunteers to operate as free agents and 'without proper accountability'. He expressed particular concern that I had allowed a VISTA volunteer, Richard Crane, to put his name forward as a candidate for the Louisiana Constitutional Convention, in violation of the Hatch Act. I knew this was a mortal sin in the eyes of Federal bureaucrats. Lastly, he expressed concern that I'd taken off to Ireland on a two-week holiday with two volunteers without the permission of my supervisors. While I knew I had more than four weeks of earned leave, and the volunteers involved also had several weeks of earned leave, I accepted his feedback. I'm not a bureaucrat by nature so I'm not good at enforcing the rules for myself or others. While I had never seen a job description, I could not pretend that I was not bound by the restrictions of the Hatch Act. I'm not a Federal employee, but the non-profit community organization that employs me received all of its funds from the Federal Government. And the VISTA volunteers, employed by the Federal Government, were clearly bound by the Hatch Act. I was guilty of acting as a loose cannon.

As I sit alone in my office, licking my wounds, I'm forced to admit to myself that I have been booted out because of my failure to behave as a proper administrator and to dot every I and cross every T. Nevertheless, I'm still blindsided.

Friends and colleagues call my firing 'Billy Graham's Revenge'. The belief is that the powerful preacher was most displeased over the protests during his Baton Rouge Crusade and put the word out with his friends in the administration. Perhaps I should have known there would be a day of reckoning. As I ponder my situation, I tell myself that no good deed goes unpunished.

I'm not the only employee given a pink slip – a handful of activist colleagues in Community Advancement are also terminated. Unfortunately, most of these have families depending on them for support. With full speed, Phillips is carrying out what he understands to be Nixon's re-election mandate. Similar firings take place in other community action agencies throughout the country. Nixon's hatchet men are hard at work.

A group of fired anti-poverty workers from agencies throughout the country file a class action lawsuit in the Federal District Court in Washington D.C., claiming their dismissals are illegal. Their argument is that government bureaucrats can't arbitrarily frustrate the will of the US Congress. It's a valid argument but, given the political climate, I'm not hopeful about a positive result.

There's nothing left to do but clean out my office at Community Advancement. My last day is a low-key affair. I make the rounds to say a personal goodbye to co-workers I've come to know and respect during my tenure with the agency. Then, I remove memorabilia from the office and retreat to my apartment on Park Boulevard to consider future options.

Within days of cleaning out the office I start getting calls from the VISTA volunteers still working in Baton Rouge. I learn that I'm the target of some kind of investigation by the Federal government. This gets me really riled up. I'm wondering what the hell is going on.

My former colleagues keep me updated.

First, there's a preliminary investigation. A special investigator is flown from Seattle to Baton Rouge. Then two new investigators arrive from Washington, D.C. The basis of their investigation appears to be the fourteen-page letter written by the disgruntled

VISTA volunteer, a letter I've been told – albeit off the record – was clearly written under the influence of alcohol.

While the investigators are going about their work, I'm at home seething and feeling helpless.

One morning I get a phone call from a secretary at Community Advancement letting me know the investigators are scheduled to return to Washington later in the day. I realize I'm not going to be offered the opportunity to answer questions, even though I'm the target of the investigation. It's clear that if I'm going to have my say, I'll need to act immediately.

I make the five-minute drive from my apartment to Community Advancement and go directly to my old office, where the investigators have set up shop. By the time I arrive they've concluded their final interview with one of the VISTA volunteers and are packing their briefcases.

'Gentlemen, I'm here to answer any questions you have,' I say, as I barge into the room.

Well-dressed and clean-cut, these guys could be mistaken for a couple of young preachers.

'And who are you, Sir?'

'I'm Ed Deevy – the fellow you've been investigating.'

They seem uncomfortable.

'We don't have questions – we're not really investigating you, Sir.'

'Don't give me that bullshit. Why are the VISTA volunteers complaining about your enquiries into my private life?'

Now I'm really pissed off. The temptation is to tell them the unvarnished truth about what I really feel about their 'inquisition,' but I keep my cool. This is an argument I'm not going to win. Having a tantrum isn't going to help. They close their briefcases and get ready to leave.

'Mr Deevy, we have a plane to catch.'

There's nothing more to say. Frustrated, I walk out and return to my apartment on Park Boulevard.

Later that day the two investigators fly back to Washington. Nothing more is heard about the investigation. Evidently my unspectacular love life doesn't provide enough ammunition for legal action. Or maybe the Nixon administration has other, more pressing concerns. Or maybe the entire purpose of the exercise was simply to let everyone see what happens to uppity activists. After all, it's less than two decades since the end of McCarthyism. The televised trials of Senator McCarthy's House Un-American Activities Committee may seem like a lifetime ago. Learned analysis of McCarthyism's paralysing impact on American cultural and intellectual life make it seem like ancient history and the 1960s revolution may have persuaded hippies and idealistic young radicals that progressive forces are unstoppable. But political strategists look at the long game and never stop thinking about how to control hearts and minds. The best way to stamp out dissent is at grassroots level: neutralizing local activists like me is just part of the game.

Happily, the way the game is played at the top level is being exposed in all its dirty detail. The American public is just learning about the Watergate scandal. It's a story that started as a report of a break-in at the Democratic National Committee's headquarters in the Watergate building the previous summer. Now, just months after Nixon's inauguration, the story is finally exploding into the national consciousness. My satisfaction in knowing that the shenanigans of the Nixon backroom people are now being exposed is tempered by the knowledge that his administration has already gone a long way towards dismantling the anti-poverty programme. Watergate is important, but it's about the game of politics; the anti-poverty programme is about people's day-to-day lives and opportunities that poor people are losing right now that will affect their lives forever. Destroying Lyndon Johnson's anti-poverty vision is literally a matter of life and death.

In the midst of all the investigating there's one positive development. The campaign to block Howard Phillips in his efforts to dismantle various anti-poverty programs is successful. Federal

Circuit Court Judge William Jones stops the bulldog in his tracks. He orders Phillips to cease and desist from phasing out programs mandated by Congress. Furthermore, his order specifies that all dismissed employees be reinstated and given full back pay.

On foot of the reinstatement order, I return to Community Advancement, ready to pick up where I left off. However, I am informed that my old position as VISTA supervisor has been eliminated. I'm offered a job as Youth Program Coordinator, which I accept. It doesn't take long to realise it's a job in title only. I'm left in limbo, with nothing to do.

It is clear Community Advancement is no longer the organization I'd joined in August 1969. The new agency administrators are determined to do everything possible to please the Washington bureaucrats. They had, for example, cooperated with the bogus investigation of the VISTA project – something that never would have been sanctioned at an earlier time. (By 1973 the man who hired me, Charlie Tapp, had moved into a position in Louisiana state government.) Not willing to take a paycheck for doing nothing, I tender my resignation at the end of May 1973.

19.

'Goodbye, Mr VISTA'

It takes a while for it to sink in that I'm unemployed and that I don't have a clue what I'm going to do next. An on-off girlfriend, Betty, suggests I take advantage of the pool at her apartment complex while I'm considering my next move. I accept her offer. At Betty's swimming pool I'll be able to soak up the summer sun and reflect on what's happening in my life. It will be as if I'm on vacation.

Betty was someone I met in my early years in Baton Rouge. Initially, I was attracted by her friendly personality. With her long, wavy, auburn hair, Kentucky accent and seductive eyes she could be mistaken for a Southern belle, but she combines traditional Southern charm and values with a very enlightened social conscience. When we first met she was teaching counselling skills at predominantly black Southern University.

Over time it became clear that Betty saw me as more than a casual boyfriend. But I was not inclined to get involved and resisted her efforts to get me to share real feelings about our relationship. A few years on and now I realize my reluctance to respond to her back then may have had something to do with my puritanical upbringing and seminary indoctrination. I'm glad there are no hard feelings and as I work my way through this major life transition, I'm grateful to still have Betty as a friend.

The weeks pass. At first I enjoy the carefree lifestyle. Unemployment doesn't pay much, but the hours are great. No reports to write. No meetings to attend. No problems to solve. When I get bored lounging at the pool I watch the Watergate drama unfolding on TV. This exposure of arrogance and corruption in the Nixon administration provides a certain satisfaction. Selfishly, I'm thinking that this exposure offers some measure of vindication.

Before long I start to feel guilty about doing nothing – when we were growing up, idleness was considered sinful. It's certainly true that idleness makes your mind wander. Now, free for the first time in years, I have the luxury of time to reflect on the changes in my life since leaving the priesthood.

Sitting by Betty's pool, I try to figure out where I am in life. On one level I'm thinking that I've done a pretty good job of adjusting to my new lifestyle as a single man. But, being honest with myself, to some extent I've been trying to live the life of a recent graduate instead of an uptight, late-developing Irishman in his mid-thirties. I'm inventing myself as I go along and not everything I try is a natural fit. For instance, that trip to the Celebration of Life festival with Sondra. After a couple of days of 'liberation', I was ready to get back to work. The reality is that I was born before the invention of the teenager and youth culture.

Discovering southern culture and music has been a joy. I make regular trips to New Orleans and spend nights in the French Quarter listening to jazz in bars or enjoying Creole cuisine. On one of these trips to the Big Easy in July 1971, I'd joined thousands dancing in the streets at the funeral of Louis Armstrong. A memory to savour. I've come to love Motown and country and Cajun folk music. So my cultural horizons have certainly opened up, and that's something that will stay part of my life.

During the years after arriving in Baton Rouge I'd also undergone an evolution in political consciousness. To some extent Congressman Rarick had been right in labelling me an agitator. Through work as a community organiser I'd come to believe some

144

agitation is necessary and I viewed my work in patriotic terms. I came to see American democracy as a work-in-progress and considered myself fortunate to be in a position to make a contribution. I rationalized it by telling myself that America was in the process of becoming the promised land, of becoming the land we had always dreamed of and aspired to live in.

One other personal change from the VISTA years is more problematic. The various campaigns have taken an emotional toll and I'm beginning to experience mental fatigue. In response to the stress of work, my intake of alcohol had gradually increased and I've got into a habit of binge drinking. On my visits to the local Irish bar I sometimes end up drinking more beers than I can handle (about six is my limit).

A veteran newspaper reporter had given me some heartfelt advice late one night at the Press Club: 'Ed, don't fight too many battles – it'll destroy you. You've got to think of the long road.'

His advice had an unsettling effect. I had a hunch he was talking from personal experience and I recognize that I have these tendencies. I spent so long wanting to make a difference but doing nothing about it, I still feel like I have something to prove, to myself more than anyone. Perhaps I should pace myself.

Looking back on the intense activity of the past few years, I wonder if maybe I've escaped into work and neglected the personal side of my life. Maybe I've been too caught up in saving the world at the expense of myself? I recognise I need some separation between work life and personal life.

To change my life as fundamentally as I feel I need to, I briefly consider the possibility of returning to Ireland. In several transatlantic phone calls with Andy, I get a feel for what's happening in my homeland. Andy thinks I should focus on opportunities in America. He's thinking about the economy, I assume – we talk often enough about the state of the country – though perhaps he is also concerned about my status as an ex-priest. That's not something he would raise unless I raised it first. There is a diplomatic silence around that issue and I don't want to put him on the spot. The question is on my mind though: I know that attitudes are changing in Ireland, but I wonder if my background will prove problematic. There's a voice inside telling me I can make it anywhere, including Ireland. However, with almost daily reports of sectarian violence in Northern Ireland, I decide I don't want to get near another battle zone.

After concluding that returning to Ireland is not a viable option, I start considering other possibilities. One day Betty asks what I'd really like to do with my life. I don't have to think long to come up with a response. The years with VISTA have left me with a keen appreciation of what a skilful human rights lawyer can accomplish. And I have also developed an appreciation for the work of progressive journalists. I tell Betty I'd love to be an advocate on behalf of the disadvantaged, as a lawyer or as a journalist.

'Well then, why not go back to school and get the credentials?' Betty asks.

A very good question.

During my VISTA years I had also developed an interest in group and organizational psychology. I'd worked as a facilitator with the LSU Psychology Department for workshops on the racial integration of Baton Rouge schools. In doing this work I discovered a natural talent for group facilitation. I look into it and discover that I need a doctorate in psychology to pursue a career in this area.

The more I explore academic options, the more I realize that I can't afford to spend several years at university. I'd left the priesthood with less than $5,000 in my bank account. My current savings of less than $10,000 will not go very far. I conclude that back-to-college plans will have to be deferred.

After weeks of ruminating I decide I want to leave Baton Rouge in order to get a fresh start somewhere else. One evening Betty arrives home from her work at Southern University and I tell her about my decision. It's an uncomfortable moment. We both know that my moving away may foreshadow the end of our relationship.

I begin to think of where I might relocate. Washington D.C. is on the list. A friend has offered me her spare room if I want to move there and explore opportunities. But I'm thinking a place with less heat and humidity might be a welcome change. As would somewhere with greater racial tolerance. While I'm debating the possibilities, I get a letter from Frank Stewart. After Frank was vindicated, he married VISTA volunteer Sharon Jones. I assisted with the ceremony, which was held at the Martin Luther Centre at Southern University. Frank and Sharon have since moved north, to Massachusetts, where Frank is pursuing graduate studies in the School of Education at the University of Massachusetts. Sharon is doing volunteer work with the local Mormon Church. They invite me to come and stay with them in their new home in Holyoke, Massachusetts, while I figure what to do next.

I accept their offer. I'll go with an open mind and see what unfolds. It may turn out to be a temporary stop on my journey, but at least I'll be moving forwards again.

The final weeks in Baton Rouge are spent getting organized for the move and making the rounds of old friends. I also make a trip to Mexico with my old colleague from Bunkie, Father Bill Provosty, and some friends. I'm going to miss the companionship and positive energy of my extended family in Baton Rouge. Lynne Devine, a VISTA volunteer from Connecticut who is just completing her year, invites me to dinner. A typical New Englander, I'd always appreciated her blunt and sometimes challenging way of giving feedback. Over dinner she gives me an unexpected compliment.

'Ed, when I came down here, I had no idea what to expect. I was fearful. You made me feel welcome. You were always a cheerleader – not a boss.'

Given what I have been through, Lynne's comments are a welcome confidence boost before I set out into the unknown.

One morning, as I'm trying to stuff a few more personal belongings into my already packed Oldsmobile, a local reporter with photographer in tow shows up at my house.

'Jesus, Ed, why didn't you rent a trailer?' he asks.

'Jim, all I'm taking is books, clothes and a few things that have sentimental value. But you're right – maybe I should have got a trailer.'

He's an old friend. We chat for about an hour as I load the car. He wants to know if I still think Billy Graham is a hypocrite. He wants my comments on the Nixon administration. And, of course, he wants my opinions on Baton Rouge law enforcement and politicians. I give him my version of the unvarnished truth. I'll be more than a thousand miles north before the story, titled 'Goodbye, Mr VISTA', appears in print. The reporter writes: 'Ed Deevy left Baton Rouge the same way he came in, with a few hundred dollars in his pocket and all his possessions in the trunk of his car. In the four years that he stayed, he whipped VISTA into a cohesive, effective organ of social action and performed a little mischief besides, befitting his Irish temperament.' A copy of the article will be waiting for me when I arrive in Holyoke, compliments of Betty.

The night before departure David and Roberta Madden open up their home for a going-away party. As usual, David and Roberta are wonderful hosts. The party leaves me full of sadness at the thought of leaving so many valued friends. I keep telling everyone that I'll be back at some time. But the evening is not all about loss. I'm also beginning to feel excited about the future. I'm thinking that my time really is up: I've done my share of 'agitating'.

One morning in late July 1973 I have breakfast with Betty. Not much is said. I have all kinds of mixed emotions. I tell Betty that as soon as I get settled I'll invite her to come and visit. Of course, I have no real idea where I'll end up living. After a hug and a clumsy goodbye I head out of Baton Rouge. The Oldsmobile is loaded with all my worldly goods. I stay off the Interstate highways so that I can appreciate the cities and towns along the way.

As I travel north I tune in to the Senate's Watergate hearings on the car radio. They provide high drama and great listening. Driving endless hours, I'm struck by the vastness and beauty of the American landscape.

On a Friday evening in late August I drive into Holyoke in western Massachusetts. First impressions are not that favourable: the city centre looks like a bombed-out Dresden. I make my way to the rundown tenement building where Frank and Sharon rent an apartment. Part of the attraction of Holyoke is cheap rentals. Frank and Sharon and several neighbourhood teenagers help transport my personal stuff from my car up the staircase to their fourth-floor apartment. It's a humid evening, with the temperature over 100 degrees. Though their apartment is large, it is without creature comforts like air conditioning. We have a lot of catching up to do and we talk late into the night. I go to bed knowing that tomorrow truly will be a new beginning.

20.

Living in the world of the mentally ill

With my eleven years living in Louisiana in the rear-view mirror, I start to consider a future life in Holyoke. The city is situated on the banks of the Connecticut River and was built during the Industrial Revolution around the manufacture of paper. The original paper mills were driven by hydropower generated by a dam on the Connecticut River. Many Irish emigrants who fled poverty and the Great Famine in the middle of the nineteenth century made their way to Holyoke. According to local mythology, the Irish labourers who built the original dam proceeded to blow it up after it was completed – something to do with getting revenge on the Boston investors who had exploited them. Yet the city still has a strong Irish connection and is proud of having the second largest St Patrick's Day parade in the world.

However, Holyoke's glory days have long passed. As in other American cities, the whites have moved out to the suburbs, leaving the centre to the immigrants. In Holyoke there is a huge Puerto Rican community. The streets are teeming with Puerto Rican children. This could be a neighbourhood in San Juan, Puerto Rico, not New England. Almost every night one of the old redbrick tenement buildings goes up in flames. Some say the fires are set deliberately in order to collect on insurance.

Within weeks I accept a position as director of a residential mental health program called Maple House, located in the dilapidated downtown area. Maple House looks like any other four-storey tenement except for its renovated exterior and modern glass-door entryway. No name – just a street number on the building. Part of the attraction of Maple House is that it's located in a rundown neighbourhood where no one notices former mental health patients, however erratic or anti-social their behaviour. Across the street is a large Catholic church built with the donations of Irish and French immigrants several generations earlier. The rundown church looks like just another abandoned building.

I move out of the Stewarts' place and into a staff apartment at Maple House. The facility is designed to provide a transitional living experience for individuals discharged from Northampton State Hospital, or local people who have been in mental institutions further afield. The idea is to provide an independent living environment for residents, with support from in-house staff. They are expected to move out to live on their own within one year of residency.

Almost immediately I learn that I have sole responsibility for the program. No staff – just myself. But I've been given assurances by the man who hired me, Andy Phillips, representing the Massachusetts Department of Mental Health, that additional staff will be hired in the very near future.

I know almost nothing about psychiatric illness but that doesn't seem to matter. Clearly the health department is desperate for someone who will take the low-paid, high pressure job. Growing up in rural Ireland in the 1940s and 1950s I was aware of the stigma associated with any kind of mental health problem. In Carlow there was a mental hospital, St Dympna's, surrounded by a high walls, much like a jail. When considering the position I talk to my brother Michael, who works in St Fintan's, the mental hospital in Portlaoise, and he explains that psychotropic drugs have revolutionized the care of the mentally ill. However, I have no medical training so I know nothing about medicating people. I take on the new challenge in the hope that I'll be moving on to something different in the not too distant future.

Working with the residents of Maple House I'm immediately struck by the flat, empty look on people's faces. There are few smiles; most residents seem to be in a drug-induced stupor. Many of them have been warehoused in Northampton or other hospitals for years. They represent different forms of mental illness, including schizophrenia and manic depression.

Residents come down to the recreation room at the basement level when they get bored or depressed in their apartments. Some watch television and chain-smoke all day long. Others sit for hours and stare into space. One seventy-five-year-old, diagnosed with schizophrenia, has spent his entire adult life in Northampton. He shouts out to no one in particular, 'They're all fuckers! They're all fuckers!'

Tony is a chubby, middle-aged man, also diagnosed with schizophrenia, who confuses winter with summer. He has the habit of standing on the street corner during winter snowstorms applying suntan lotion to his naked upper body.

One day a young woman resident, diagnosed as manic-depressive, comes into my office. She's clearly in a manic state. She starts talking about her sexual exploits.

'Mr Deevy, I've fucked half the men in this house ... and you're on my list.'

I tell her I've no intention of getting involved with her or anyone else at Maple House.

'Sharon, are you taking your lithium? I know you hate the stuff – but you got to take care of yourself.'

She promises to take her medicine. I give her a hug and she happily goes on her way.

One young man, believing he's one of Hitler's paratroopers, spends endless hours marching up and down the recreation room with a goose-step. Nobody takes any notice. Another resident wears a chain around his neck, brandishes a large crucifix and claims to be Jesus. Again, nobody seems to notice. After a few months I begin to see all this behaviour as fairly normal.

Some residents make regular morning visits to a neighbourhood honky-tonk lounge bar. They return by late morning, ready to sleep the rest of the day away. Alcohol and psychotropic drugs are not a good mix.

Every effort is made to screen out individuals with violent tendencies. However, we're never completely successful in this regard. There's Fred, a young man full of rage, who seems ready to explode at any moment. He's diagnosed with paranoid schizophrenia and he scares me. 'I'll kill that fuckin' Puerto Rican,' he repeats, referring to the boyfriend of another resident. One day he punches our consulting psychiatrist, Doug Cooper, as he walks down the steps outside the front door. Doug is traumatized but fortunate to escape with no major injuries.

Even with all the pressure and unpredictability, as the months pass I begin to connect more meaningfully with the work at Maple House. It is rewarding to see residents who had spent thirty to forty years in mental hospitals move into their own apartments in the community. We find a significant number of 'burnt-out schizophrenics' can cope with independent living. These are people who have spent years, decades sometimes, living in hospitals and other institutions and whose symptoms have abated with time. Unfortunately, we also find some stop taking their medications and end up back in hospital, or in the local jail.

Despite the failures I cling to the belief that residents can go on to live normal lives in the community. Maybe I am still in the business of redemption, after all. Doug Cooper smiles approvingly when he hears me talk of 'curing' our schizophrenic residents, although he knows the prognosis isn't good. He encourages me to keep believing in what we are trying to accomplish. It takes a while to accept that few are actually cured of their mental illness. I learn to have modest expectations about what we can accomplish.

Apart from those weekends when Frank and Sharon kindly volunteer to step in and provide weekend coverage so I can take a break, living and working in the world of the severely distressed is a 24/7 proposition. The work is even more draining than anything I experienced in Louisiana. I quickly realize that I'm still suffering from battle fatigue from the years in Baton Rouge – this despite the fact that I'd taken a three-month break after leaving Community Advancement. I'm like a war veteran, suffering from some kind of post-traumatic stress. And now I'm discovering that I'm alone doing the work of several people.

Six months after accepting the position I am already experiencing the symptoms of burn-out. Finally, the Massachusetts Department of Mental Health responds to my pleas for additional staff. I hire Carol, a recent graduate of Smith College, and Valerie, a recent graduate of the University of Massachusetts. This welcome development means that I'll be able to take some time off without having to worry that something serious will happen while I'm gone.

ONCE THE NEW STAFF ARE IN place, it's time for a holiday. I call my brother Tom in London. Growing up, Tom and I were separated by nearly seven years and so we were not close companions. After doing his Leaving Cert in 1963, Tom spent a short time in the seminary before training as a nurse and moving to London in the early 1970s. Our relationship has matured in recent years. We exchange long letters. Andy's job as a night telephonist means that we have regular phone conversations too. We share the experience of making our lives in socially and ethnically diverse settings far removed from the farm in Drumagh. Despite being older, I have always looked up to Tom. There is a matter-of-fact quality to his personality – he says what he means and he means what he says. One month after my phone call he arrives in Holyoke. He's immediately drafted to help Carol, Valerie and me in managing a weekend trip for house residents to Cape Cod.

Tom immediately gets into the spirit of things, even volunteering to barbecue the hamburgers.

After the weekend on Cape Cod we are ready to set out on our own two-week road trip that will take us to visit our aunt in Pompano Beach, Florida, and my old friends in Louisiana. We start out from Maple House in the early morning and by nightfall we have already reached North Carolina and are well on our way towards our destination in South Florida.

Driving through South Carolina late at night we're stopped by state troopers. With the flashing lights of two police cars, one in front and the other behind, a state trooper approaches me on the driver's side.

'Where are you from, buddy?' he asks.

I explain that I'm originally from Ireland but I'm living in Massachusetts. He's not too friendly.

'Mister, don't you know you were exceeding the speed limit?'

He tells me I have a choice: pay the fine or spend the night in custody and appear before a magistrate the next day. I shell out the cash and we continue on our journey.

Tom has a smirk on his face as we leave the state troopers behind. 'That reminds me of a scene from an American movie where the cops are arresting two notorious criminals.'

I decide to keep a close eye on the speedometer. We take a nap in the car in North Florida before arriving at our destination at noon the next day.

After a few days with our Aunt Irene, and a night with a cousin, Father Eddie Condren in North Florida, we head for Baton Rouge, where we stay with Betty. I had continued a long-distance relationship with her by letter and phone. Since I was reluctant to make a commitment, the relationship has remained open-ended and unresolved. Betty had joined me for my first Thanksgiving at Maple House. Together, we cooked dinner for those who had no families to visit.

On Sunday morning we join Betty at a service at the Unitarian Church. This is the church where social activists – both black and white – gather on Sunday mornings and where I'd occasionally worshipped during my years in Baton Rouge. The pastor, the Reverend Toby Van Buren, is an old friend and Tom is made to feel very welcome. On the way out of the service he turns to me and says, 'The best sermon I've ever heard.'

After our sojourn in Baton Rouge we set out on the 1,500-mile return journey, hoping to make a brief visit to Washington D.C. en route. Within a few hours, driving on Highway 85 through the pine woods of Mississippi, disaster strikes. The car comes to a complete standstill. A burst piston. There's not a human in sight except the cars whizzing past at 70 to 80 miles an hour. I set out on a three-mile walk down the highway while Tom stays with the car. I finally find a garage owner who is willing to help. He tells us it will take a couple of days to get the parts and to get us back on the road. He offers us the hospitality of his home.

After a couple of days we're back on the road, feeling very fortunate at having met such a generous family. We used our unscheduled free time in the backwoods of Mississippi to do some forward planning. Tom had been feeling stressed in his job as a charge nurse at Whittington Hospital in north London. And I'm feeling burned out in my career as a social activist-turned-mental health advocate. Our brainstorming leads to a grand plan to work as partners in a new business venture. I'll be responsible for organizing charter flights from New York to Dublin, primarily targeted at Irish-Americans. Tom will organize a complementary program in Ireland to provide low-cost accommodation and a culturally enriching experience.

We set out early and continue travelling north, but the gods are not on our side. After taking a nap in the car at night we resume travelling the next day ... but all is not well. On an early Sunday morning, traveling through beautiful Virginia countryside, the car again comes to a complete standstill. This time we're not so lucky.

We are ripped-off by the garage that carries out the repair work. It becomes clear that, travelling at twenty miles an hour, we are not going to be able to make it back to Massachusetts without further repairs.

Low on cash, we decide to skip Washington and get to Holyoke as quickly as possible. We abandon the car in a rest area, grab our stuff and start hitchhiking. A truck driver gives us a ride that takes us all the way to western Massachusetts. We arrive home in Holyoke after three weeks on the road, completing what we'd planned as a two-week trip.

Not long after I manage that trip to Washington D.C. where I join Betty for a week. The last time I'd been in Washington I'd challenged the Nixon administration to provide support for one of my VISTA volunteers. This time the circumstances are very different. The city is bubbling with excitement and anticipation. Strangers on city buses are weighing in on when 'Tricky Dick' will resign. It seems like the whole city is anxiously awaiting the end of what has become a lengthy national scandal. And then, on 8 August 1974, it happens: Nixon tells the nation he is resigning. We no longer have Richard Nixon to kick around!

Betty and I are among the watching crowd outside the White House the next day as Nixon boards the helicopter for his flight back to California and a life as a writer and after-dinner speaker.

'Bye, bye, Richard,' I say as the presidential helicopter disappears into the clear blue August sky. We listen on a small transistor radio as Gerald Ford is sworn in as the 38th President of the United States.

'You must be sad to see him go,' says Betty, with a smirk on her face.

'Yes, Betty. I'll be wearing a black arm band for the next month – that's what we Irish do when we're in mourning!'

I'm happy the Nixon era has come to an end. I'm still bruised from my treatment by Nixon's hatchet men in Baton Rouge, so now I'm feeling vindicated.

After the short break in Washington I return to Holyoke feeling re-energised. Carol, Valerie and I work as a team and share responsibilities for evening and night duty at Maple House. The job no longer feels as onerous as it did a year previously. I'm feeling more settled than I have in a long time.

21.

An office romance

One evening Carol is on duty in Maple House and I wander over to a neighbourhood Irish bar for a few glasses of beer. At the pub I play pool and hang out with the regulars. Later, around 10.00 pm before going to bed, I check in with Carol to see if everything is okay.

She says she has just put down the phone from a woman who said she was a friend of one of our residents, 'Susan'. 'She asked me if Susan was okay.'

From Carol's description of the caller, I immediately realise who it was. She's someone I have come to view as a bit of a nuisance. Over the previous months I have had several conversations with Susan's mother and others – including this caller – regarding Susan and her suitability for Maple House. It does not strike me that this call is any different.

'Don't mind her. She's just a busybody,' I say.

I make my usual late-night rounds, walking up and down the two stairwells to check on residents, before going to my apartment. I make a point of stopping outside Susan's apartment. The television is playing as usual.

Next morning Carol and I cross town for a meeting at an agency that provides day care services for discharged mental health patients. Someone interrupts us, asking us to call Maple House

159

immediately. Susan's mother has been on to say that she is not getting a response from her daughter's apartment and wonders if anything is wrong. Carol and I rush back and dash up to Susan's second-floor apartment. There's no answer when we knock on her door. Using a master key we gain access to the apartment and find Susan lying on her bed in a pool of blood.

Within minutes the ambulance arrives and Susan is on her way to the Emergency Room at Holyoke Hospital. Both Carol and I breathe a deep sigh of relief when we find out she's going to recover.

Susan is in her early thirties and is a member of a wealthy local family. She had been in several private psychiatric institutions before the family gave up hope that she'd be cured. She has been diagnosed as schizophrenic and has a long history of suicide attempts. Though inappropriate for Maple House because of her psychiatric history, she's been admitted because of her family's political connections. In putting her in Maple House, the family washed their hands of financial and other responsibility for her care. She has become the responsibility of the Commonwealth of Massachusetts.

We reconstruct the events of the previous evening. Susan had taken an overdose. We don't know if it was deliberate or accidental. While on the phone to her friend she had fallen and hit her head on the open door of her oven. The line then went silent, leading the woman on the other end of the phone to call Carol and ask her to check on Susan. Carol had just put down the phone when I arrived back at Maple House. Naturally, she left it up to me to take over the situation. I then made a terrible misjudgement by dismissing the caller out of hand, a misjudgement that could have had tragic consequences. We were very lucky to find Susan in time that her life could be saved. The fall-out if we hadn't would have been catastrophic on a number of levels.

Later in the day Susan's mother shows up to pick up some personal things to take to her daughter in the hospital. I accompany her to the apartment. She tells me she knows about the call to Carol the night before.

'You know, I could sue you for malpractice, Mr Deevy,' she says.

Her threat doesn't sit well. I hold my tongue, but I don't like her attitude. I'm thinking: *Good, blow a ton of dough on a lawyer and maybe you'll win the rights to my beat-up car and a few boxes of books* – the sum of my worldly goods.

She says Susan will be back in Maple House in a week. She sees a little of the temper that I usually keep carefully under control.

'Over my dead body!' I say. 'Your daughter is not appropriate for this program and that's final!'

As I'm about to go to bed that evening I call downstairs to Carol on the intercom to ask if she's okay. She says she'd like to come up to my first-floor apartment for a visit.

We sit on the couch in my living room and talk. Carol tells me she's having flashbacks to her father's suicide. Says she saw him put a gun to his head. Earlier that day she had volunteered to take Susan's blood-drenched sheets and blankets downstairs to the laundry room. I sense the intense hurt she's feeling and we hug. We continue to talk late into the night. We both feel the need for each other's support at this difficult time. Carol stays the night and it is the beginning of a very intense relationship.

A slim, shapely woman of medium height in her early twenties, Carol is quiet, thoughtful and reserved. Her long brown hair is pulled back off her face and she wears wire-rimmed glasses. A soft-spoken person, Carol seems almost too frail to confront the challenges posed by acting-out residents. But her shy smile belies a strong, determined personality. Carol shares with me a book of poetry she'd edited at Smith College that includes some of her own work. She's more poet than social worker. That, combined with her experiences growing up, lends her a serious demeanour that can be slightly off-putting to those whose style is easy-going and less intense.

161

The relationship with Carol is different from anything I've experienced before. She is very sexually liberated and likes to experiment. Sometimes during the workday she suggests that we go to her bedroom and make love. Love-making provides an escape from the constant stress and tension surrounding us. Her attitude is a gift that educates, thrills and scares me a little. She is not long out of college and knows twenty times more than I do about sex.

Carol tells me about a secluded reservoir in southern Vermont that her family had discovered. We decide to spend a camping weekend at this hidden retreat. When we get there on a Friday afternoon there is just a handful of people on the beach. This may have to do with the fact that it's late September and most tourists have gone home. My big surprise is that the people on the beach are all naked. Carol hadn't mentioned that we were going to a nudist beach. Another first!

We're an unlikely couple. She's eccentric and unconventional in a way I find attractive. When one of my friends tells me that Carol is 'strange', I consider it a huge compliment.

After several months, however, I begin to worry about the consequences of having a love affair with a co-worker. We try to hide the relationship from the residents of Maple House. I'm thinking these people are already too confused and don't need to deal with a sexual relationship between two staff members. One day a female resident asks me if I'm having an affair with Carol. Says she has seen Carol leave my apartment in the early morning. I worry that other residents will become aware of what's happening.

Our age difference contributes to my guilt. My Irish Catholic conscience starts giving me a hard time. Clearly, I'm not as liberated as I'd hoped I was.

While it's an intense sexual relationship, I'm not sure about the level of emotional commitment on my part. I wonder if this might have something to do with the unresolved relationship with Betty. I feel as if I'm cheating. Or maybe my fear of commitment has something to do with unconscious hang-ups going back to semi-nary days.

Carol senses my lack of commitment to the relationship and we gradually conclude that we should go our separate ways. For me it's a decision based largely on guilt. We end the relationship with lots of hurt feelings on both sides.

I AM BEGINNING TO SEE WHY psychologists advise against get-ting involved with co-workers. I quickly learn how difficult it is to work with an ex-lover. Despite efforts to be gentlemanly about the situation, my behaviour reveals a side of my personality that's not attractive. I have intense feelings of rejection despite the fact that I initiated the break-up. Working together in the same office is dif-ficult for each of us. One day Valerie tells me she's really bothered by the tension in the office and is considering leaving. I ask her to stay and promise that I'll try to work things out with Carol.

A few days later I ask Carol if we could meet for a chat at the coffee shop down the street. She agrees. I begin by telling her how much I've been upset by the fact that her new boyfriend stays over-night at her Maple House apartment.

Quite reasonably she points out that this is none of my busi-ness. I can see from the look in her eyes that she is annoyed and upset. She reminds me that our relationship is over.

'That's the way you wanted it. You have your life to live and I have my life to live.'

I agree with her and say that I'm not proud of myself. I promise to make more of an effort to manage my feelings.

Somehow this venting helps reduce the tension between us. We agree that as mature adults we should be able to work together. In an attempt to cope with the situation I move to an apartment com-plex outside the city, halfway between Holyoke and Northampton. Slowly, the office becomes a more congenial place to work.

22.

My dark night of the soul

Perhaps it's part of the negativity resulting from my break-up with Carol, but I become increasingly frustrated with the whole process of rehabilitating former patients. The honeymoon period at Maple House is over in every sense. I begin to wonder if what we are doing is futile and if the exercise is doomed to long-term failure. The theory is that after a few months with us our residents can live independently in the community. While this sounds good, as time passes I realize just how many former patients are ending up homeless or in jail. The network of community support services promised by state bureaucrats and the politicians isn't materializing. I wonder if 'de-institutionalization' is just a way for state government to wash its hands of responsibility for the mentally ill.

I write to Governor Mike Dukakis expressing concern about the lack of support for mentally ill individuals living in the community. The response is a page of bureaucratic jargon. I start to understand why the mentally ill are at such a disadvantage. The jail cell is replacing the hospital ward as a 'home' for those with mental illness and there wasn't much they themselves could do about it.

With Christmas 1974 approaching I have a party for co-workers and friends at my apartment. At one point Carol and I retire to my bedroom where we have a row. It's not long since we broke

164

up and feelings are still raw. Both of us have complaints about perceived hurts inflicted by the other party. The confrontation ends with a mutual agreement to be more considerate of each other. Despite the stormy end to our personal relationship, we promise to remain friends.

A few days later, on the Sunday evening before Christmas, all the pressures I'm experiencing seem to come together. I'm alone in my apartment and feeling abandoned. It's like I've hit a bad curve in the road but I'm not sure how to navigate through it.

I ask myself how I can get out of this dark place. There are still intense feelings of rejection from the break-up with Carol. There's also the unresolved relationship with Betty. I'm emotionally exhausted. And it's not just my personal life. I'm beginning to feel burnt out again. The work at Maple House, coming after my experiences in Louisiana, has taken its toll. It feels like I'm running on empty. I worried that late night beer drinking at a local bar is becoming my antidote to stress.

I find myself sitting on the couch in the living room feeling confused and looking at a pile of unopened Christmas cards from family in Ireland. I call Doug Cooper at his home.

'Doug, I'm at the end of my rope – I'm not sure what to do.'

After a brief discussion he suggests a rest and arranges that I be admitted to Holyoke Hospital. Within a couple of hours I'm checked-in.

It's strange to be in a hospital bed with no physical ailment and nothing apparently 'wrong' with me. I'm wondering what I'll tell people who ask about my hospitalization. And then a perky, smiling nurse comes into the room.

'Now tell me, what's the matter with you, young man?'

She's obviously having a good day while I'm having a bad one.

'I'm here for a few days rest – it's my mind that's screwed-up, not my body.'

The nurse looks puzzled. Most patients are checking out to be with their families for Christmas.

Back in Carlow College I'd read about various mystics and saints who experienced what was described as the 'dark night of the soul'. I assumed this was some kind of emotional or existential crisis. Now, as I lie in my hospital bed, I'm thinking this might be my 'dark night of the soul'.

In the hospital bed my thoughts go back to childhood years growing up in Drumagh. We worked all the time, but work was a practical necessity of farm life. There was no time to think about the meaning of life or any concept of having a 'quality of life' or a 'work–life balance'. Who you were was defined by how hard you worked. I wonder if, because of these early experiences, I've become a workaholic. It seems as if work both defines me and has become my escape – but also my trap. I know I'm now operating on low energy. I'm thinking maybe this breakdown is nature's way of telling me to take a look at my personal priorities.

There's not much to do in the hospital but ruminate and daydream. After a couple of days resting I begin to think of this hospital stay as offering a welcome opportunity for serious reflection. Maybe I'll be able to unscramble some of my muddled thinking and make some helpful resolutions for the New Year.

On Christmas morning Carol drives in a snowstorm from her family home in the Berkshires to visit me. It's a much appreciated surprise. She sits on the side of my bed and we chat for over an hour. Later in the afternoon there's a telephone call from Betty. Those who I care about are reaching out to me and I'm no longer feeling quite as alone in this world.

On Christmas evening I'm experiencing cabin fever and need to get out of the hospital room. Since there's a snowstorm blowing outside, my options are limited. I put on a jacket to go for a stroll around the hospital. A nurse tells me how to get to the chapel. There's nobody around and I sit quietly on a pew.

I'm homesick and feeling nostalgic for Christmases past. Despite the culture of unrelenting work, Christmas was a special time of year in our home. In my memory the small choir at midnight

Mass in Mayo on Christmas Eve is as good as the Sistine Choir. On Christmas morning we were up before dawn to find out what Santa Claus had brought. Despite limited financial resources, my parents always managed to buy something special for each of us. Mammy, with the girls helping, made a big dinner with turkey or a goose and all the usual trimmings, followed by the traditional plum pudding that would have been made weeks in advance.

Even Daddy seemed to get into a joyful mood at Christmas-time. He did all the farm work on Christmas morning and allowed us to enjoy a warm fire in the parlour. This was a big treat since we only got to sit in the parlour on very special occasions. When electricity came to our house in the late 1940s and we got a radio we were able to listen to the Pope's Christmas message, *Urbi et Orbi*, 'to the city and the world'. The memories bring peaceful feelings. It's as if I've been transported to that rural community that was so much part of my childhood years. I begin to feel more grounded in my past.

Back in my hospital room I get to thinking about that first lonely Christmas in north Louisiana and the journey travelled since. I'm also thinking that maybe I've lost something along the way. I'm a nomad in a world where I'm surrounded by people who are settled and getting on with their lives. Perhaps I've strayed too far from my roots. Maybe I need to recapture some of my uncomplicated childhood innocence. Or rediscover the core religious values that were part of my upbringing.

Lying in bed, I'm feeling envious of people who appear to have things figured out. Why has my life become so confused and complicated? There are lots of questions and few answers. One explanation for my emotional turmoil is the so-called 'mid-life crisis', experienced by many men in their forties. I'm nearly 37 so could it be that I'm having it just a few years ahead of schedule?

The hospital stay is a blow to my ego. I'm stripped of feelings of invincibility. I wonder what happened to the 'can do' drive of earlier years. In Baton Rouge I'd challenged the local political establishment. I'd even challenged one of America's most influential religious leaders. But recently the challenges have felt overwhelming. I've been fighting an endless, uphill and thankless battle on behalf of the mentally ill. It's clear that more than half a decade of advocacy work has left me drained of energy. And my self-esteem has suffered.

During the remaining days of my hospital stay I continue to search for the causes of my anxiety and depression. I keep asking myself what I've done to get to this point – and what I need to do to put joy and energy back into my life.

'Ed, find a psychotherapist to help sort through the personal issues,' advises Doug Cooper on one of his visits. This suggestion makes me a little nervous: I've never gone down this road before.

As I leave Holyoke Hospital I realize that while the rest in hospital has helped uplift my spirits, it has provided only temporary relief. There's still work to be done if I'm to recover my old self. I know I'll need to follow Dr Cooper's advice.

On my release from hospital I'm given a prescription for antidepressants – pills to make me feel better. After a few days taking them I feel like a zombie. Now I understand why the residents of Maple House hate taking their psychotropic medications. I say to myself, *Enough of this stuff!* – I'd rather be miserable and depressed than feeling nothing. The pills go into the bin.

As I go about my work at Maple House I put up a brave front, but I'm still hurting inside. Sometimes late at night, in the privacy of my apartment, I find myself in tears – and this scares me. I'm worried about my behaviour and my mental health. I'm confused. Is this just a case of burn-out? Was the break-up with Carol just a trigger revealing a more serious pathology? I turn inward as I attempt to regain lost energy and confidence. My intake of alcohol and nicotine increases. And then I wonder if my drinking is masking an underlying clinical depression?

The months pass and I try to refocus energy on my work.

One day Betty calls and tells me she's getting married. I wish her well, but again I can't help wondering about my own inability to make a commitment. I suspect our long-distance relationship may have ended in disappointment for her. She gave me several years of emotional support that I sorely needed and now I'm feeling guilty about my response. It seems there's no end to my wellspring of Irish Catholic guilt.

TOM AND I HAVEN'T FORGOTTEN the grand plan we had cooked up in the wilds of Mississippi. Our charter company. This will be my first venture into entrepreneurial activity. Our plan is to initially operate two flights to Ireland. I decide to put all of my spare energy and most of my savings into this project. I study the Civil Aeronautics Board requirements for operating a charter. I obtain a surety bond and depository agreement from Chase Manhattan Bank and, after numerous delays, I sign an agreement with Pan Am to provide the Boeing 707 jet for the initial charters.

Our timing could not be worse. A serious economic recession has hit the USA and our window for selling the 178 seats (per flight) is very narrow. In desperation I make a last-minute trip to New York City in March 1975 for St Patrick's Day to promote the flight. I had already placed ads in a number of Irish-American newspapers. I visit dozens of Irish pubs all over the Big Apple. I pass out leaflets promoting the charter. I find myself standing beside representatives of the IRA outside Carnegie Hall at the annual St Patrick's Day concert. They are hustling money for guns and I'm trying to sell a few seats on my charter flights. It's a frantic, desperate effort and it fails.

In the end, the charter flights never get off the ground. I abandon the project and chalk up the financial losses to experience.

23.

Facing the past

Acouple of months after checking out of Holyoke Hospital I'm
feeling better, but recognize that the skills of a professional
might help me sort out the issues that had driven me there in the
first place. I sign up for sessions with a psychotherapist in the Psy-
chological Services Department at the nearby University of Massachusetts.

The weekly meetings with Roz force me to ask honest questions about my relationships with women. Why am I afraid of
commitment? Why do I fear losing my 'space'? I acknowledge a
yearning for intimacy, but also a fear someone will invade my privacy. Roz says there's nothing abnormal in wanting personal space.
She assures me that people in long-term, committed relationships
experience the same need.

The work environment at Maple House has improved as a result of the last confrontation between Carol and me. And these
sessions with Roz reinforce the healing process. As I come to better understand the nature of my attachment to Carol, it becomes
easier to let go. I come to understand that there was something
addictive about our sexual relationship. In one session I explore
lingering anger towards Carol. Roz has a way of challenging me
without provoking defensiveness.

'Edward, who feeds the anger?' she asks.

There's a long silence.

'Well, I guess I'm doing my part,' I say, attempting to be honest.

'You're not Mr Nice Guy after all?'

She has hit on one of my hot button issues.

'I like to have people think well of me, to see my good side,' I say.

I begin to recognize a 'good guy syndrome' in my past relationships. Not wanting to be perceived as negative, I'd failed to be totally honest. Now I'm realizing that may be what frustrated Betty and the other women I'd dated. The most painful discovery is the realization that, in failing to be truly honest, I may have used women. Ironically, I'd fancied myself as a liberated person, free of male chauvinism.

In one session we address my attraction to women in their early twenties rather than women closer to my own age who would be more suitable girlfriend material.

'You may be trying to compensate for missing normal courtship experiences when you were a younger man,' says Roz. It's a helpful insight.

In another session I explore how the admonitions of school and seminary years are still affecting my ability to develop intimate relationships. At Knockbeg College our annual retreat always included sermons designed to instil a fear of Hell. Dire warnings regarding 'impure thoughts' and masturbation were part of the package. The constant warnings got under my skin and my major preoccupation during teenage years was the prospect of damnation. The fear of dying in a state of sin and going to Hell was very real.

While the wording might have been slightly more sophisticated, the message in the seminary wasn't much more complex: sex equals sin and sin equals damnation. Women, of course, were the occasion of sin. Nothing was ever said about attraction to men because the training was predicated on all of us being heterosexual. Yet the ban on visiting each other's rooms, and the stern warnings about the dangers of 'special' relationships with other students, indicate an awareness of same-sex attraction.

As much as I'd wanted to believe – indeed, congratulated my-self – that I had walked away from the priesthood without psy-chological scars, the reality is different. Roz brings me to a point where I recognize the obvious: five years in an all-boys boarding school followed by six years of seminary life and seven years in the celibate priesthood was not ideal preparation for living a well-adjusted sexual life. This insight allows me to be more accepting of my shortcomings.

But the most painful topic of all to explore is my childhood ex-periences. In one meeting with Roz I acknowledge residual angry feelings over things that happened during my early years growing up in Ireland.

'Edward, why don't you come clean – tell me what you really felt. You're not going to surprise me by anything you say.'

If only it were that easy.

UNTIL RELATIVELY RECENT times I had not thought of growing up in Drumagh as happy or unhappy. I conformed to the expectations of my parents and worked hard in support of the family enter-prise. I enjoyed the give and take of growing up in a large family. I experienced Mammy as kind and supportive. I saw Daddy as a strict and demanding taskmaster – someone to be feared at times. I sometimes wondered if he was typical of fathers or if he was one of a kind, but I had no basis for comparison. I was never around other families long enough to observe interactions between par-ents and children. I assumed my situation was no more difficult than that of other children. In fact, I realized that in material terms we were better off than some of our neighbours. In lots of ways I considered us lucky.

One afternoon – I think around 1945 – when we arrived home from school Mammy told us to check in one of the out-buildings for a surprise. We found a spanking new blue Ford van. No words could adequately express our excitement. This was special because only a few other families in the parish owned a car or a van. As

Daddy had driven buses in New York, he didn't have to learn to drive like other neighbours who taught themselves at great risk to both humans and livestock. The arrival of the van meant Sunday 'excursions' could be extended to a wider circle of relatives, to towns further afield than Carlow, and to significant Catholic shrines around the countryside.

The other great use for the van was going to hurling matches locally and in Croke Park, in Dublin. Daddy rooted for his native County Kilkenny and somehow expected his Laois-born children to share his enthusiasm. We regularly got to see Kilkenny in action, but rarely had the opportunity to see the team from Laois play. I would go along and fake my enthusiasm for Kilkenny – a day out was a day out after all. Once when Laois was playing an important game, my father announced that we were going on a pilgrimage to Knock, the Marian shrine in County Mayo. Our Lady might have had my body that day, but the local hurlers had my heart and prayers.

When the rural electrification scheme reached our area our home got a major work-over. A new stairwell and bathroom were installed. The radio connected us to the outside world. Before the radio a wind-up gramophone was brought out to play records, mostly at Christmas and other special holidays. The small collection of scratchy records included the great tenor, John McCormack, singing Irish ballads. The new radio was mostly turned to Radio Éireann. Many of the programmes were in Irish – a language I didn't understand. While we could pick up the BBC and European stations, Daddy didn't want us corrupted by 'foreign' influences. When he and Mammy went to visit relatives we would switch over to Radio Luxembourg or one of the other stations that played modern music. We just had to remember to retune the radio before they got home.

When friends or relatives came to visit we were all lined up for introductions and Daddy would always present me as 'the shy member of the family'. I was a quiet, introverted child, partly, I think, to avoid drawing attention on myself. And this is where the memories become difficult. What frightened me most growing up was Daddy's tendency to lash out at my mother and my brothers, particularly Andy. Of the four boys, I managed to escape a lot of the verbal abuse because I went out of my way not to cross him in any way. For reasons I didn't fully understand the girls generally escaped his wrath. Perhaps he considered that their domain was domestic and he was happy to leave their formation to their mother. Also, as the boys were outside with him doing farm work, there was far more opportunity for us to annoy and frustrate him.

If Daddy was 'cross', we all wore long faces. On occasions when things would go wrong on the farm, Daddy would erupt into a rage. He was a person to be feared when he lost his temper. One day a farmyard tool was missing and everyone was called into the kitchen. Daddy implied one of us was guilty of stealing – as if we had some secret place to go with one of his implements. On this occasion he removed his leather belt and threatened to beat the guilty party. No one came forward with a confession and nobody got beaten, but the whole episode was bizarre and threatening, and I was shaking in my shoes.

While incidents like that occurred only occasionally, they had a chilling effect. A lot of our good times were conditioned on not crossing our father, whether wittingly or unwittingly. There was always the real danger something unexpected would go wrong and he would get upset and everyone would be punished. These incidents built, brick by brick, the wall that separated my brothers and me from our father.

I internalized the hurt I felt at his displays of impatience and temper. I hated conflict and as a quiet youngster, all I wanted was for everyone to get along. I did everything in my power to keep the peace.

THE DISCUSSION WITH ROZ brings some deeply repressed feelings to the surface. What I try to explain is that there were times I'd felt deeply hurt when I heard Mammy or Andy subjected to one of Daddy's tirades.

'I wanted to shout, "Stop the bullying!" But I wouldn't have had the courage to say anything – no matter how upset I was feeling.'

'You obviously experienced your father as a fairly intimidating person?'

I explain to Roz that the first of the Ten Commandments that I'd learnt was 'Honour thy Father and thy Mother'. Daddy had been fond of reminding his family of this mandate first delivered to Moses. And one of his own commandments was that 'children should never contradict their elders'. None of us, including our mother, would ever challenge his authority.

Roz reassures me that childhood feelings of hurt are not unusual, but they should be addressed. In order to get me to vent repressed feelings, Roz role-plays my father. She encourages me to verbalise past hurt feelings.

'Okay Edward, tell me exactly how you feel about the way I treated your mother. Tell me how you feel about the way I treated Andy.'

I freeze – unable to vent my feelings.

'Just say the words. Try telling me what an S.O.B. I am.'

Despite gentle coaching, getting in touch with repressed anger is traumatic. I'm humbled to realize that as a middle-aged man I'm still feeling intimidated by an aging man living three thousand miles away. The simple act of conjuring up memories of those early experiences causes anxiety. Usually I just break down in tears. I'm inclined to rationalize certain things: my father was a product of his time, of his background, of a struggling new state, of a repressive and punitive religion. He sincerely thought he was doing his best for us. And not only for his own family, but for the country he had gone out and fought to bring into being.

Despite my reluctance, Roz is determined to get me to deal with repressed feelings. One day she asks me to punch a pillow as if I'm punishing my father. Again, I freeze, unable to respond.

These psychological workouts sometimes leave me exhausted. But I begin to understand what Roz is trying to accomplish. She is helping me negotiate my emotional crisis by dealing with the painful 'baggage' from childhood years that is affecting how I live now. In a firm but gentle way she has been forcing me to confront the issues that I've conveniently ignored. I am learning I have to let go of some stuff from the past in order to move forward. I conclude that these therapy sessions are only the beginning and that I'll need to do more work to be free of the sense of helplessness that dominated my childhood.

In one of our sessions Roz had suggested I find a support group to further my self-exploration. I join a group engaged in a process called Re-evaluation Counselling. I'm attracted to this group by the emphasis on building self-esteem and getting in touch with inner strengths and resources. I meet weekly with one of my fellow members and we counsel each other. I learn that I have to be patient and give myself time to recover. It took a while to get myself into a bad place, and it will take time to get out of it again.

ONE EVENING I ARRIVE home from work to find a large envelope with 'Diocese of Alexandria' listed as the return address. I have a queasy feeling about what is inside. I prepare myself with a glass of Jack Daniel's. When I open the envelope I realize this is the response to a letter I sent the Bishop indicating that I wouldn't be returning to the ministry. The envelope contains the forms to be completed to formalize my 'divorce' from the priesthood. The Church, like all large organizations, has a bureaucratic machine in need of constant feeding.

The package includes a couple of surprises. As I scan through one questionnaire I realize I'm expected to swear that I was coerced into becoming a priest. *What the hell do these people want?* I am surprised by the intensity of my response. A few bureaucratic questionnaires arrive in the mail and here I am, getting totally worked up.

The forms touch a raw nerve. As I review them I recall how, when I was still in the ministry, I would ask people seeking annulments to sign statements claiming that they didn't intend to marry the first time. Completing these statements was a requirement for getting a marriage annulled and for getting the Church to bless a second marriage. Now I can see the same line of reasoning behind the documents I've received: if I was coerced into becoming a priest, then I was not validly ordained and the Church is just verifying this fact. I won't be an ex-priest, I'll be a never-was-a-priest. Now that I'm on the receiving end, I properly understand why people get angry at this kind of ecclesiastical legalism. It's a dishonest game and I don't want to play it.

As I read through the documentation I find another unwelcome surprise. There's a questionnaire to be completed by my father in which he accepts responsibility for coercing me into becoming a priest. Now, my blood pressure goes off the charts. Yes, Daddy influenced my decision to become a priest, but he didn't *make* me go for ordination. And he has been through so much in recent years I have no intention of adding to his distress by asking him to swear that he screwed-up my life. Then I think, *Why am I getting so defensive and upset?* I tell myself to chill out and have another drink to calm my nerves. This is just bureaucratic bullshit.

I realize this is one of those times when I need to get out, find a place of solitude and have a good talk with myself. So I go to the summit of a local mountain, Mount Tom, and sit down to think. After calming down my emotions and thinking through everything rationally, my considered response is only slightly more sophisticated that my initial *screw-the-bureaucrats-in-Rome* reaction. I realize I'm just a tiny cog in a big machine and getting upset is not a constructive use of my time and energy. I decide I won't shade the truth for the sake of expediency, and I certainly will not add to the burdens of an old man to lessen my own. The Bishop's missive gets shredded.

Periodically after that I receive communications from the Diocese of Alexandria enquiring about the questionnaires. I simply ignore them. As far as I'm concerned the issue has been resolved between me and my Maker and doesn't need bureaucratic approval.

A WEEK-LONG VACATION ON Cape Cod helps lift my spirits. Each day I go jogging on a bicycle path between Falmouth and Hyannis. I meet a friend for a round of golf. I begin to feel like my old self, ready to become more socially engaged once again. A Jewish colleague invites me to celebrate Seder with her family in Boston. I go biking on weekends. There are occasional trips to Boston to take in Celtics basketball games. I go along to a weekend workshop on human sexuality that a friend thinks I might find helpful. The workshop facilitators begin by asking that participants remove all their clothing. It's a bit of a surprise, but soon my initial discomfort disappears.

The country is a year out from the celebration of the American Revolution and already excitement is mounting. Concord is considered the birthplace of the revolution and an official event is organised by the government's Bicentennial Commission for 19 April 1975. Various groups on the left, including the anti-war movement, establish the People's Bicentennial Commission. It will be sponsoring an alternative event.

Three friends and I drive to Concord for the People's event. With the rain and the muck, it reminds me of the Festival of Life I had attended in the backwoods of Louisiana. I listen to Pete Seeger sing out songs of liberation. His rendition of 'This land is your land, this land is my land' brings back memories of anti-war rallies in Baton Rouge. Woody Guthrie's version of the song was part of the soundtrack of my years working with the anti-poverty programme.

After the event in Concord we go to a friend's place. Our host is the proud owner of what he describes as a collection of 'the saddest country and western songs ever written'. We drink beer, smoke some weed, and I find out how enjoyable it can be to listen to songs of heartbreak on a rainy New England afternoon. I return to Holyoke feeling I've fulfilled my patriotic duty.

On a weekend visit to New York I attend Sunday morning service with a cousin at an old Lithuanian church on the Lower East Side. The beautiful Gregorian chant conjures up memories of the years spent in seminary. It has been a long journey on a winding road since those Sunday mornings back in Carlow College when I'd join fellow students in celebrating the ancient liturgy. On this Sunday morning, I'm at peace with myself and glad to get in touch with my spiritual roots.

A three-week visit to Dublin and London proves to be therapeutic. The whole family gathers in Dublin in May 1975 for Lena's final profession into the Little Sisters of the Assumption. This time I feel totally accepted as a layman. They see that I've moved on, as they have too. Andy, Lena and I go on a side-trip to stay with Tom in London. It feels like we siblings are just getting to know each other as adults after all those years. It is a relaxing visit – exploring London, chatting a lot, getting acquainted and catching up on our lives since we grew up together. We're a typical bunch of thirty-somethings, more caught up in the present moment than bothered about looking back.

After years of intense activity I find myself in a reflective mood. I read the book of the moment – Robert Pirsig's *Zen and the Art of Motorcycle Maintenance* – and it really resonates. Like Pirsig's character, I see myself as a traveller on the journey through life. My friends are telling me that I should be settling down, making some money and having a family. I know this is the road followed by most self-respecting middle-class people, but at this time the journey seems more important than the destination.

As my energy returns I start getting excited about the possibility of doing something different with my life. Almost every week one of the old factory buildings Holyoke burns to the ground. I live with the fear that I'll drive into the city one morning and find

Maple House burnt to the ground. That's just one of my concerns. For a variety of reasons I want out of this situation. I start to look into graduate school programmes.

When I finally find my new direction, it comes about through my work in Maple House, which feels rather ironic. In the spring of 1976 I get a call from a professor in the University of Massachusetts, Jack Wideman, who is looking to relocate his sister from Washington D.C. She developed schizophrenia in her early twenties, is now in her late fifties and has been living in a private psychiatric facility for decades. The family trust supporting her care is becoming depleted and he is looking for a less expensive option.

Jack and I have long conversations about the suitability of Maple House for his sister. We wonder if she'll be able to cope with the kind of independence offered in the Holyoke program. We decide it's worth a try.

Jack comes to visit regularly and occasionally, after he's spent time with his sister, we go for pizza and a few drinks. He works in the university's School of Education where he is a professor of counselling psychology, and I find our conversations stimulating and thought-provoking. Jack is a big hulk of a man with an endearing, shy smile and a deep gaze that makes you feel like you are a very special person. He is one of the most gifted and empathic men I've ever met. On one of his visits I share my intention to move on from Maple House as soon as I can find a suitable graduate program.

'Ed, why don't you come and join us at U Mass?' he says. 'You could build on your civil rights experience in Louisiana as well as the experience at Maple House.'

My heart almost skips a beat at his suggestion. As I listen to him describe the School of Education graduate programme, I realize it is perfect for me. The idea that I can design my own program and build on past life and work experience has special appeal.

After that, things happen quickly. I am accepted into the doctoral programme commencing in the fall of 1976. I convene a meeting of Maple House residents and tell them of my intention to leave and pursue new challenges.

When I am leaving a few months later, there's a tinge of sadness about the occasion. I give the residents a pep-talk about believing in themselves and demanding to be treated with respect. Then I walk out, knowing a burden has been lifted off my shoulders. Not for the first time in my life, I feel like a freed man.

Carol and I decide to spend a week camping together in southern Vermont. We go as friends, not lovers. A mutual friend says the plan is crazy, but it turns out to be an enjoyable week – a chance to end our relationship on a good note. And then we go our separate ways: Carol becomes the new executive director of Maple House, and I get ready to move on to a new life as a graduate student.

(It will be thirty-seven years before Carol and I meet again, in autumn 2013, when she is close to 60 and I am 75. On a trip to New England I am doing a tour of the people and places that were significant to me during my life there. Over dinner in Holyoke we remember Maple House and swap stories of where life has taken us in the intervening years. Earlier that afternoon I had discovered that the building that was once Maple House has literally vanished – it is now a vacant lot, a gaping hole in the row of tenement buildings.)

In August I get an invitation from the man who hired me at Maple House, Andy Phillips, to join him and his wife Donna for dinner at his home in Northampton. When I walk in, I'm somewhat stunned to see so many friends and colleagues. They present me with a Waterford Crystal decanter and the evening is an enjoyable and positive closure to my career as an advocate on behalf of the mentally ill. I'm excited to be moving on and to be doing something for myself rather than for the rest of humanity.

24.

Making peace with my father

The transition from psychiatric halfway house to the University of Massachusetts brings some changes in lifestyle. One of these changes involves moving from Holyoke to Northampton, about eleven miles away and home to Smith College, the elite third level institution for women. I receive an invitation to join a group of graduate students who share an old house. I'm told it's a commune, with three male residents and three women residents. I've never fancied living in a commune but this place suits my budget. The interview with the residents, all mature graduate students, leaves me with a few concerns. There seems to be a lot of rules. Despite niggling reservations I accept the invitation to join the group.

I have a small room in the attic with just enough room for a bed. The other room in the attic is occupied by one of the guys in the house and his girlfriend. Every night I can hear their loud lovemaking. But as I feared, it's the rules that really get under my skin. Our dinners often end with booze-influenced arguments. I tire of the hassle and pettiness. As a student at Carlow College I didn't like the fact that every facet of my life was dictated by rules. Now, as a middle-aged man, I feel like I'm back in the same situation.

One evening Margaret, a member of the household, asks me privately if I would like to go out with her for a drink. By the second drink I realize that Margaret hates living in the commune as much as I do. We decide to find our own apartment and move out. On a Friday afternoon we move to an apartment two blocks away, leaving a note for the other residents. I'm relieved that four months of misery are over.

Margaret and I enjoy the personal freedom provided by our new place, a second-floor apartment in a family home. Margaret has an on-off relationship with a graduate student living in Amherst. I have an on-off relationship with Margaret. Bill, a counsellor at a local program for delinquent boys, becomes the third resident of our apartment. Margaret decides to move to her boyfriend's place and Kathy, a nurse from Maine, comes to share the apartment. Kathy, Bill and I are happy campers.

Kathy bubbles with positive energy and makes our place feel like a real home. The highlight of each evening is *Mary Hartman, Mary Hartman.* This wildly over-the-top soap opera parody provides us with a necessary daily dose of laughter.

One late night, after an evening of drinking at a friend's birthday party, I'm driving home when I crash my Volkswagen Beetle into a roadside sign-post, causing major damage to my car. A friend travelling in the car behind me stops to check that I'm okay. She calls Kathy to come and get me. When Kathy arrives she's obviously pissed-off.

'What the fuck are you up to, trying to kill yourself?'

I'm feeling humiliated as Kathy cleans the blood from a gash on my forehead.

'Ed, do you have any injuries? Are you hurting?'

I assure Kathy that I'm okay. The tow truck takes my car to the garage. We drive back to the apartment.

Next morning I'm still feeling ashamed of what happened. And Kathy is still upset.

'You could have killed yourself last night,' she says. 'You're supposed to be an intelligent person!'

'Well, I just had a few glasses of wine at Joan's house in Florence. I guess I had too many.'

'Ed, I grew up in Maine with a father who was alcoholic. It caused an awful lot of pain in our family. You have no idea of how much fuckin' abuse my sister, my mother and I had to endure. Take my advice – be careful.'

I tell her it won't happen again.

I remain upbeat about my new life as a college student. Each day I commute the ten miles between Northampton and Amherst. The university, surrounded by farmland, including tobacco fields, provides an ideal setting for time-out after what seems like a life-time of in-the-trenches advocacy work. I'm having time to regroup – and I'm enjoying it.

Because of my background the faculty at the university treat me more as a colleague than as a student. It feels as if I'm on a care-free vacation, with nobody to be concerned about but myself. And there's no guilt about my new stress-free lifestyle. I tell myself I've paid my dues. I relish the opportunity to recover from 'battle fatigue', as well as to enrich my life with new ideas.

My university idyll is interrupted by developments back in Ireland. Towards the end of 1976 I start getting calls from Andy indicating Daddy is in deteriorating health. In mid-December he is blunt: 'Eddie, this would be a good time to come home – Daddy is not going to be around much longer.'

I arrive in Drumagh a few days before Christmas. By this time the old homestead is receding from memory, having passed from our family's ownership nearly a decade earlier. I've come to accept the house built in the 1960s as my Irish 'home'.

It's immediately apparent Daddy has changed. He is now seventy-two. Gone is the drive and obsession with work. As always, though, he's eager to talk politics and world affairs. Each morning I go down to the local shop to fetch him whatever newspapers are available. A news junkie with a voracious appetite for information, he sometimes complains that the different papers carry identical stories. I'm guessing he doesn't realise that all these newspapers get most of their stories from the same wire services.

During the weeks preceding my return Daddy had been bed-ridden and had received the Last Rites of the Church on several occasions. I'm not sure how worried I should be. I learn that on one occasion, when he thought he was dying, he demanded that Maura summon the parish priest to administer Last Rites. When the priest arrives a couple of hours later he's met at the front door by Daddy, fully dressed and demanding to know the purpose of the visit.

Patricia is delighted I've come home to join in the holiday festivities. She has just turned eleven and is full of energy and determined to turn Christmas into a joyful celebration. Together, we go walking around the fields to cut down holly to decorate the house. It's obvious she wants to do everything in her power to make my visit enjoyable. Maura is welcoming and hospitable. If she is feeling anxious about the future – and given the state of Daddy's health over the past few months, she must be – she doesn't show it.

We all attend midnight Mass on a moonlit night in Mayo parish church. Since Daddy has stopped driving, I'm given the job of chauffeur. All kinds of memories come rushing into my mind. Memories of that first lonely Christmas in north Louisiana. Memories of another lonely Christmas spent in Holyoke Hospital. The small choir singing Christmas hymns in the dimly lit church evokes memories of Christmas Masses attended in this church as a child. It's as if time has stood still. After Mass, in the darkness, neighbours exchange Christmas greetings. Back in the house Maura and Patricia make tea and we eat Christmas cake and reminisce about Christmases past.

Christmas morning is special. Daddy and I chat as Maura and Patricia prepare dinner. We watch the Pope on television deliver his annual *Urbi et Orbi* message. I'm fascinated by how relaxed and sociable Daddy is being; he's obviously very pleased that I've come home. As for me, it's my first family Christmas in fifteen years, one of the nicest Christmases I've had in years, and I am very happy to contrast it with Christmas two years previously when I was on a hospital ward wondering if I was going out of my mind. It feels like I have come a long way in recovering my mental equilibrium. Apart from all that, the days are easy-going and relaxing – not something I ever thought I would say about spending a lot of time in close proximity to my father.

I had been told that the relationship between Maura and Daddy was strained but there is no apparent tension between them. And the relationship between Daddy and Patricia seems particularly warm. Clearly, he's not the demanding man I'd experienced during childhood years. I'm a bit envious of Patricia, but I'm happy that she's experiencing a man who has mellowed with the years.

One day Daddy asks me to drive him to Carlow. On our way he tells me he wants to visit the solicitor to make changes in his will. He asks my ideas about the future of Drumagh – a surprise request.

'Well, it's Maura's home, and Patricia will need an education,' I say.

I'm not used to giving my father advice on such matters. He listens and keeps his opinions to himself.

I park the car on the street outside the solicitor's office and wait while he transacts his business. When he returns to the car he asks if I'd like to go for a drink. Another surprise. For the first time in my life I'm joining my father for a drink in a pub. We walk over to Reddy's, on Tullow Street, and order two whiskies.

'I had a fall in the mart and hit my head on the ground. I haven't felt right since,' Daddy says. And then, after a few moments of silence he says, 'I may not see you again, Eddie.'

I'm stunned by this statement and at a loss for words. I do the only thing I can think of – bluff. 'Daddy, I know you haven't been well. Andy calls regularly and he's been keeping me posted. But you look like you're doing pretty good right now.'

We sit in silence, each of us lost in our thoughts.

As I sit in the dimly lit pub I think that though my head is full of stories and ideas about him, really I hardly know this man who has so profoundly shaped my life. Nearly forty years of memories rush through my mind. As a child I'd listened to stories about his experiences as a young man in New York. One incident – told as a funny yarn – was about his arrival at Ellis Island. He was little more than a teenager at the time. Every new arrival had to be claimed by a 'sponsor'. Sitting alone on a bench, he watched and waited as welcome parties greeted all his fellow passengers. Finally, he was the only passenger left unclaimed. After a couple of hours a policeman asked him for his last name and matched it to some form of 'Deevy' ID in the wallet of a man sleeping behind the wheel of a parked car. My father's uncle, in anticipation of the arrival of his nephew from Ireland, had gotten drunk on homemade whiskey.

Daddy always told stories like this about his time in New York as tales from a heroic adventure. It was the place that made him. But I wonder now what it was like to get off the boat in a foreign country and find nobody waiting. For a young lad who'd grown up in a rural Irish community, it must have been extremely distressing, though he never admitted to any fear.

I had always interpreted the Ellis Island story as a metaphor for the tough experience he had in New York. From early on he had to keep his wits about him and fend for himself. I inferred that there was a lot of hardship during his early days in America. Once he spoke of what it was like working ten hours a day in a stone quarry. He also spoke about the 'temptations' associated with living in big bad sinful New York City. He was particularly proud of the fact he'd remained steadfastly faithful to the values of his Catholic religion. Perhaps it was his faith and strongly held conservative moral views that enabled him to survive this experience.

Daddy is a slim man of medium height but he always had extraordinary energy and drive. Some neighbours refer to him as 'the bossman', and it's not a title of respect or endearment. Daddy could be authoritarian and self-righteous in his dealings with people. For starters, he took a very dim view of anyone who didn't work as hard as he thought they should. And if he had a falling-out with a neighbour or a relative, the rest of the family was expected to follow his lead. When I'd arrive home from school or college for holidays I'd ask the others, 'Who are we not talking to these days?'

Some saw him as overly ambitious. He was a 'blow-in' in our community, a young fellow from the neighbouring county who had turned up out of nowhere to buy a property from a Protestant landowner and proceeded to develop it with relentless drive. When my parents moved in the house hadn't been completed and was in a state of serious disrepair, and though for the time the farm was substantial in size, it was difficult to work because of the poorly drained, heavy soil. It comprised of several smallholdings that had been merged together over a period of several decades.

Daddy believed 'an idle mind is the devil's workshop', so he kept us busy all the time. We were a family in constant motion. As a youngster, each morning I'd go with Andy to fetch the farm horses from the fields before going to school. We used a bucket with oats to apprehend the horses and then would ride back to the farmyard at full speed. In due course Michael and Tom also performed that duty. From about the age of eight the boys were involved in driving cattle into the mart in Carlow on a fair day. We would be awakened at three o'clock in the morning. Mammy would have cooked a boiled egg and made tea. After breakfast we'd set out with the cattle on the eight-mile trek to town. With no traffic at that hour, the only sound would be the clip-clop of cattle hooves as we walked under the bright stars and the moonlight. Daddy would meet us at eight o'clock and we'd watch as he and a cattle dealer haggled over the price. After the sale we'd go to a local eating-house for a feed of steak and onions. It always seemed like good compensation for the long day's effort. A bag of sweets was also part of the bargain – as long as we agreed to share them with whoever was at home.

There was a predictable rhythm to life on the farm. Spring was the time for planting crops – Daddy would head out with the horse at daybreak to plough the fields. Summer was the time for making hay. As we were often competing against the rain, we worked from dawn to dusk when the weather was fine. On sunny days Mammy would bring ham and tomato sandwiches and tea to the fields so that we wouldn't have to waste time going back to the house for a midday meal. Sitting in a pile of new-mown hay, eating sandwiches and drinking tea from a mug was one of the simple but delightful pleasures of summertime.

In the autumn, there was potato-picking and a major event was the annual threshing. There was tremendous excitement as the threshing machine, drawn by a steam engine, made its way slowly along the long driveway leading to our house. Neighbours came from all directions to lend a helping hand. Mammy would cook a big dinner of cabbage, potatoes and bacon for the whole crew. The barley, wheat and oats would be stored in different farmhouses, to be used as feed for cattle and horses or to be sold in Carlow.

Work continued throughout the winter. When there was nothing else to do we kept busy cleaning and painting barns, sheds and outhouses.

Sometimes Daddy would hire a workman to help with farm work. These were usually men who travelled the countryside and worked for a while with different farmers. The workman lived in a room in one of the farmhouses and would eat meals with the family.

During the long winter evenings we would sit around the open fireplace in the kitchen. For fuel we used turf from a local bog or coal mined just a couple of miles from the farm. At night-time Daddy would read the newspaper and share his views on the news of the day. During the war years there was plenty to comment about. He supported de Valera's policy of Irish neutrality. Rationing meant that certain products, including tea and sugar, were difficult to get, but under our staircase we had several large plywood containers of Indian tea. I never knew how this rare merchandise was obtained and even as a youngster knew better than to ask. Relatives who came to visit were sometimes treated to some of the tea. Despite the rationing we always had enough food on the table. Mammy made bread every day. The butter was homemade. We grew vegetables in the two gardens that were at either side of our house. Periodically, pigs were slaughtered to provide meat. Sunday dinner regularly included a home-reared roast chicken. Occasionally, Daddy would invite us along as he took his shotgun to shoot pheasant or other game. On one occasion he offered to let me shoot a rabbit and I almost fell over from the kickback of the gun. My hunting career ended that day with a dead rabbit, a sore shoulder and a bruised ego.

Our extended family included cows, calves, bullocks, horses, pigs, chickens, turkeys, a dog and an assortment of cats. Riding bareback on horses was part of everyday life. The dog and the cats got names and were our pets. Sometimes farm animals would perish, but Daddy took these setbacks in his stride. The death of an animal or the loss of a crop was considered 'the will of God' and accepted as one of the givens of farm life.

On the farm we lived close to Mother Nature. I saw cows calving and horses giving birth to foals. I saw chicks breaking out of eggs. We always had a bull that serviced the cows. Because my mother left our home several times a week to help women in childbirth I knew where babies came from at an early age.

We were a self-contained community, to some extent removed from the world around us because of our distance from the public road. We could go for days without seeing anyone from the outside world. As young children we always found ways to entertain ourselves – we made the farm our playground, whether hunting for rabbits, or fishing, or picking hazelnuts or blackberries. A favourite game in winter was hopscotch on the kitchen floor. We also played board games such as Ludo and Snakes and Ladders. We played cards for small stakes but the game frequently ended abruptly when Daddy, a sore loser, was at the wrong end. At these critical times he would announce that we were about to say the rosary. I don't know that it's a particularly Irish thing, but in our house bad things seemed to happen when we were having a good time. Even so, good times were frequently had.

The effort to improve the homestead was unending. Flowers were planted, hedges were clipped and farmyards were paved. A new glass porch in front of the house was built as a special entrance for visitors. Even the outside farmhouses underwent constant repair and improvement. The original neglected two-storey house that my parents had purchased began to resemble a handsome, albeit small, country home. Visitors frequently commented on the transformation. There were no limits to Daddy's ambition, his energy and his willingness to drive his family to realize his vision. What his vision was we could only intuit from his actions, but it seemed it was to be a man of substance and status in the community. That substance and status would come from being a successful farmer, a stalwart of the Church, and the head of a household whose members served – and were seen to serve – Church and State in an exemplary fashion.

I remember as a child how we'd have visits from relatives returning from faraway places. These would spark a frenzy of improvements. Daddy wanted to impress people with his achievements. One of most significant visitations was by Daddy's older sister, our Aunt Lena, who had entered religious life in the 1920s after her fiancé was killed by the Black and Tans during the War of Independence. She lived in Western Australia and was known to us as Sister Paschal, her name in religious life. Months of preparation preceded her visit in the early 1950s, her first back to Ireland in nearly thirty years. Windows were washed, doors were painted, floors were scrubbed and hedges were clipped. My brothers and I joked that it must be the Pope who was coming to see us, not a mere nun.

When she turned up, Sister Paschal fit the stereotype of the severe Catholic nun: strict, pious and cold. She was patronising and bossy with my father, which was startling, and a reminder that in his family he was the baby brother. No wonder he needed to impress. (What little enthusiasm I had for Sister Paschal was diminished even further when I discovered that letters I'd sent her from school were re-mailed to my father. From her convent in Subiaco, sixty-odd years before the invention of e-mail, she started operating a primitive version of mail-forwarding, sometimes to extremely mischievous effect.)

Inevitably, Daddy attracted traditional Irish begrudgery. He didn't exactly help himself with his dry humour. When he was annoyed with a neighbour whose cattle broke into our land on a Sunday morning the neighbour, knowing Daddy's staunch religious beliefs, reminded him of the urgency of getting to Mass and of Christ's injunction to 'leave all and follow me'. To which Daddy replied, 'Well, he didn't say, "Leave all in Michael Deevy's field and follow me"!' However, it's fair to say that he was also admired by other neighbours and he formed deep and lasting friendships with some very fine people.

Our closest neighbours in every sense were the Delaneys. We could get to the Delaneys by walking through the fields and crossing the river. Like my parents, Minnie and Michael Delaney were raising a young family. Minnie would come and help when Mammy was away for several days delivering babies or when a new baby arrived in our house. Michael Delaney was Daddy's most loyal and devoted friend. A man with big watery eyes, a warm smile and a gentle personality, he was always there when my father needed him. He was called upon when a cow had difficulty calving or it was time to break a young horse into farm work.

Among other things, we loved Michael because of his calming influence on Daddy. I recall an incident when I was just five or six years old. A horse had broken out of a yard and Daddy started shouting at Andy for leaving a gate open. Daddy was getting himself more and more worked up when, fortunately, Michael Delaney came on the scene and managed to talk him down. Michael had the magical touch in these kinds of situations. 'That's okay, Mike, everything will be fine,' he would say. And somehow that diffused the situation.

Despite his own strong Catholic convictions and his insistence that his children follow the same path, Daddy was extremely and genuinely respectful of our Protestant neighbours. (Though not to the point of disobeying the Church's injunction not to enter a Protestant church – when we attended a neighbour's funeral, we remained outside.) In later years I suspected that his time in America had left him with an appreciation of the Protestant ethic as an admirable approach to daily life. He certainly considered our Protestant neighbours reliable, hard-working and decent.

In his day Daddy was considered a progressive farmer who embraced the latest advances. Daddy believed in using technology to improve efficiency. The arrival of our first John Deere tractor transformed the farm operation. But being the driven man that he was, the tractor didn't reduce the workload – it just made it possible to do more work.

Daddy's interests weren't limited to farming. Though he had gone no further than primary school, he passionately believed in the value of education. He was an avid student of politics and world affairs and among his prized possessions was a small library he'd brought back to Ireland from America. It included several large hardbound volumes on Catholic theology.

Despite his austere personality, a softer side sometimes emerged. Seared in my mind is the memory of him tearfully carrying the tiny white coffin of my baby sister Brigid, just a few weeks old, out of our family home. I was six years old at the time. When he and Mammy brought me to Knockbeg College in September 1951, he made a point of telling the Rector that I wasn't in the best of health since I had just recently recovered from pneumonia and he enquired about what I would be eating. (The Rector, with an attempt at dry humour, said that after a couple of weeks I'd be prepared to eat gravel from the drive.) He and Mammy were both in tears when they left me. And he cried when Mary and Rita left home to go to the convent. And he cried when I left for America. For a hard man, he cried a lot.

As a child I treasured those rare occasions when Daddy revealed the social side of his personality – when he put his mind to it, he could be warm, witty and charming. There were lots of photographs from his years in New York. They show a smiling young man, dressed stylishly in well-fitted suits and jaunty hats. Or kitted out for a game of hurling with other ex-pats. Or in swimwear, enjoying the pleasures of Jones Beach on Long Island. He's usually in the company of a large circle of friends, including plenty of good-looking girls dressed in the height of 1920s and 1930s fashion. They're just like any bunch of young twenty-something Irish emigrants with the means and the opportunity to have fun in ways unimaginable at home.

I wondered why, after returning to Ireland for good the year he turned thirty, he had changed from that apparently sociable and easy-going young man who enjoyed life. Maybe it was the responsibility of fatherhood. Maybe, having started life as a carpenter's son, he got caught up in a dream of making something of himself. Perhaps he believed if he acquired a social standing greater than that he had been born into, it would give him security and protect him from loss and misfortune. In that respect he was not unlike many of his generation who came from humble origins, who knew the chaos of civil strife and who had a deep sense of mission about creating a successful, independent Ireland. Sadly, their definition of success was narrow, rigid and fearful. It was formed by their early religious indoctrination and the conservative politics arising from such an intellectually impoverished and morally controlling view of humanity. It was the frugal, inward-looking 'ideal Ireland' of de Valera's famous speech, 'The Ireland That We Dreamed Of', and the pure and chaste Ireland that seemed to obsess the Church.

'Your father was a hard man – made of steel.' That's how an elderly relative would describe Daddy to me years later. It was intended as a compliment. But I was left wondering how hot the fire had been to create this steely personality. I got the impression Daddy had grown up in a home devoid of love and tenderness. It was something he never talked about.

His mother never recovered from his birth and died a few months later. His father remarried, but the stepmother wasn't nurturing. According to a cousin, she was downright mean. The fact that my grandfather had effectively 'divorced' this woman because of her unsuitable temperament speaks volumes. (Details are sketchy, but family legend has it that some sort of court settlement was worked out in Kilkenny and she was paid off to stay away from her husband and stepchildren.)

Not only did he not talk about his background, neither did he talk much about his involvement in the War of Independence. He and his older brother, just teenagers at the time, were IRA volunteers. His sisters were in Cumann na mBan, the republican women's paramilitary organisation. It's likely that they all became adults before their time.

If life experience had made him a hard man, he wasn't one to complain. Single-minded and fiercely determined, Daddy was not inclined to seek sympathy – and was unapologetic for anything he did in pursuit of his goals. He answered only to that higher presence he called 'the Man Above'.

SITTING IN THIS PUB WITH my father, I'm aware there's nearly forty years of unresolved issues between us. And I'm conscious time is running out if these issues are ever to be resolved. As if reading my thoughts, Daddy suddenly holds out his hand.

'Eddie, I hope there'll be no hard feelings.'

We shake hands. It takes a few seconds for it to sink in what he's said. Given that Daddy passionately believed that he had God-given responsibilities as head of the family, his implied expression of regret for events of the past is totally unexpected. I appreciate it and I'm at a loss for words. We're both teary-eyed. It's a genuinely cathartic moment. I look around and realize we're the only two customers in the pub.

'Everything is fine, Daddy,' I say. 'The past is long gone – we have to live in the present.'

It's a clumsy response, but it's the only thing I can say. There seems no point in revisiting the past. I'd always believed there was a line between us, but I'd also known that line was invisible to some of my siblings. We sit quietly, just looking at each other. In that brief exchange much of the hurt is drained out of our relationship. As I observe tears roll down his face, I know that I can't continue to hold negative feelings against this man who's worked so hard for my siblings and for me. He'd always been motivated by good intentions and it seems small-minded to fault him for using the only methods he knew.

We order a second drink. And then he makes an unlikely request. He asks me to promise to keep our family together after his death. I assure him I'll do my best. However, unlike Daddy, I realize there are limits to the ability of one individual to control the behaviour of others.

The thought runs through my mind that here I am, a thirty-eight-year old man, and I'm having the first truly personal conversation with my father. Finally, we're relating to each other adult-to-adult. I am thankful for this precious hour. Just sitting and talking, he seems to value our time together. I'm surprised but pleased he's taken me into his confidence – despite the relatively friendly tenor of our relations in recent years, I know that my decision to leave the priesthood was a difficult blow. Perhaps as he gets closer to death he realizes that family ties are more important than anything else.

Walking out of the pub I notice that I'm taller than my father. In every sense, Daddy is no longer that larger-than-life figure who was such an overpowering influence during my childhood years.

196

As I get ready to travel back to Massachusetts, I'm feeling a heavy burden has been lifted from me. There's been some measure of reconciliation with my father and with my past. I've come to understand that I'll never fully understand my father, an extremely complex man. It's enough that we part with a measure of mutual respect. As I reflect on our conversation I'm thinking that while he's been the most forceful influence in my life, it's my mother's values that I've inherited. At least that's what I tell myself. Maybe I'm reluctant to admit to myself that I've also embraced some of his values – his work ethic, certainly.

On the return flight I'm feeling fulfilled. I know it will be only a matter of weeks or months before I'll be back in Ireland for a funeral, but somehow I'm at peace. The thirty-eight-year relationship with the most powerful person in my life has essentially come to an end, and I know my life will be different from now on.

25.

The passing of the patriarch

After working hard on the front lines for fifteen years, graduate study doesn't feel like real work. I've designed a program of study that will allow me to become licensed as a counselling psychologist after obtaining my doctorate. But I'm still not convinced this is the ideal career plan. My experience in Maple House has left me ambivalent about a career in psychotherapy – I'm just not sure I want to spend my future listening to the problems of distressed people. However, through my work with faculty members, I'm discovering a real passion for organizational psychology.

In a sense, I've been engaged in organizational psychology since my days as a social activist in Louisiana. The theoretical aspects of my studies are complemented by practical applications: graduate school provides an opportunity to explore strategies for effecting change in the culture of both community and business organizations. (Later, during my career as a consultant, I'd come to refer to myself as a 'change agent'.)

My academic life revolves around the School of Education. I'm offered the position of Teaching Associate, with responsibility for finding internship placements for graduate students. The salary is small, but it goes a long way given my scaled-down lifestyle. A special bonus is the fact that I get to participate in the Wednesday morning faculty meetings. I feel like I'm part of an extended family that includes faculty as well as mature students like myself.

As I get into graduate studies I find myself thinking of my earliest classroom experiences with a sense of amazement that I am now in this position. For the first four years in Mayo National School, every morning started with a rosary and various other prayers. 'The Mistress' was cranky and mean and instilled fear in all of us. The experience when we graduated to 'The Master' for our remaining four years in primary school was not much better. He was an alcoholic who took out his frustrations on the kids, sometimes through physical punishment.

When I got to Knockbeg College I was well behind where I should have been academically. In class I was scared to ask questions that might reveal my ignorance, and I was regularly on the list of students making trips to the Dean's office for poor grades. In other ways, though, Knockbeg was a positive place. The teaching staff was made up of diverse personalities who were generally well liked by students. There were no mean or abusive teachers and there was a shared *esprit de corps* between the small student body and teachers. It was only when I got to Carlow College and seminary life that I started to understand what it was to learn. This was not because of the culture there but in spite of it – the library offered an escape from the suffocating rules, and I discovered that I enjoyed reading and discovering new ideas. And now, finally, in U Mass I feel like I'm hitting my academic stride.

THERE'S A NOTEWORTHY development in my social life. My on-off relationship with Margaret is on again. From the beginning we have a turbulent relationship. We both come to the relationship with baggage and wounds from previous relationships. She's in her mid-thirties and divorced. Passionate sex becomes the antidote for our arguments and misunderstandings. When I'm seriously upset with Margaret, she always comes back with the same response: 'Eddie, let's just fuck each other.' I'm in my fortieth year and I realize – yet again – that I'm not nearly as liberated as I thought I was. I don't expect women to think or talk like that.

One day I discover that Margaret has secretly started a relationship with one of my friends and colleagues in the School of Education. Not surprisingly, this leads to a complete breakdown of trust between us. Our brief relationship ends with both of us seeking therapy at the Campus Health Centre. My only regret is that we never say a proper goodbye. Margaret disappears completely out of my life.

Happily, this bump on the road doesn't send me off-course the way it might have in the past. I'm relishing the work at the university. I hang out for hours at the coffee bar in the local 24-hour Howard Johnson's restaurant, engrossed in work, carving out a solitary space amidst the bustle. Sometimes I hold forth with fellow students in the cafeteria of the Campus Newman Centre. We're always willing to pitch in and help with each other's projects. And each student has his or her own interesting story. As the School of Education has a distinguished national reputation, the program attracts students from all over the USA and abroad. Some, like myself, are veterans of the civil rights struggle.

I get up each morning excited about what I'm going to discover. As a full-time doctoral student I'm discovering that learning can be enjoyable, enriching and truly stimulating. I come to appreciate why some become career graduate students. It's a seductive lifestyle.

A requirement for the doctoral program is a Comprehensive Examination that includes a major theoretical paper. The decision as to the subject I shall explore emerges out of conversations with my favourite professor – Jack Wideman. One day Jack gives me a copy of the dissertation he'd written at Harvard. I'm intrigued by his concept of the 'Authority of Experience', the idea that significant influences from early life shape our counselling theory. Maybe Wideman's thesis resonates with me because it validates the insights I've gained from real-life experiences.

I decide to write a paper illustrating Wideman's proposition. The paper, titled 'Counselling Theory as Autobiographical Metaphor', provides an opportunity to revisit past experiences. I include a narrative account of my early years as part of the documentation submitted to my Comprehensive Examination Committee, a group consisting of three professors and one fellow graduate student. Committee members agree that the autobiographical material would be treated 'for their eyes only'. I'm not ready to share the personal material with a wider audience. I schedule my presentation before the Comprehensive Examination Committee towards the end of the spring semester of 1977.

Then I get a call from Andy: 'Daddy has just a few days left. If you want to see him before he dies, you better come immediately.'

Within twenty-four hours of receiving the call I arrive at Dublin Airport, rent a car and go directly to Michael and Elsie's home. I learn that Daddy has been lodged at St Fintan's, the mental health hospital in Portlaoise where Michael works. He was moved there after becoming unmanageable at the General Hospital. Daddy in a mental hospital? This is shocking. Later, Michael told me that his irrational behaviour was the result of brain cancer.

(A few years earlier Daddy had gone to a folk healer to deal with skin cancer on his ear. The 'healer' applied some potion to the cancerous lesion and then set out a treatment regime. As a result, in his last few years Daddy had a noticeable hole, about the size of a two cent coin, in the middle of his left ear where the lesion had been removed – by Maura, in the kitchen in Drumagh, using a bread-and-hot-water poultice. After weeks of 'treatment' a lump had detached itself from the middle of his ear. At a later date he was sent to the Dublin cancer hospital, St Luke's, for tests and came home vowing never to go back. For a sensible man it was an irrational response, but perhaps his fear of cancer went back to the trauma of watching Elsie's death from the disease a decade earlier.)

The plan now is to send Daddy home to Drumagh by ambulance, to die. I leave Michael's home with the intention of meeting the ambulance when it arrives. En route to my destination I pass through Timahoe and stop at the same pub where, several years earlier, VISTA volunteer Mike McCarthy and I had led the locals to believe we were on a mission to find Richard Nixon's ancestral home. The joviality of that occasion contrasts dramatically with the gloomy anticipation I now feel.

It's mid-afternoon. I go into the pub and there's nobody there but the bartender. I order a shot of Paddy's whiskey. I'm trying to brace myself for what's ahead. After a short time I decide I have to pull myself together and deal with whatever faces me. I continue on my journey. I'm relieved to arrive at the house before the ambulance.

The decision to bring Daddy home is in accord with his final wishes – he'd always said he didn't want to die in a hospital. We're fortunate to have our sister Rita on hand to take charge. She is an experienced public health nurse and has supported many families confronting death.

Daddy is carried into the house on a stretcher. I attempt to speak to him but he doesn't recognize me. Rita treats him with the utmost consideration. I'm consoled by the fact that Daddy is getting first-class nursing care as his life is nearing its end.

As I watch this frail, confused man being carried into his house, I realize this isn't the same man I'd known in my youth. It's a scene that makes me consider the futility of personal ambition. Here's a man who'd worked himself to the bone in order to achieve his goals. He'd done everything in his power to control his own destiny and the destiny of his family. And he'd constantly driven himself and everyone around him to achieve success. No obstacle would deter him. Yet now, lying on a stretcher, he's reduced to total dependence. It is a salutary lesson about the limits of worldly ambition. Of course, this is how the story ends for us all. I know this will be my fate one day.

My three sisters and I support each other for the last few days as we keep watch for the end to come. Maura seems to have gone into a world of her own. Late at night we decide to get a few hours rest, leaving Rita to keep vigil. Maura goes to bed in another room.

In the middle of the night the household is disturbed by loud shrieks coming from Maura, who is out in the hallway. I rush out to her. This is not a normal outpouring of a wife's grief. She seems to be having some sort of fit. I try to calm her down, but it's as if I'm not even there. I know that whatever is going on with her, the situation will take more than a few reassuring words. I'm concerned Daddy will hear the commotion and even more concerned about the distressed state Maura is in.

I try to soothe her though my efforts are futile. All I can do is stay near to make sure she is physically safe. Finally, she runs out of steam and goes back to bed. In shock, my siblings and I adjourn to the kitchen to figure out what to do: Daddy's death is imminent, we have a funeral ahead of us, an eleven-year-old child in the middle of it all, and now we are panicking about what prompted Maura's meltdown and how to prevent it recurring.

I'm standing in the kitchen with my arms around my three sisters. Four of us in our thirties, all with experience in roles of responsibility, all working to some extent in caring capacities, and all completely bewildered. Though Daddy spoke to some of the family (though not to me) about difficulties in the marriage when we visited all seemed fine, and of course we agreed he wasn't an easy character himself. Up to now we've only ever seen Maura be welcoming, good-humoured and mild-mannered.

One of the girls says, 'Eddie, you're the psychologist, you should know what to do!'

In our frantic state this comment makes us burst out laughing and the humour breaks the tension. It is definitely not the way Daddy would have planned his final hours.

There is no phone in the house, so early in the morning Lena goes off to call Michael to ask his advice. He suggests contacting the family doctor. I drive to the doctor's practice a few miles away, explain the situation and he agrees to come right away. He gives

Maura a sedative. We hope for peace and quiet, for both Maura and Daddy, in the hours to come.

Daddy dies peacefully on the evening of 6 April, the Wednesday of Holy Week.

The next day Andy arrives and goes directly to where the body has been laid out for the wake. I'm walking up and down outside the house, smoking a cigarette, when he comes back out.

'It's strange, Eddie – I feel free in a way I haven't felt before,' he says.

I tell him I feel exactly the same.

The sun is shining. The daffodils Daddy had planted are blooming. The countryside has the fresh look and smell of springtime. There's a strange stillness as each of us stands there, lost in thought, thinking about the man who has passed away and what his death means for us. Like Andy, I'm experiencing a strange sense of liberation with the passing of my father. And I'm having difficulty admitting – even to myself – the degree of my father's influence over me well into adult life. It seems almost pathological and I wonder, as I have my whole life, whether ours is a typical or atypical patriarchal Irish family. It certainly feels like a defining moment in my life. And as I continue to ponder the implications of Daddy's death, I whisper a silent prayer, hoping he will find peace and rest beyond the grave.

The funeral is to be on Good Friday and the local parish priest explains that the church doesn't allow a funeral Mass to be said on a Good Friday, the day commemorating the death of Jesus Christ. I'd already come to understand that Father Kennedy was not known for excessive flexibility or charm. On this occasion he more than lives up to his brusque reputation. There is no talk of rescheduling the funeral. There are no other options and it's simply unthinkable that we would challenge the priest's decision. I'm thinking, how ironic: my father, who prided himself on being a stalwart of the congregation and a leading contributor to the parish coffers (to the extent of providing a stained glass window for the church), being denied a traditional Catholic funeral Mass.

The church is packed. The funeral for another local farmer is scheduled to run simultaneously. The other man was a father of nine. So, two large families, extended families and mourners from near and far are packed into one small church. In addition, the funerals are being combined with the normal Good Friday ceremonies for the parish. The situation is somewhat chaotic to say the least. Shambolic would be closer to the mark. Daddy's brother struggles to get into the church. Father Kennedy, dressed in black vestments, drones his way robotically through the funeral prayers and other liturgy. The organist and choir-mistress, Mrs Looney, leads the choir through a couple of interminable dirges. It's all about sin, bloodshed, dying, darkness and despair and how we sinners have nailed Jesus to the cross. In other parishes a modernizing Church is starting to bring the faithful a more uplifting message of God's love and redemption. But this is a blast of the old Ireland – not a word of hope or forgiveness. The atmosphere is certainly funereal.

After the ceremony Andy, Michael, Tom and I, with assistance from a couple of neighbours, carry Daddy's coffin outside and walk slowly to the grave just inside the gate of the adjoining graveyard where Mammy, Elsie and our baby sister Brigid are already buried. It's a cold, dark, miserable and rainy afternoon. A large crowd of parishioners and relatives watch silently as the fresh wet clay is shovelled into the grave. As I hear each shovel of clay drop onto the wooden coffin, I'm thinking how different this is from the sanitized burials I've attended back in the USA.

After Father Kennedy has finished reciting the traditional graveside prayers someone leads the assembled mourners in reciting a decade of the rosary.

In that country graveyard, in the midst of the large gathering of neighbours and relatives, I think how different my feelings were fourteen years earlier when I'd presided at the burial of my mother.

On that occasion there was a great sense of loss. Now, it's more of a sense of relief that this extraordinary man has finally found peace.

As we're walking away from the gravesite I turn to Andy. 'He went fast in the end,' I say.

'Death always comes as a bit of a surprise,' says Andy.

We return to the house in Drumagh for the usual hospitality. Being a Good Friday there is no meat – we'd had to press chicken and ham sandwiches on visitors the evening before so they would not be wasted. The truly observant are staying away from alcohol. Thankfully, Maura is more like her normal self as she accepts condolences from those who have come to mark her husband's passing. (In years to come we get to know more about Maura's life before marrying our father – in 1945, in her early twenties, she had had a baby, at that time a disaster for an unmarried woman from a respectable family. The depth of her unacknowledged and un-processed trauma and grief is an ongoing source of suffering. Her levels of emotional resilience are low. So her odd fit when Daddy was dying finally makes sense to us long after the event: the atmosphere of crisis and sense of impending loss set off something very deep in her psyche.)

A FEW DAYS AFTER THE BURIAL I return to Massachusetts. I plunge myself immediately into preparing for the presentation to the Comprehensive Examination Committee, which had been originally scheduled for early May. This presentation is designed to provide a platform for the graduate student to stage a serious discussion of the topic he or she is exploring.

I reschedule the presentation for a conference room on the tenth floor of the Campus Centre on 10 June 1977. The room overlooks the surrounding countryside. I invite twenty close friends to join us for the presentation. Wine and cheese add to the informality of the occasion.

After my presentation the chairperson of the Committee, Dr Ena Nuttall, invites each of the other members to make any comments they might wish. One member, Dr Donald Banks, says he has a few things he'd like to say about the autobiographical material.

'Ed, I hope you'll decide to share your story with a wider audience. Because I'm Afro-American, I'm deeply interested in your work in the South. A young Irishman doing some hell-raising for civil rights is a good story.'

I'm flattered by the compliments, but I'm not sure I deserve them.

With this important milestone passed, it's time to move on to selecting a subject for a doctoral dissertation. I start to focus on identifying a dissertation project. Colleagues and friends tell me not to get carried away with an overly ambitious research project. They remind me that the dissertation is only a rite of passage. I heed their advice and my project focuses on the development and formative evaluation of a curriculum for training laypeople in psychotherapy skills. It's a practical, manageable project that doesn't require advanced statistical analysis.

In early June 1979, dressed in traditional cap and gown, I join the procession of other doctoral students in the University of Massachusetts football stadium to receive my degree. Most of my friends in the School of Education don't bother with the graduation ceremony. For me, though, it signifies the accomplishment of an important personal goal. I need to soak up this moment before moving on to new challenges.

26.

My Camelot years

While still a student at the University of Massachusetts, I and a fellow doctoral student, Paul Powers, worked together analysing data from a graduate research project on behalf of another graduate student. Paul is an Irish-American Vietnam veteran, a former Marine. As a result of our collaboration we become good friends.

He tells me about a friend, an alumnus and former U Mass administrator, who has just bought a big property near North Andover in eastern Massachusetts, just 35 miles northwest of Boston. Paul invites me to come along for a weekend visit to the sprawling mansion, a former Jesuit retreat house located on beautiful Lake Cochichewick.

As we drive through the gates I realize we're entering another world. Driving down the tree-lined driveway, I understand why the Jesuits selected this lakeside mansion as a retreat house. The location is breathtaking.

The mansion had been built in the early twentieth century by a wealthy German owner of several woollen mills in the local city of Lawrence. Originally known as Hardtcourt, it was renamed Campion Hall by the Jesuits when they purchased the building in the 1950s. Edmond Campion was an English Jesuit martyr. The new owner, John Warlick, has reverted to the original name. Inside there is a huge rotunda and a carved wooden staircase leads to a second-floor balcony. I'm stunned by the size and grandeur of the place – it's over 21,000 square feet and sits in ninety acres of grounds.

John is a thirty-something Texan who has left behind the boring life of a university administrator to seek entrepreneurial opportunities. A generous bank loan enabled him to purchase the mansion.

'Deevy, we have more than forty rooms in this building and about sixty in the dormitory,' says John. 'Find a place to put your stuff.' He makes me feel right at home.

Most of the rooms still have beds and mattresses from the days when the place was used as a busy retreat house. The dormitory was an addition by the Jesuits.

Later I meet the rest of the household. There's Rich and Dana, both friends of John going back to his days at the university. And there's Peter and his partner Helen, who also knew John from his days in Amherst. John's brother and his partner live in the guesthouse.

Visits to Hardtcourt become a weekly affair, with Paul and I leaving the university campus on a Friday evening and not returning until the following Monday. When possible we extend weekend visits an extra day. We become part of the Hardtcourt family. What we all have in the common is the U Mass connection. And we all consider ourselves to be 'in transition'.

Typically, on Friday and Saturday evenings we pool resources and someone volunteers to make the short trip into North Andover for pizza and beer. We gather in a second-floor room to watch reruns of *M*A*S*H* and smoke some weed or hash. On Sunday mornings someone will go into town to pick up the *Boston Globe* and the *New York Times*. We have lively discussions about the op eds in both newspapers as we drink coffee and watch the Sunday talk shows.

Sometimes other friends from the university will drive down for the weekend. One weekend, one of John's friends shows up with magic mushrooms. While living in Baton Rouge I'd tripped on acid – nervously – a couple of times. I'm reluctant to participate.

'Try them, Deevy,' says Warlick.

Behind closed and locked doors we share the mushrooms. With the music of Roy Orbison blaring out throughout the mansion on John's large speakers, we enjoy the afternoon in a world of our own. It's definitely a psychedelic experience.

As the months pass Hardtcourt becomes my home, though I still maintain my apartment in western Massachusetts. I become the self-appointed groundskeeper. And I occasionally do a barbecue or cook up a pot of Irish stew. John opens up the house for huge Hallowe'en and New Year's Eve parties. On these occasions dozens of friends stay overnight.

One year our immediate neighbours, Jack and Diane Caldwell, decide to come to the Hallowe'en party as President and Mrs Carter. I collaborate with them on the staging of the arrival. Nobody else in the mansion is aware of our plans.

While the party is in full swing, I climb to the stop of the grand staircase and, megaphone in hand, I get the attention of the partially inebriated crowd.

'My friends, we're about to be honoured by a special guest – the President of the United States.'

There are a few seconds of silence.

'Deevy, you're drunk!' shouts Warlick, who is as taken by surprise as everyone else.

Within moments it's obvious from the flashing lights and the sound of rotor blades that a helicopter is landing on the front lawn. There's a mad rush out the front door. Out steps 'President and Mrs Carter'. They're ushered into the main hallway and proceed to the top of the staircase to read a proclamation. Then, while everyone is still in shock, they're exit and get back on the helicopter. They disappear into the night, leaving some at the party stunned and wondering if they had just imagined the whole episode.

I come to love the splendid isolation that Hardtcourt offers. While there are just a few holy statues to remind us of the mansion's recent history, it offers a unique feeling of retreat. I come to think of this mansion on Lake Cochichewick as my Camelot.

AFTER GRADUATING IN THE summer of 1979, I spend some spare time preparing for the state examination to become a licensed psychologist in Massachusetts. I take on a few small consulting projects and pursue several academic opportunities.

One day I get a letter from a friend in Dublin containing a newspaper advertisement for a position at a third-level college. The job is something for which I might be a fit, but I later discover that my application didn't arrive in time. The reason: a postal strike in Ireland.

In the summer of 1980 I'm offered the position of executive director of a social services organization based in Northampton. It's not my ideal career opportunity – the task is to salvage a non-profit organization in serious financial trouble – but I accept the offer, knowing it will help with cash-flow. The board of directors understand that it's only a temporary commitment on my part.

Life in Hardtcourt stops me returning to my work-obsessed ways. There is always something going on. On the eve of one Fourth of July celebration John Warlick turns up a pig to be cooked for the gathering. Everyone is looking forward to whole roast pig. We dig a pit in the lawn behind the mansion and build a fire. Around midnight most people have drifted back to their rooms. The father of one of my housemates volunteers to keep watch over the fire until the next morning. I volunteer to stay up with him. We sip beer and trade stories as we douse the fire with water when it flames up. Somehow we both drift off to sleep about three o'clock.

I wake up at eight o'clock in the morning to discover the fire has turned into a raging inferno and our poor pig has been burnt into a cinder. When John comes down from his room we have to share the bad news. What we get is a typical Warlick response: 'Not to worry, guys, I'll pick up some steaks.' I never live it down.

One summer John goes away for Army Reserve duty and returns with Diane Trace. Diane studies law at Boston University. She adds an extra woman's touch to the Hardtcourt 'family'. John and Diane have their wedding at the house.

One Friday evening as we're having our usual pizza supper, John asks me if I'll be around on Monday at noon. On Monday morning he tells me that he and Diane have purchased a ticket for me to attend a stop-smoking clinic in nearby Lawrence General Hospital. The clinic is to be conducted by a hypnotherapist. As a two-pack-a-day Marlboro Man with repeated failed efforts at going cold turkey, I'm pessimistic about the possible outcome.

At noon I walk into a smoke-filled room that's filled with 20 individuals, mostly nurses at the hospital. A tall, slim young man named David Bader enters the room and invites everyone to extinguish their cigarettes.

Thirty minutes later I walk out of the room with an audiotape and instructions to play it twice daily for two weeks. Almost miraculously, the nicotine desire is gone. I'm so pleased that after a couple of days that I decide to direct the hypnotic self-suggestions to another behaviour that's damaging my health. I decide I'll use this 'magic cure' to give up alcohol. I had grown up in a home where alcohol was never produced except for visitors or on special occasions and high holidays. And then it was just a glass. Unlike many Irish families, there were no alcoholic role models in my formative years. I was almost thirty years of age before I had my first alcoholic drink. However, I became addicted within a couple of years of having that first drink. Now, I knew the problem of abuse needed to be addressed, particularly my tendency to binge drink as a response to stress.

I listen to the hypnosis tape and substitute stop-drinking suggestions for stop-smoking suggestions. I tell myself I can have a fulfilling life without alcohol. That I can get up in the morning feeling free of nicotine and alcohol. That I can live a healthy life. That I don't need to sedate my nervous system. John and Diane have given me one of the best gifts I've ever received. At the end of two weeks I've become a non-smoker and a non-drinker. It will be fifteen years before I have another drink of alcohol and over thirty before I smoke another cigarette.

Jack Caldwell is a long-time political activist in Massachusetts and a close friend of Ted Kennedy. In 1980 Kennedy is challenging Jimmy Carter to be the Democratic Party candidate in the presidential election. That spring we decide to put on a fundraiser to help his campaign. It is a memorable night. After an inspirational speech delivered from the steps of the staircase Ted leaves, observing that he still 'has places to go, people to see and things to do'. The fundraiser is a major success, but we know that the odds are stacked against him. He's carrying some heavy baggage – questions about his behaviour following the 1969 car crash on Chappaquiddick Island, in which a young colleague, Mary Jo Kopechne, lost her life after he crashed the car they were in, have haunted Kennedy for the previous decade. Knowing that he would not be able to get past questions about Chappaquiddick is the likely reason he didn't run for the presidency in either 1972 or 1976. At the Democratic National Convention in August he bows out to Jimmy Carter. In his concession speech, he concludes with these words: 'For me a few hours ago, this campaign came to an end. For all those whose cares have been our concern, the work goes on, the cause endures, the hope still lives, and the dream shall never die'. Even in defeat Ted Kennedy is inspirational.

By the summer of 1982 I've resigned my position at the social services agency in Northampton and accepted the position of Visiting Professor in the College of Food and Natural Resources at the University of Massachusetts. The Hardtcourt group disbands, with John and Diane relocating to an island in the Caribbean and each of us going our separate ways. Years later I would come to think of my time in the lakeside mansion as a charmed and carefree period on my life's journey. But I knew life at Camelot could not last forever.

27.

Out on my own for the first time

My new job involves teaching undergraduate courses in communications and organizational behaviour. It's an exciting opportunity and I'm delighted with the response from the students. While I've become licensed as a psychologist in the Commonwealth of Massachusetts, I feel I've found my true vocation in academia. My friends tell me that the psychology licence will serve as 'insurance' in case I find myself looking for a new source of income.

By the end of my first academic year I'm feeling that I'm hitting my stride. In addition to teaching, I'm providing supervision for a number of students doing off-campus internships. With regular breaks in the academic calendar I can make short visits to Ireland, where I have started a training and consulting practice. In a short time my life is filling up with interesting work experiences. One in particular leaves a lasting impression. I spend a weekend assisting Ken Blanchard with a graduate course in leadership at a ski resort in Vermont. His book, *The One Minute Manager,* had just hit number one on the *New York Times* bestseller list. Blanchard is the most charismatic educator I have ever met. I learn one of the keys to Blanchard's success is hard work and extraordinary dedication. One night I stay up with him as he edits a training video that is being produced to tie-in with his book. He views the material over and over, paying close attention to every detail, working until five in the morning.

It is not just the professional work that I find rewarding. Having given up smoking and drinking I feel as if I have a new lease on life. Biking, jogging and regular visits to the gym add to the feelings of well-being. I decide to reward myself by spending the summer of 1984 in Dublin. It will be the longest visit to Ireland since emigrating twenty-two years earlier. Though I plan to do a little work, I'll use the trip mostly as an opportunity to get to know Dublin and to spend time with friends and family.

As I fly in over north Dublin, the distinctive towers and blocks of the Ballymun flats are clearly visible. Ballymun was built in the 1960s to relieve inner-city overcrowding by providing low-cost accommodation. Like many such 1960s experiments in social housing, it hasn't been properly resourced and the estate has become an area of great deprivation. Ballymun is to be my home for the summer because I'm staying with Lena in her congregation's two adjoining flats on Shangan Road.

Lena picks me up at the airport and drives the short distance to Ballymun. We enter the eight-storey block and the hallway smells of urine and rotten food. The elevator is out-of-order so we trudge up the stairs and finally arrive at our destination on the sixth floor.

After that, walking into the flat is like entering another world. It's warm and cosy and provides a panoramic view of the city with the Dublin Mountains in the distance.

I quickly come to enjoy life at my new 'home'. For many years I'd admired the Little Sisters of the Assumption for their work on behalf of the most disadvantaged families in society. Now I will have the chance to observe their work up close. Each evening over dinner the sisters compare notes on their various projects. Knowing my background as a social activist with some expertise in psychology, they welcome my input.

I soon become aware of an impending visit by President Ronald Reagan. He'll be visiting the home of his ancestors in Ballyporeen, County Tipperary, in June. I try to ignore the media hype as Reagan, with his Thatcherite policies, is not my favourite politician. On the weekend of his visit I'm in Cork to deliver a workshop to staff at the Bon Secours hospital. I return by train to Dublin on Sunday evening. I walk out of Heuston Station and realise something big is happening. Police and security people are everywhere and there are no buses or taxis in sight. I'm told that Reagan will shortly be travelling down the quays on the Guinness side of the Liffey, on his way to a reception at Dublin Castle. I cross over the river and start walking towards the city centre. The city is in lockdown. Hundreds of gardaí and security personnel line the presidential route on the other side of the river. And then I hear sirens and see flashing lights. I see the President's large limo, shipped in from the States, moving slowly. Even from where I am on the other side of the river, I can see Reagan waving his hand robotically. I wonder if he notices that there is no one to wave at. In the distance I can hear the roar of a crowd. It's coming from a huge anti-US foreign policy demonstration on O'Connell Street. Lena and fellow members of the 'Sisters for Justice' group have been busy all weekend as part of the broad coalition of left-wing, social justice and Church groups protesting against Reagan's visit. Some of the sisters have been on hunger strike for the duration of his stay. I presume she is participating in the march.

Since I'm going to be around for a bit, Lena asks me to design and conduct workshops on leadership and stress management for community groups. Like other members of her congregation, she is very committed to the idea of empowering people within their communities. One of these workshops is designed for single mothers and I convince two local women to join me in running and presenting the events. The work with Phyllis and Aileen becomes the highlight of my summer. Both are warm, straight-talking and smart, real down-to-earth Dubliners who are not at all impressed by the blow-in from the States. Aileen, in particular, takes great delight in teasing me. Phyllis and I occasionally go jogging or walking together. In just a few weeks we all become life-long friends.

At the end of summer I travel back to Massachusetts. By this time I'm teaching two of the most popular courses in our department and I'm feeling very confident that the department chair will deliver on her promise to create a new tenure track position for the courses I've developed. I'm beginning to envisage a future working at the university.

And then I become a victim of academic politics. A tenured professor from another department exercises her prerogative to claim the newly created position. This is a huge disappointment. One colleague suggests that I put up a fight. The idea of fighting the university bureaucracy has no appeal, however. I've already seen a couple of academic colleagues fight self-destructive losing battles.

While I've really valued the security provided by the university salary, I decide that I'll become self-employed. Training and consulting work will become my major focus. I know that self-employment offers less security, but I'm hoping I have what it takes to make it on my own. And so I embark on a full-time career helping organizations address such issues as teamwork, employee empowerment and the management of change. After opening an office in 1985 in North Andover, I team up with another consultant, Kate Gilligan, and we begin marketing management services under the name Deevy Gilligan International.

Working as a freelance consultant proves to be both demanding and rewarding. My whole life becomes absorbed in the business. Both Kate and I draw on our backgrounds in the behavioural sciences. Each new client organization brings exciting new challenges and opportunities. We're both on a steep learning curve. We specialize in helping mature organizations manage change and address employee morale problems. And we help fix broken organizations. While most clients are based in New England, our work also takes us to the Midwest and to the West Coast.

I continue to make regular trips to Ireland to conduct training workshops on leadership for the staff of both voluntary and business organizations. The client list includes a major bank, the Institute for Industrial Managers, the leadership teams of several religious organizations and many second-level schools. My Dublin-based colleague, Denis McGrath, a lecturer in Bolton Street College of Technology, and I travel together throughout Ireland providing one-day workshops on leadership for secondary school teachers. It's an opportunity to get to know Ireland in a way I'd never known it. Typically, after a day-long workshop Denis drives me to the next town where we're scheduled to offer the next workshop. We often travel late into the night. One evening on a long drive from a school in Waterford to the West of Ireland I tell Denis he'll be exhausted from driving.

'Eddie,' he replies, 'I'd rather wear out than rust out!'

That's a sentiment that resonates. On our tours around Ireland we both experience the kind of exhaustion that energizes.

With each flight from Boston to Dublin I'm feeling more connected to my roots and increasingly feeling like a citizen of two countries.

IN THE LATE 1980S I BEGIN to research a book to help popularize the concept of employee empowerment. The core message of the book, based on in-the-trenches experience, is that employees who feel that they have an ownership stake in the organization will be more productive and deliver better services to customers. It will show how worker participation benefits both the employees and the company, and will suggest strategies for promoting organizational resilience.

The book will reflect convictions that evolved over several decades. I'd gone from civil rights advocacy in the late 1960s and early 1970s to advocacy for individuals with mental disabilities. Now, at a new stage in a winding journey, I've found opportunities to advocate on behalf of working people.

In the meantime, Lena has embarked on a new life direction, too. She worked flat-out in Ballymun for well over a decade, but now feels she needs a career break and a change of scene. With the support of her order, she moves to Boston in 1989 and embarks on a Master's Degree in Harvard's School of Education. Her move to Boston means we get to see a lot more of each other and can meet regularly for lunch. She listens as I tease out my ideas for the book and is hugely encouraging and supportive. It is very impressive to see how quickly she adapts to American life. Before long her drive to make something happen where she sees people in need and her dynamic organizing instincts kick in again: after completing her degree she starts running a project to help Irish emigrants.

At the dawn of the 1990s I'm feeling very satisfied with my life, both personally and professionally. In north London Tom is working on a house that he has gutted and is now renovating and he invites me for Christmas 1990. The renovation part of the project is at an early stage but in spite of the Spartan living conditions, it is great to be with him. I have had some diverse Christmases and this looks like being right up there with the more memorable ones. When I ask Tom about our plans for Christmas Day he is vague and politely declines my offer to go shopping for the ingredients of a traditional Christmas dinner.

Christmas Day delivers on its promise. Tom decides to use the occasion as an opportunity to gather his friends to consider some of the important issues confronting humanity. The group is diverse – academics, business people, individuals with New Age-type beliefs. He dispenses with the turkey or any of the usual trimmings. Instead, he cooks a big hearty omelette that includes potatoes, onions, peppers, grated Cheddar, milk and a dash of nutmeg. He tells us it has everything necessary for good nutrition. We sit around an improvised dining-room table in a setting not too far removed from a construction site, and discuss everything from psychology to politics to the environment and other world affairs. It is as if the rest of the world is getting on with its gaudy celebration while we serious-minded folk are considering the Big Questions. This is indeed a very different Christmas – simple and unconventional. Tom is forty-five and obviously is searching for answers and a way of living that makes sense to him. Having been through some searching times myself, I hope he finds what he's looking for. At this stage of my life, at the age of 52, I feel I have found contentment and I'm eager to see those I care about finding it, too.

28.

A bomb goes off in our family

On the morning of 25 August 1991 I receive the kind of call every emigrant fears – news of a death in the family. Andy has taken his own life. It's like I've been hit with a sledgehammer.

It's Elsie, my sister-in-law, who must convey the news to me. I tell her I'll take the first available flight to Dublin. I put down the phone and I sit numbly, my body paralyzed and my mind racing. Where did it happen? How did it happen? How are Mary Ann and the children? What are they going to do? Why did it happen?

Why? Why? Why?

Finally, I move. I call the airline. I book the ticket. Then I try to talk to my siblings. I can't reach Lena. She should be in Boston but she's in Washington D.C. for the weekend and hasn't left a number. I call Tom. He's out of London for a few days. He hasn't left a number either. I think I'll go out of my mind. On one of many calls to Ireland I find out that in rural Kenya, Mary has heard the news. Thank god. She'll make the funeral.

The funeral? For Andy?

Within twenty-four hours I'm in the air. On the red-eye flight I sob quietly all the way to Dublin. I'm feeling devastated. By the time the flight nears Dublin I've managed to get a few thoughts on a couple of pages of a yellow notepad. I'm thinking that if I get the opportunity, I would like to pay tribute to my brother. As I stuff the yellow pages in my pocket I suddenly realize I won't need notes. I'll only have to say what I'm thinking and feeling.

The wake is held in Andy and Mary Ann's home on Longwood Avenue. Andy is laid out in the front room. He looks different – his normally thin face bloated and out of shape. I'm disappointed – but then I think, what difference does it make how he looks? He's gone and that's that. The age-old rituals keep us going – a house full of mourners to reminisce with, a funeral to plan.

In his note Andy said he'd understand if he couldn't have the usual Catholic funeral. Maybe he was thinking of the man, a distant relative, who'd hanged himself in his barn when we were children. There was no church ceremony for him. In the old days in Ireland suicides weren't buried in consecrated ground. Thankfully, times have changed.

As Andy's coffin is carried down his street and along the canal bank the city traffic, just a block away, seems muted. We slowly make our way towards the parish church on Harrington Street. The only sounds are birdsong and the footfall of hundreds of mourners, bearing testimony to the number of lives my brother touched. It reminds me of my mother's funeral nearly thirty years earlier. She too was walked to the church in stillness and reverence.

The next morning before we leave for the funeral Mass a message of sympathy arrives from the Fianna Fáil leader, Charles Haughey. *Andy would have loved it,* we keep saying, *he would have absolutely loved it.* He was so addicted to politics and dedicated to the party that you were sure to get into a good-humoured row if you criticized Fianna Fáil. We loved to provoke him. It's as if he's having a laugh at our expense.

I have permission to deliver a eulogy. In the front pew are Mary Ann and her seven children, aged nine to nineteen, two still at primary school, the eldest midway through university. They are pale and strained and silent. So are my brothers and sisters behind them. The huge church is crowded. He was – is – beloved. Old neighbours have come from Drumagh, Mary Ann's family and friends from the Aran Islands, cousins from all over, Fianna Fáil people, phone company colleagues, the Lord Mayor of Dublin. I speak about Andy's courage. I speak about his commitment to family and community. The nodding heads in every row tell me they already know. I thought a eulogy would honour Andy; it dawns on me that the honour is all mine.

Early in their marriage, Andy and Mary Ann rented rooms to young gardaí. They became friends. Now these gardaí are older and in positions of authority. For Andy they stop the traffic. We seem to glide from the city centre to the cemetery in Shanganagh.

After the burial, family and friends gather back at the house. We have given Andy a good send-off and now everyone is in the mood to celebrate his life. We drink tea, tell stories and conclude Andy had gone as far as he could go with his life – given the extreme pain he lived with as a result of the spinal injury.

Evening comes, the crowd disperses and I decide to escape for some time alone. Within a couple of minutes I'm walking down the path along the canal. In the late summer warmth, young couples holding hands pass me by. I watch children riding bicycles, dog walkers, older people taking their nighttime constitutional. Minutes to cherish alone after all the intense emotions of the past couple of days.

I remember my last visit with Andy, just a few months earlier. We sat on two stools at the breakfast bar in his kitchen chatting as we had a cup of tea. For the first time I really appreciated the pain that he was experiencing. Constant, excruciating pain. And I sensed the despondency he was feeling. He had had high hopes for an operation that might relieve the pain, but it had left him in worse shape. It was the only time I had ever heard Andy sound defeated.

I recall my conversation with Mary Ann on that visit. We'd talked about Andy's deteriorating physical condition. It seemed obvious he couldn't go on the way he was. He had pain written all over his face. Even the slightest movement seemed to result in jolts of pain. We wondered whether a spa or whirlpool might grant him a measure of relief. Now I'm thinking that despite limited financial resources, I could have offered to help in some way. I'm experiencing a heavy dose of guilt. Not a damn thing I can do about it now, I say to myself.

After walking more than a mile my mind is still racing. Why did this have to happen? Why did Andy end his own life? I know the kind of hurt I'm feeling inside isn't going to go away in a hurry. I wonder, clinically, how long I'll wear this grief. Walking back towards the house I keep trying to convince myself that Andy has done what he believed was best for his family. I try to see his death in a positive light. Still ringing in my ears, I'm hearing the refrain from the burial service: Rest in peace.

Back at the house I find the remaining mourners have left. It's just Mary Ann, her brother Patrick, myself and other members of the immediate family. The conversation becomes lighter and sprinkled with humour. My youngest niece, Noreen, a week off her tenth birthday, looks across the living room.

'Uncle Eddie, are you pregnant?'

Her question results in howls of laughter. My exercise and nutritional regimen – or lack of one – has left me with a 'beer belly'. (Noreen is now a fitness instructor: I like to think I was an early source of inspiration.)

After a couple of hours family members leave for bed and there's only Mary Ann, Patrick and myself. We have another cup of tea. As we sit quietly and reminisce, I think about how Mary Ann has held up through this difficult experience. Despite her own pain, she clearly communicates the message that life must go on. She simply assumes this is what Andy would want her to do.

The day after the funeral Andy's GP comes to the house to share his thoughts. I assume Mary Ann invited him. Gathered in the living room, we listen intently to what he has to say. I already know the basics – his accident, his serious spinal injuries and his defiance of doctors' predictions that he'd never walk again or have a family. Instead, he left the hospital with steel callipers on his legs and a wheelchair that he abandoned as quickly and as often as he could.

Andy was a rock of common sense. He was conservative when it came to traditional values – too conservative for my way of thinking. He was a good provider for his large family and because he was a skilled craftsman and very good with his hands, he supplemented his salary by carrying out home improvement projects for neighbours.

The doctor began by giving a brief description of Andy's deteriorating condition over the previous months. He pointed out that the pain-killing medications had mostly lost their effectiveness. The operation intended to provide relief had only aggravated the situation.

The doctor then went on to share his perspective on how an individual can reach the decision to commit suicide. He said that during the weeks or days preceding the suicide the individual enters a 'black tunnel'. In this place, according to his doctor, Andy would have seen suicide as the only escape from his intolerable situation and, by implication, would have seen others as unable to offer any solution that would make life worth living.

The visit by the doctor and his compassionate words help us to start making sense of Andy's decision. Though it will be a very individual journey for each of us and there is a long road ahead.

AFTER THE FUNERAL I RETURN to Haverhill feeling drained. The days and weeks that follow are torture and I can think of nothing else. Intellectually, I understand Andy's decision. Our last chat made me aware of Andy's sense of hopelessness about his deteriorating physical health. Emotionally, I feel like I've been punched in the head and in the heart. There is a pain that accompanies my every waking minute.

Tom's reaction to Andy's death is fury. He returns to London deeply angry. He sends a letter to other siblings, and to Mary Ann, advancing his theory that mistreatment by our father when Andy was young was a significant factor in his decision to end his life. He does not send the letter to me. Afterwards I conclude that was because he thought we were on the same wavelength and I would not need things spelled out.

Mary and Lena are particularly upset by Tom's letter. I call him to say that the letter has only added to his sisters' grief and ask him to 'cool it'. The call is made in the heat of the moment and I haven't really thought through what I'm going to say. It is not a calm conversation. This intervention from the person he considers his closest friend in the family backfires. His response is to express his hurt and bewilderment that I am now on 'their' side. Immediately I regret making the call: it's obvious that the breach between us won't heal quickly.

The trauma of Andy's death, including Tom's response and my handling of that response, challenges my most basic assumptions about life. I find myself exploring the big existential questions. I'd made a study of the question for my doctorate, but now I wonder anew how childhood influences really affect our decisions as adults? How have my early experiences growing up on a farm in Ireland impacted on my life? Does life have a purpose? Is there a God? Is there an afterlife?

29.

Epiphany on Salisbury Beach

Back in Massachusetts the hurt is there every hour of every day. It feels as if all the energy has been sucked out of my body. Andy's suicide is on my mind all the time. I scarcely sleep at night and drag myself from bed each morning exhausted. I try to get back to work. But it's not easy. Kate's background is in psychotherapy and she suggests I see a counsellor. She is clearly worried about my mental condition.

My inability to get a handle on my emotions knocks me off my high horse. Somehow the image I've had of myself has changed. Over the years I'd come to think of myself as a person with the fortitude to deal with tough situations. I had made difficult decisions, put myself on the line for things I believed in, and even when I'd experienced a mental health crisis, I had faced it head-on and come out the other side believing myself to be stronger and more resilient. But now the feelings of invincibility are gone.

My therapy is long walks on Salisbury Beach, a seaside community just twenty-five miles north of Boston. With its shabby, weather-beaten beach houses it looks like Coney Island or any other blue-collar seaside resort, packed at summertime and abandoned during the winter months. Just a short twenty-minute drive from my Haverhill apartment, it becomes a favourite retreat during the months after Andy's death.

On cold winter evenings I walk for miles on the deserted beach, alone with my thoughts. With the rhythmic sound of ocean waves in the background, it's a place to consider the existential questions that are now plaguing me. I remind myself that Andy's was a considered decision. That's clear by the manner in which he had died. He'd gone to work on a Saturday evening and when his shift was over he had driven to a quiet spot on Dollymount Strand, where he had died in his car. He left a note encouraging family members to take care of each other.

Tom's response to Andy's death forces me to consider what Andy felt deep inside about his childhood experiences. He never voiced anger to me about anything that happened when we were growing up, but that wasn't the kind of thing I would have expected to hear from him. He had a strong sense of family loyalty and if he believed our father had bullied him, he wouldn't have spoken about it. Andy preferred to focus on the positive things that happened in the past and to pass over the negative stuff. He would have defined the ups and downs of his life growing up as simply the 'will of God' – he was more into religion than psychology.

Andy's death brings me down to earth and forces me to ask what life is all about. My reading tells me it's normal to have feelings of anger towards the family member who dies by suicide. However, I don't experience this anger towards Andy. I believe he had a right to put an end to his unbearable pain. (Whether he had a right to put his wife and children through the resulting trauma is simply too big a question for me to grapple with.) Andy, one of the most sensible and prudent individuals I'd ever known, entered the 'black tunnel' and saw no other options. I must respect his choice, however much I might wish it were otherwise. In my mind, it's that simple.

But if I have come to accept Andy's decision and see it as a release from pain, why am I trapped in this valley of darkness? I think back to an expression I'd heard growing up: *There's no hurt that time won't heal.* I very much want to believe this is true.

As I mull over these questions, I realize that the lesson to take from Andy's life is the appreciation of how he bravely picked up his life after his near-death experience as a young man in Drumagh. There never was a word of complaint when he was dealt that cruel hand. Indeed, he cherished life. I knew I was just one of many who admired his personal courage. I could imagine his advice if he were around: *Get over it and get on with your life.* He wasn't one to dwell on 'what might have been'.

The weeks and months after Andy's death continue to be filled with sadness and it's a challenge to get through each day. I'm still trying to write my book, but it's a struggle to get anything done. Then, on one of my walks along Salisbury Beach, I have an epiphany: I decide to dedicate the book I'm writing to Andy's memory. I can be inspired by how he defied the odds after his accident to make a good life and a positive contribution to the world. Somehow that simple decision unleashes the creative energy I need to pick up on where I'd left off on the manuscript. This is a part of Andy's legacy that I can take forward.

The book project gets a major boost after Jack Caldwell, my old Hardtcourt friend, suggests I stay at his house in the Virgin Islands to do some writing. The light and the heat do me a power of good. Each morning my toughest decision is whether to locate myself by the pool or make the short trip down to a mostly deserted beach. Ideas flow non-stop. I find unexpected inspiration in thinking about Drumagh. Daddy strongly believed in the concept of continuous improvement and embraced new technologies. On the farm we had no meetings or formal strategy sessions. However, we functioned as a self-organizing system with information about the farm operation freely shared. Everything just seemed to happen spontaneously. And every family member contributed to the success of the family business and had a vested interest in the outcome. On a day when Daddy had been to the cattle mart or out doing other business, he would tell us over the evening meal how things had gone. We got ongoing data on turnover, profit and loss. Lessons would be learned and new goals set. I've never made the connection before, but these are the very tenets I have been trying to get organizations to implement. My message is simple: treat workers as insiders. Sharing information with employees is the key to their motivation. Employees need to develop a sense of ownership for the success of the organization. I return from St Croix a few weeks later with a suntan and a completed manuscript.

After I have secured a literary agent and a publisher, Kate and I dissolve our business partnership and Gilligan Deevy International is no more. I downsize the consulting practice and go to work full-time on revising the manuscript.

ON 19 JUNE 1995 A LARGE group of friends, as well as Lena, and Mary who is on a visit to America, gather for the launch of *Creating the Resilient Organization* in the Colonial Inn in Concord, Massachusetts. Jack Caldwell helps organize the event. He has a phenomenal contacts book and he invites his friends Richard Goodwin and Doris Kearns Goodwin to host the occasion. I have met the Goodwins from time to time through Jack and given their influential roles in American political and intellectual life, I feel greatly honoured that they agree. Dick Goodwin was not only a speechwriter and advisor to JFK and Lyndon Johnson, but also one of the architects of the War on Poverty program. Since leaving politics, he has had a prolific and distinguished career as a writer. His memoir, *Remembering America: A Voice from the Sixties*, is the inspiration for the movie *Quiz Show*, which he coproduced. Doris is an equally distinguished historian who has just been awarded a Pulitzer Prize for *No Ordinary Time*, her book about the Roosevelts during the Second World War. (Years later *Team of Rivals*, her book about Abraham Lincoln's civil war government, is also the inspiration for a movie – Steven Spielberg's *Lincoln*.)

The idea is to organize the launch as a New England-style town hall meeting where people can exchange ideas about the future of the workplace. Since Concord was the birthplace of the American Revolution, it seems like an ideal place to launch a book on worker empowerment. Dick Goodwin leads off the discussion by castigating both major political parties for neglecting the interests of working people. He refers to me as 'a harbinger of the new workplace' – a nice compliment, if not fully deserved.

A year later the Massachusetts launch is followed by one in Dublin attended by family, friends and professional associates.

The publication of the book provides a major career boost and creates opportunities for overseas work during the late 1990s. There is an invitation to address an international conference of human resource development professionals in Dublin. I travel to Taiwan to share ideas with civil servants. I lead a team of consultants working on a three-year culture change project for Hawaiian Airlines. After completing the Hawaiian project a colleague invites me to accompany him on a visit to Johannesburg to do some work with South Africa Airlines.

As countries around the world usher in the New Millennium I'm already focusing on a new book project, a book that will build on the 1995 publication. This book will offer a critical exploration of corporate practices as they relate to the treatment of employees. It will include a critique of CEOs who are paid obscenely high salaries while outsourcing American jobs to low-wage countries. The book will also explore the consequences of corporations avoiding taxes through the use of off-shore tax havens. The hope is that this book will address the scandals starting to emerge from corporate America.

After six months of research I've completed a full draft of the proposed book. While the book clearly has an anti-corporate bias, I'm hoping some publisher will be interested. One editor expresses interest but ultimately rejects the project, explaining that the timing isn't right. Another editor offers a similar response. I realize the message may be too radical. Now that I'm into my seventh decade I'm wise enough to know when to let go. I decide to abandon the project. *You win some, you lose some*, I think, and I move on.

Part 3

THE WAY HOME

30.

The fading of my American dream

On 1 March 2001 Maura passes away at the age of seventy-seven. Over the years I had come to value the welcome and hospitality she always extended before she became incapacitated by poor health in her mid-sixties, and I looked forward to her updates on what was happening with neighbours.

In the years after Daddy's death our understanding of Maura's past helped to explain her occasional vulnerability. Her son, and then his family, were always in the background of her life, but the relationship was not as open as would have been desirable for either of them. It is a sad reminder of how harsh Irish society was in the past. Maura had remarried in 1986 and her second husband, Tom Kennedy, also predeceased her.

Her death represents the closing of a chapter in our family story. With Maura's passing it feels like the book is finally closing on my father's life. At the wake someone jokingly remarks that my father had emulated his own father by getting married three times (Daddy was the product of my grandfather's second marriage). This father-son combination could clearly lay claim to some kind of record for number of marriages in pre-divorce Ireland.

Maura's funeral is held in her home parish of Raheen. Patricia organizes everything and gets permission from the parish priest to have a college friend of hers say the funeral Mass. Father Christy makes it a meaningful and touching liturgy that honours Maura's life and marks the significance of her passing for her son and his family, for the Deevys, and for the Kennedys. Raheen is also the home place of Patricia's mother, Elsie Ryan, who is remembered in the prayers. It is a service with dignity and grace and there is a healthy sense of closure as we bring Maura to her place of rest on this beautiful spring morning. The contrast with Daddy's dismal funeral could not be greater.

At her son's request, Maura is buried with her mother in the graveyard in Raheen. Afterwards we adjourn for a reception in the local pub, Eamonn A'Chnoic, and honour this important family milestone in the traditional way. Not only that, but all over Ireland in rural farming communities like Raheen there has been a sense of siege, bordering on panic, since the outbreak of Foot and Mouth Disease among livestock in the UK a couple of weeks earlier. Now that everyone is 'on message' and the country is mobilized to prevent the spread of the disease, a gathering like this is a time to appreciate neighbours looking out for each other through the crisis and the whole country rising to meet a challenge. The atmosphere in the pub on that Sunday afternoon is warm and good-humoured, and the afters of Maura's funeral end up being an uplifting expression of family and community solidarity.

WITH THE FAILED BOOK project behind me, I refocus on the work with client organizations. And then one day as I go about my routine, life in the United States is suddenly changed. On a beautiful clear September morning I'm at my computer when I learn about a plane crashing into the one of the towers at the World Trade Centre in New York. As the details unfold that first plane turns out to be American Airlines Flight 11 from Logan Airport to Los Angeles. I'd taken that flight on my way to Hawaii numerous times over the previous four years.

There is an outpouring of patriotism that I have not seen since arriving in the United States almost forty years earlier. The whole world rallies behind President George W. Bush and the American people. All of this is short-lived, however: Bush will snatch defeat from the jaws of victory.

While 9/11 is a great tragedy for the American people, it will become an even greater tragedy for the world as it is exploited by right-wing demagogues. Almost immediately the neoconservatives unleash a campaign of fear-mongering and war-mongering that has a poisonous effect on American society. The neocons see the attack on the Twin Towers as a golden opportunity to go after their arch-enemy, Iraqi president Saddam Hussein. The two top figures in the Bush administration – Donald Rumsfeld and Dick Cheney – are obsessed with invading Iraq. They had both been members of the disgraced Nixon administration in the 1970s. Though there is nothing linking the events of 9/11 with Iraq, within weeks they are clamouring for an invasion of Iraq.

Despite intense opposition in many parts of the world, Bush obliges his advisors and his administration leads America into a war based on neocon propaganda and hysteria. Tony Blair, a politician I had admired, joins in the war-mongering and the instigation of a war based on lies. Blair ignores the hundreds of thousands who march on the streets of London protesting against the war. For the first time in almost four decades I feel less than proud of my American citizenship. Instead I feel anger and despair. After being part of the movement to end the war in Vietnam, I'm sick at the thought of young Americans being shipped out to fight another war based on propaganda.

Increasingly I become psychologically disengaged from American society as the Bush administration wages war on basic American freedoms. The world learns about the barbaric treatment of prisoners in Iraq. The so-called 'war on terror' has become a convenient excuse for all kinds of abuses. I'd lived through the abuses of the Nixon years, but this seems to be a much more serious attack on the freedoms American cherish.

JUST WHEN I THOUGHT I could not be more disillusioned, my disenchantment reaches a new level. On 27 August 2005, the City of New Orleans drowns as a result of Hurricane Katrina. It is one of the worst natural disasters in the history of the USA. Almost 2,000 people lose their lives. The whole world sees the horrific images of thousands of hurricane evacuees seeking refuge in the Superdome and the Convention Centre as their neighbourhoods are washed away. In the privacy of my apartment, I weep as I observe the suffering of people who've lost everything except the clothes they are wearing.

Three months after Hurricane Katrina I travel to Louisiana to see for myself the results of the destruction. It will be a homecoming of sorts, returning to Louisiana more than forty years after I'd first set foot there as a newly ordained Irish priest.

I arrive in Monroe, the city where I'd spent my first two years in America, in the early afternoon on the Friday after Thanksgiving. I'm filled with all kinds of mixed emotions – happy to be 'home', but fearful of what I'll discover when I get to New Orleans.

My first stop is a visit with Father Patrick Murphy, an Irishman and an old friend who'd spent almost fifty years working in north Louisiana. He's semi-retired and serving as a chaplain at an assisted-living facility. Patrick tells me that the current mayor of Monroe is an African-American. I'm somewhat stunned by this information. When I'd served as an assistant pastor in a downtown parish back in the early 1960s, an African-American would not have dared set foot in our parish church. I was aware that there had been major changes in the Deep South, but this I could never have expected.

We talk about Ireland and the changes that have come about there as a result of the economic boom. The old country has been dubbed the Celtic Tiger and has become one of Europe's wealthiest economies. That's also something we could never have imagined as young men leaving Ireland behind. As we talk about our families back in Ireland, I sense that Patrick is homesick for his native County Cork.

It's already getting dark when I drive downtown to visit St Matthew's Church, the church where I'd celebrated a memorial Mass for President John F. Kennedy after he was assassinated. I walk around the dark, deserted inner-city streets and it seems as if time has stood still since I left this city in the fall of 1964.

The next morning I travel south on Highway 165 towards Bunkie, the central Louisiana town were I'd worked as an assistant pastor after leaving Monroe. There isn't much traffic as I drive for hours through the flat, open countryside. Driving into Bunkie I realize that not much has changed since I'd first driven into this town in September 1964. A nondescript southern town of about six thousand residents, Bunkie is situated in corn and cotton country. And the differences in living conditions are still as obvious as night and day: like many small towns in the Deep South, the white people live on one side of the railroad track and the black people live on the other side.

Bunkie was my home for five years. After an hour of driving around old familiar neighbourhoods I stop off at St Anthony's Church. Sitting in a pew at the back of the church, my thoughts go back to the personal transformation that I'd undergone during the years serving in this parish. I'm remembering that Sunday in July 1969 when I'd preached my farewell sermon at all the Masses, breaking the news to parishioners that I was leaving the ministry. Now, I'm remembering the intense emotions of that day and the sense of relief as I drove into the red sunset that evening.

Before leaving Bunkie there's a visit with another old friend – Harriet 'Booby' Reed. Booby treats me to a crawfish dinner at a local restaurant. 'You know, Father Deevy, you've called me every Mother's Day since you left Bunkie. Isn't that amazing?'

What I find amazing is that she still calls me 'Father' after all these years.

239

'Booby, you were like a mother to me when I came to Bunkie. I've great memories of barbecues at your house.'

'Father, you still have a lot of friends in this town – and it's been a long time.'

After the whirlwind visit to Bunkie, I travel south on Highway 71 towards Baton Rouge. The landscape is marked by marshes and bayous, fertile swamplands filled with alligators, crayfish and lush plant life.

Driving down the long, straight, two-lane highway I sit back, relax and tune-in to a station playing traditional Cajun music. I'm only half paying attention when the station plays the Rockin' Dopsie Jr. version of 'I'm Coming Home'. This zydeco classic, regularly played at musicians' funerals in New Orleans, suits my mood. It seems appropriate since I am coming back to a place that was a home to me after an absence of thirty-two years.

As I approach Baton Rouge I can see the huge oil refinery in the skyline and crossing the Mississippi I'm thinking about the profound personal changes I'd experienced in this city more than three decades earlier. The four years of work as a social activist had transformed my view of American society. My work with LBJ's War on Poverty had allowed me to identify with the struggle of African-American people. I'd been radicalized and by the time I was booted out of the anti-poverty program in 1973, I was a profoundly changed person. Visiting familiar places and catching up with old friends provides an opportunity for lots of reminiscing.

Early on a Sunday morning I head southeast on Interstate 10 towards New Orleans. I'd made the trip from Baton Rouge to New Orleans many times years earlier on the old Airline Highway. Cruising down the almost deserted expressway I think about all the good times in New Orleans. The visits to Mardi Gras. The late-night partying in the French Quarter. As I drive towards the Big Easy I'm in a nostalgic, melancholic mood.

Driving through the western suburbs of Kenner and Metairie I see the blue tarps of the Federal Emergency Management Agency

(FEMA) that are the first signs of Hurricane Katrina's devastation. And as I approach the city I remember those television images of hordes of hurricane survivors camped on this highway without food or shelter.

Coming off the ramp of the downtown exit I see the Superdome. Thousands of people had been herded into this building after the levees broke and the city flooded. They had suffered indescribable indignities. On this beautiful sunny November morning, three months after Hurricane Katrina, the area is almost totally deserted.

My next stop is the Convention Centre. Seared in my mind are those television images of a deceased person lying for several days in a supermarket shopping cart and covered with a poncho at the entrance of the Centre. It was an image broadcast all over the world. In a call from Laois my sister-in-law Elsie had wondered why nobody was removing the abandoned body.

After breakfast at the St Charles Tavern, a downtown diner, I'm ready for the serious business of the day. Almost 80 per cent of the city had been destroyed by the floods that followed the hurricane. Now I want to see for myself. The tour of devastated areas begins with a drive through Centre City to the area called Lakeview. I join more than a thousand parishioners who'd come home from temporary homes hundreds of miles away for the first Mass at St Dominic's Church since the hurricane. In the church I see lots of evidence of Katrina's damage. There are no lights. The pews are gone – they rotted when 12 feet of water flooded the nave.

As I drive around Lakeview, a formerly middle class community, I see block after block and street after street of total devastation. Houses sit empty behind brown lawns and foothills of garbage. On Lake Pontchartrain Boulevard I see a trash mountain that's two storeys high. Even the trees that had been submerged in the 'toxic gumbo' have turned brown.

After spending a couple of hours touring Lakeview and Gentilly, I drive to the Lower Ninth Ward. Again, what I see is block after block of total destruction of the so-called shotgun houses in what had been primarily an African-American working class community. There's no sign of life, human or animal. There are piles of debris and abandoned cars in front of what remains of the houses. A huge rusty barge, washed ashore by the hurricane floods and sitting in the middle of an abandoned neighbourhood, is a reminder of what happened when the levee broke.

I park the car on Claiborne Avenue and walk down a side street. Outside what remains of one house I get a putrid smell. An African-American policewoman comes by and we have a friendly chat. She shows me some photos she'd taken with her digital camera. She tells me they are still finding bodies in the neighbourhood. I wonder about all the people who had been washed away. And I wonder about the thousands of survivors, who are scattered across more than forty states.

As darkness falls over New Orleans I abandon my tour of devastated neighbourhoods and retreat to a hotel room in the French Quarter. I can't help thinking that the people – people belonging to a community that is so close to my heart and that I feel a part of – were screwed by this terrible storm and the failure of the levees. I feel a sense of deep anger over the failure of the Bush administration to respond to the needs of this devastated city. In my state of heightened emotion, the word 'genocide' keeps coming into my mind.

Regaining control over my emotions I set out on a walking tour of the downtown area. On Canal Street I see huge piles of trash and several ransacked stores. After a bowl of sausage gumbo at Pearl's Oyster Bar, I walk over to Café Du Monde in the French Quarter. This was a favourite hang-out when I visited New Orleans as a young man. On this night the crowds are sparse. The city is still mostly a ghost town. Across Jackson Square I can see historic floodlit St Louis Cathedral. I sip on a cup of strong creole coffee. I'm feeling exhausted but glad that I've made this 'homecoming' trip.

I pull a notebook from my pocket and start to make notes. A woman sitting at a nearby table interrupts my note-taking.

'Excuse me, if you don't mind me asking, are you writing a book?'

'No, I'm just taking a few notes to capture the memories. I used to live in Baton Rouge and I've come back to see for myself.'

'That makes two of us. I'm from Philadelphia, but I did undergraduate studies here at Loyola. Like you, I needed to come back to see for myself.'

She's in her forties so she lived here two decades later than me. We compare notes on our Louisiana pasts and chat about our experiences in visiting the devastated parts of the city. And we share our anger over the failure of the Federal government to come to the rescue of this historic city. I'm comforted to know this stranger shares my anger.

I stroll back through the dark, deserted streets to my hotel room. I keep thinking about my activist days in the early 1970s and how full of optimism I was for America. Lately, I've been feeling somewhat disillusioned and the response of the government to the plight of the flood victims has only added to the disillusionment. For the first time the idea of returning home to Ireland enters my mind.

31.

Leaving the promised land

By the fall 2005 I'm experiencing burn-out and reduce my consulting practice. I start drawing on my savings. In August 2006 I begin to experience mild discomfort in my chest when walking up hills. This first becomes evident on the golf course. Initially I'm thinking that I'm just out of shape. On a visit to Ireland to attend my niece Lena's wedding the discomfort becomes more noticeable. The morning after the wedding I go for a walk with Elsie and her sister, May, and find myself struggling to keep up with them.

I keep hoping the chest discomfort will go away. By early October it's clear that this is not going to happen and I schedule a visit with my physician. He sends me to a cardiologist. When I walk into Dr Goldman's office I notice the ring in his ear and warm to this little touch of non-conformity. He is a friendly, personable man and immediately instils confidence.

Dr Goldman schedules an early morning angiogram at a local community hospital. After the test he comes and sits on the side of the gurney.

'These four charts show blockages of 80 per cent to 95 per cent on four major heart arteries. I guess you know what this means?'

I do: we had already talked about by-pass surgery. An hour later I'm in bed upstairs and the reality of my situation is beginning to sink in. And then Dr Goldman shows up in my room.

'Ed, you have the luck of the Irish! I have a room for you at Massachusetts General Hospital. I've arranged for an ambulance to transfer you to Boston at six o'clock.'

I feel fortunate – I know of the international reputation of Mass General for cardiac care. The following afternoon a nurse gives me the 'happy juice' and then wheels me down to the operating theatre. As the doors of the operating room open I realize it is just like on the TV shows. The nurse gives me a hug and wishes me good luck.

The next thing I remember is waking up in Intensive Care. The surgeon, standing at my bedside, tells me the seven-hour operation has been successful. He asks how I'm feeling.

I tell him I feel 'great', and I mean it.

The following Monday I leave the hospital feeling deeply appreciative for the wonderful care. After a few days at the home of my friends Paul and Linda Powers, I return to my apartment in Haverhill to begin several months of recuperation.

The operation has left me with a profoundly changed view of life. Gone is the obsession with work and with the future. Now I just want to live in the present and appreciate every moment. As ever when I'm trying to figure something out, I find myself taking regular solitary walks on Salisbury Beach. I'm seriously thinking of moving back to Ireland. In conversations with myself I explore the pros and cons of such a life-changing decision.

A brief visit to Michael and Elsie three months after the surgery provides an opportunity to explore the practical issues. In his typically blunt way Michael simplifies everything: 'All you need to do is take a one-way flight from Boston to Dublin. Don't worry about bringing stuff. You can get everything you need over here. Just pack up and leave!'

This all sounds like pretty good advice, though I know that making this move after living in the United States for forty-six years will be somewhat more complicated than that. But Michael's words make me think seriously about how I can simplify the business of relocating from Massachusetts to Ireland.

Unlike some returning emigrants, if I move back to Ireland it won't involve a major culture shock. Over a period of twenty-five years, for a combination of social and work reasons, I've made the transatlantic flight between Boston and Dublin numerous times, sometimes a couple of times a year. I am familiar not only with Ireland's rapid social and economic transformation but also its evolution into a multicultural society.

A more influential factor in my thinking is how I feel about leaving America. What about my friends? Some of my friendships go back decades. I conclude that with modern communication technologies it will be possible to maintain these friendships. What I won't miss about America is its changed political culture. Public discourse has become angry and polarized. 'Hate media' – extreme right-wing radio talk-shows and Fox TV and its imitators – are toxic, promoting Islamophobia and fear and division within society. I've found pundits' and politicians' racist campaigns against non-legal immigrants to be repulsive. And I've grown tired of the relentless war-mongering. The same pundits who had acted as cheerleaders for the Iraq war are now advocating the bombing of Iran.

Despite intense negative feelings about the Bush administration I still feel great admiration for the American people. When I'd first set foot in the United States in the early 1960s I'd encountered an energy, vitality and hopefulness that I came to believe was unique to American society. That unique 'can do' spirit of optimism defined, and still defines, America. As I consider relocating to Ireland, I know I'll miss all that energy and vitality.

Ironically, after experiencing the depression of the Bush years I find myself suddenly believing that America might yet deliver on its promise. A young Chicago politician named Barack Obama is looking like a viable candidate for the presidency. I'm hoping Obama will win and at a personal level I'm thinking that his election would make those of us who had even a modest role in the civil rights struggle feel vindicated.

MY CONVERSATIONS WITH myself on Salisbury Beach lead to a definite decision to return to the country where I'd spent the first twenty-four years of my life. I confide my decision to Paul Powers.

'Eddie, it really doesn't make a difference where you live. You've dual citizenship. You'll be able to commute back and forth. And besides, after all these years, you don't owe this country a fuckin' thing.' A typical Powers statement! Paul picks up on my concern that I am somehow abandoning my adopted country and in his usual no-bullshit manner he gets to the heart of the matter.

When I set out for America in 1962 I thought of myself as going to 'the Promised Land' – a country offering unlimited opportunities. I thought of it as a society where each individual had, as it said it the country's Declaration of Independence, 'inalienable rights'. Now as I look back I realize I was somewhat naïve and unrealistic in the vision I had for my adopted country. I understand that America is a work-in-progress.

In early 2008 I begin taking the practical steps towards relocation. A friend of Lena's agrees to rent me her house in Dublin, so I have a place to live. The process of getting rid of 'stuff' takes several months and involves a lot of trips to the Salvation Army. While the process of downsizing is intensely emotional, it's also liberating. I can now look forward to starting a new life in Ireland without the burden of a lot of unnecessary baggage. One day Paul shows up with his pickup truck to help me take twenty boxes of personal belongings to the docks in Boston for shipping.

'You may never see this stuff again,' he says, as the freight company takes possession of the boxes. Frankly, I'm not concerned.

The final, emotionally draining months include lots of lunch and dinner dates with friends and professional associates. On 1 April 2008 I board an Aer Lingus jet in Boston for the red-eye to Dublin. It's a flight I have taken so many times before, but this time I am going back for good.

32.

Still journeying

One day, several months after returning to Ireland, Michael and I make the fifteen-mile drive from his house to Drumagh. We park the car at the entrance to the long winding driveway that leads to where our home once stood. Large, locked, prison-like gates block access and we're not going to be able to drive in. Whatever nostalgic impulse had drawn us to the site of the old homestead is quickly extinguished.

I knew that the two-storey house where we had grown up was destroyed in a fire in the mid-1980s. On a visit home a little while after Andy's death in 1991 I had come to Drumagh seeking ... I don't know what. One afternoon I had walked through neighbouring fields to find an opening in a hedge where I could view the spot where the house had stood. There was nothing to see but a crater. Though I'd known the old place had gone up in flames, I never imagined the empty space would look so desolate. And where once there was a beautiful lawn and bountiful gardens, now there was just weeds and rubble. I couldn't even read the landscape. In our day the vista from the front of the house overlooked several fields that each had a name. One was called Ward's Hill. We used to roll down the steep hill and then run back up to do it again until we were so dizzy we couldn't stand up. But because most of the hedges had been removed it was impossible to get my bearings or to figure out where the fields had been.

I'm saddened that I cannot walk around the place where I'd grown up with my brothers and sisters. I still can't help peering across the fields in the direction of the old homestead. Memories of childhood years flood back. Memories of living in our own world, somewhat isolated from the outside world. For a moment, I see myself upstairs as a twelve-year-old in bed, battling to recover from life-threatening double-pneumonia. Each night I'd hear the family downstairs, led by Daddy, recite the rosary for my recovery. Thanks to the loving care of my mother and a dose of penicillin, I was back on my feet in a couple of months.

Next stop on our tour is our two-room primary school, though I don't feel any sense of nostalgia for a place in which I was never happy. Near the school is Mayo church and the graveyard where our parents, our sister Brigid and our stepmother Elsie are buried. The following day we visit our alma mater, Knockbeg College.

A few weeks later I take the train to Carlow. Many shops are boarded up, the devastation caused by the collapse of the Celtic Tiger economy obvious. As I approach the main entrance to Carlow College I can see that the high walls are gone, but as I walk in off College Street it looks like very little changed in the last forty-odd years. Looking up towards the big Georgian building, I'm struck that the grounds are still beautifully maintained. Then I notice a contemporary building on my left, in a space occupied by handball alleys when I was a seminarian. I go to investigate and discover an impressive, light-filled building – a modern art gallery and theatre.

After checking with security inside the front door I walk into an environment that is very different from my student days, with male and female students rushing around in all directions. In my day the atmosphere would have been sober and a visitor would have seen seminarians walking around in their soutanes, full length, black fitted garments with a row of buttons from neck to hem. In the 1990s the college ceased to be a seminary and became a regular third-level institution, specializing in the humanities and social studies.

I walk down the corridor in the direction of the Senior Chapel and notice the class photos from the college's seminary years hanging on the walls: a record of the young men it sent to all corners of the English-speaking world every year for decades. The pictures are composed of individual headshots of that year's crop of young priests. The 1962 class photo has thirty-eight individual headshots. (A few years later, in 2012, I'll join a small group of these classmates in Carlow to mark the Golden Anniversary of our ordination.)

I open the door of what was the Senior Chapel and walk into a magnificently designed library. Named the P.J. Brophy Memorial Library, it seems like a fitting tribute to a professor who inspired generations of students and eventually became president of the college. He greatly expanded my parochial views at a formative period and it was always a pleasure to reconnect with him.

Outside again, I take a seat on a bench looking out over the town. I admire the manicured lawns, the colourful shrubs and blooming flowers. In the distance I can see the Killeshin Hills. I'm remembering those Wednesday afternoons when the entire student body, dressed in black with hats and canes, walked in pairs up these hills. And I'm remembering the many trips over these hills on the way home to Drumagh – just eight miles away.

My thoughts drift to all the experiences I had on this campus. I remember the isolation that came from having no access to newspapers or radio. I think about all those conversations with myself, years ago, on solitary walks around these grounds. I remember my bouts of anxiety about my sexual urges, the conversations with the spiritual director about them and telling myself that once I was fully trained and ordained, I would probably not be as troubled by them.

We had an entire term devoted to sexuality – not our own, of course. Instead we made a special study of the Sixth Commandment – 'Thou shalt not commit adultery' – so as to be in a better position to advise dating couples what not to do on a date (for fear of straying from venial to mortal sin territory) and to counsel married couples on their relationships. I'm amused to think how much my life was ultimately enriched by women – both friends and lovers – at each stage of the journey, not something I would have anticipated all those years ago when I persuaded myself I would be able to manage celibacy.

I think about the journey I have travelled from the apparent certainties of my training here. Growing up I embraced the hopeful and compassionate values expressed by Jesus in the Sermon on the Mount. These ideals have been at the core of my personal philosophy down through the years – though I have often fallen short in living up to them. After I left the ministry I became less engaged in formal religious practice, though that bedrock of values stayed with me.

I feel no bitterness towards the Church, have great respect for the many good people (including my three sisters) who worked tirelessly for others within the framework of a consecrated life, and I often go to Mass. That brings me to thinking about the radically changed status of the Church in Ireland – symbolized by the changes at this institution. Clearly, it wasn't simply modernization and increasing prosperity that made people turn away from the Church. A key factor in the Church's diminished role and reputation in Irish life is the shocking breach of trust revealed in the series of the abuse scandals over two decades. (One such was close to home for me: in 2006 allegations of sexual misconduct with minors 'in his early priesthood' were made against my old boss in Bunkie, Monsignor Fred Lyons, and he was suspended from all priestly duties. In 2013 Church authorities stripped him of the title of Monsignor and 'sentenced' him to 'a life of prayer and penance.')

ONE YEAR AFTER SETTLING BACK in Ireland I travel back to Boston for work on my aorta. I arrive back in Dublin with an infection.

Rita helps restore me to good health. Rita and I, having had lives that took us in very different directions for so many years, now meet regularly for lunch in Cork city. We have become very good friends and there is great enjoyment in rediscovering this sibling who is endlessly kind, sometimes unexpectedly funny and hides a sharp intelligence behind her low-key personality. I come to appreciate more fully Rita's unselfish dedication to helping people in need.

In late July 2009 I receive a call to say that Rita has died suddenly. She collapsed as she was locking the doors of the hospital chapel after evening devotions and died later in hospital in Cork, with Mary at her side. A massive brain haemorrhage.

The large funeral procession through Midleton, from the hospital where she was assistant matron to the parish church, becomes a moving expression of community affection. It reminds me of Mammy's funeral, people coming up to family members with stories of the good she has done. More than one person refers to her as 'Midleton's Mother Teresa'. Rita, I know, would be mortified by the entire thing. She was self-effacing and incredibly private. At the funeral Mass the next day, in a brief eulogy, I describe my sister as 'her mother's daughter'. It is the highest praise I can bestow.

Two years after Rita's death, in May 2011, I get another telephone call. Another sudden death: Tom has been found dead in his bed in London. More devastation. Since I was now fully settled into life in Dublin and in easy reach of London, we had been making various plans for spending more time together. The post mortem reveals he died of a heart attack. He was just sixty-five.

In 2004 Tom had legally changed his name from Tom Deevy to Christopher Condren – combining his middle name and our mother's family surname. It was his way of publicly shedding an identity he experienced as a source of pain and that he felt no longer fit the man he wanted to be. Initially, it had felt a little strange calling him Christopher, but I got used to it. After arranging Christopher's funeral service I spend the next eighteen months in transit between Dublin and his home in Muswell Hill, sorting out his affairs.

The most interesting discovery I make in going through Christopher's papers is a journal he'd kept over the last fifteen years of his life. Several times each week he'd type his reflections on what was happening in his life. There were thirty-three ring-binders covering that period. One particular journal entry grabs my attention.

In 2007 Christopher had attended a workshop on creative writing in Wiltshire. He left the workshop at noon and returned home. Immediately on his return he wrote to the woman running the course, explaining his early departure. Here, in part, is what he wrote:

> Here I am at the word processor in my north London base while you continue to inspire the participants, in so far as they are open to being inspired.
>
> Your workshop was so inspiring for me that I decided to leave after the first session. I explained to you that I was leaving because I had already gotten what I came for – I knew when I noticed on your workshop plan 'Who Are You Before Your Writing Begins' that I was in the right place. This was confirmed as you opened up your workshop and crystallized for me when you spoke of 'nurturing the creative process'.
>
> The truth is that I'm an amazing guy – in my formative years every shred of humanity in me was trampled upon but my spirit has survived. I have an amazing story to tell but there is no way in which readers could listen until I achieve sufficient self-compassion to tell that story with compassion for myself and compassion for them ...

Christopher was indeed an amazing man. For many years he battled demons stemming from childhood years. I believe it was a lonely journey. As a child he was reserved and serious and he was just seventeen years old when Mammy died. It was a lot for a sensitive boy to deal with. Nursing took him to London. Later, he completed a science degree and then retrained as a plumber and became self-employed. After Andy's suicide in 1991, and the negative reaction to him putting responsibility for it solely on Daddy's shoulders, he severed communications with family members (apart from Patricia, who dropped in on him from time to time). It took until the early 2000s before there was a thaw between us. At that point, I resumed regular contact. He soldiered on and by the time we attended that creative writing workshop in 2007, he was well on the way to moving beyond the hurt and anger. The letter to the creative writing facilitator is full of hope and promise. When Rita died he spoke to Patricia about the practicalities of travelling to Cork for the funeral before deciding that, in the circumstances, it would be too much and he'd prefer to visit in a low-key way at a later date. In 2010 he flew into Dublin for a brief visit with me. The fact that he was tentatively going about reconnecting with Ireland and family after nearly twenty years shows how far he had healed.

In his letter he says that he cannot share his story until he can 'tell that story with compassion for myself and compassion for them ...'. From everything I read in his journals I believe the 'them' he refers to – the readers he has in mind in the first instance – are his family. As I ponder his letter I'm saddened that death has deprived him of the opportunity.

Decades earlier, over a whiskey in Reddy's pub in Carlow, I was entrusted by my father to keep the family together. Andy's joust with an angry bull predetermined so much that I had no control over. Rita's sudden departure at the house of her God, after a life of selflessness and care-giving was, in a strange way, a blessing for her while a source of deep sadness for her family.

Christopher was on the verge of a life-transforming breakthrough and re-reading his letter, he knew it. I hope that in sharing his letter I am now looking after the family as I promised my father, by reuniting Christopher with his siblings. The good news is that he was on the cusp of uncovering a pearl of great price – compassionate forgiveness for himself and for others.

A few months before his death my father and I found peace and reconciliation. Now I can be at peace on the road of life, knowing that I am the means for sharing Christopher's letter that ends with its promise, however embryonic, of a healing redemptive love.

Back in Dublin, I'm still trying to make sense of all that I've experienced in closing the book on Christopher's life. A friend sends me these lines from the well-known poem 'Ithaca' by the Greek poet C.P. Cavafy. She's right – this speaks to exactly how I'm feeling on my return from London:

> Ever keep Ithaca in your mind,
> your return thither is your goal.
> But do not hasten at all your voyage,
> better that it last for many years;
> And full of years at length you anchor at your isle
> rich with all that you gained on the way;
> do not expect Ithaca to give you riches.
> Ithaca gave you your fair voyage.
> Without her you would not have ventured on the way.
> But she has no more to give you.

We're all on that voyage towards Ithaca, towards 'home'. I like to think that the lines from the poem capture something of the journeys both Christopher and I have travelled. Christopher engaged intensely and thoughtfully with his journey. Now his travelling days are over and I am still journeying, ready to anchor at the isle, rich with all that I've gained on the way.

Afterword

Apart from this afterword, my book was finished with my reflections on Christopher's death. I was in the process of editing it in spring 2014, with a view to publication later in the year, when Mary was diagnosed with terminal cancer. Though Mary was seventy-five she was the proverbial person who was 'never sick a day in her life' and she had the energy and drive of a woman decades younger.

Mary came to terms with her diagnosis in a remarkable way and lived out her short time with amazing grace, fortitude and inspiring faith. She set about sorting out the 'hand-over' practicalities of the various projects she was involved with, entertained a constant stream of visitors and made prayer, reflection and time with family, fellow sisters and close friends her priorities. She died on 14 July, accompanied by Lena, Patricia, myself, her great friend Sister Miriam Wiley RSM and Mary Byrne, one of the exceptional nurses from Marymount Hospice in Cork.

Though to each of us our story feels unique, the fates of Mary and my siblings and me are typical of those who came of age in mid-twentieth century Ireland. At the age of seventeen Mary entered religious life and in doing so she was part of the great tide of young women and men who had been flowing into novitiates and

257

seminaries for close on a century. From post-Famine times life as a religious or a priest was considered both a prestigious and a practical life choice, particularly in the farming and merchant classes.

That this phenomenon created a vast infantry that was deployed in a range of worthwhile and necessary activities that helped the state is indisputable. That it also created the conditions in which some of their number became dehumanized and ran institutions that were far removed from the ideals of loving Christian compassion and basic decency is also inescapable. I never discussed the institutional abuse scandals with my late sisters – partly because I knew what a source of immense bewilderment and pain these were to them. Historians have much work to do in teasing out the social, economic, religious and psychological origins of those scandals. All of these strands are part of the story.

Though the reason for my departure from Ireland was vocational rather than economic, I was part of the great wave of emigration of the 1950s and early 1960s that saw tens of thousands of my contemporaries emigrate, many while still in their teens. By the late 1950s the scale of the exit was staggering, with over 80,000 young people leaving in 1958 alone. They were a lost generation, sadly one of the many generations we have 'lost' since the formation of the State. A few, now in their sunset-years like myself, are returning to the country of their birth. They all have unique stories to tell.

The impetus for me telling my story dates back to the late 1970s, when I was completing my doctoral studies at the University of Massachusetts and the paper I wrote illustrating how significant personal experiences had influenced my evolving consciousness was so well received. After completing my studies I packed away the manuscript and it remained at the back of a closet for over twenty years, until it turned up one day during a bout of decluttering. Reading that old manuscript rekindled my interest in telling the rest of the story. Since then I have, at various times, updated and revised the narrative. The image of Odysseus has never left me: the classic story of the young man who leaves home and travels to faraway places and then returns to the land of his childhood and the woman who has waited for him, Penelope. My journey has also been unscripted. I have gone with the flow and in the process ended up in some unexpected places. There was no Penelope for me to come back to. In later years, that was sometimes a source of regret. But better to have loved along the way than never to have loved at all.

The process of writing the story into my late seventies helped put various experiences into a wider context. I hope I have gained greater perspective and wisdom, and insights I perhaps lacked as a callow youth of forty! I think the story is now a richer read and my modest hope is that it is an engaging record of a time of great social transition in both Ireland and America.

In America I did indeed find a promised land, though it was rather different from the one I'd envisaged when leaving Ireland in 1962. My most exciting and transformative period was my time in Louisiana. Those days were very much on my mind as I listened to Michelle and Barack Obama's inspirational speeches in Belfast in June 2013. In the Deep South in the early 1970s I would have found the idea of an African-American couple occupying the White House utterly unimaginable. On this and the Obamas' previous visit, to Dublin and Offaly in 2011, I was proud of how the people of Ireland embraced them. Though we have a way to go, it's worth remembering that we have all journeyed a very long way.

Acknowledgements

In the United States several people provided useful input on my first version of this book. These include Kate Phillips, who provided early editorial assistance, and long-time colleague, friend and fellow author, Dr. Paul Powers, who reviewed it. In Ireland, Jean Roberts, Roz Scully and Michael Roberts read more recent drafts. I appreciate the input of Vanessa O'Loughlin of the Inkwell Group and Deborah Dooley for providing a peaceful and productive environment at the Writers' Retreat in Devon. Thanks also to Rachel Pierce for copyediting.

Early on I sent a work-in-progress version of this memoir to family in Ireland. The response was lukewarm; I had put in rather more family detail than was strictly necessary for telling my own story. Their responses also brought home the realization that everyone, naturally, has his or her own version and interpretation of the shared bits of a family's history. Though some of the feedback was critical, all of it was valuable in helping to create a narrative that I hope is fair and balanced. I am grateful to members of my family for that and for allowing the book to proceed to publication. I'm especially indebted to my sister-in-law Elsie and sister Patricia for their input along the way.

Other friends who were not directly involved in the book but who have been particularly helpful to me since I left the USA are